ABUNDANT BLESSINGS FROM MY 60 YEARS OF MINISTERING

Some of the best advise on earth

REV. JOHN BOOKO, Sr.

ABUNDANT BLESSINGS FROM MY 60 YEARS OF MINISTERING
Some of the best advice on earth
by REV. JOHN BOOKO, Sr.

Printed in the United States of America

ISBN 9781626971066

Rev. John Booko Ministries
200 S. Hooker Ave.
Three Rivers, MI 49093
269-279-2672
e-mail: revbooko@hotmail.com
Website: Assyria.freeservers.com

www.xulonpress.com

Be blessed,
John Booko

FOREWORD

At the writing of this book, at 90 years of age, I thank God for my good health and strength of mind and spirit.

If someone asks me how to get to be 90 years old, I'll tell them to go to 89, and then be very careful. Another way to get to be 90 is to have a lot of birthdays.

Seriously, here is my secret for healthy living: 5 F's

FAITH — in God and believing His Word in the Bible and living it out.

FOOD SUPPLEMENTS — vitamins to fill in where you may not be getting enough nutrition from your food.

FITNESS — exercise at least five days a week along with prayer and praising the Lord.

FUN — do things that make you happy and laugh a lot.

Forgiveness — don't hold on to any grudges.

I give thanks to God, my heavenly Father, for all of His miracles in me and through me. I give my Lord Jesus Christ all of the glory for all the good things said of me and done for me; and for all the good I have said and done in His Name.

Reverend John Booko was born in Chicago, IL, November 29,1922 of Assyrian parents who came to America from Northern Iraq.

He served in the United States Navy during World War II for almost 3 years as Aviation Machinist Mate 2nd Class. He gave his life to Christ in the Navy and received his call to Christian ministry.

John met his wife, Burnell, in Chicago while attending the Moody Memorial Church and were married in Wakefield, MI, June 12, 1948. Burnell passed on to heaven April 30, 2010 after almost 62 years of marriage.

Rev.Booko holds a Bachelor of Theology degree from Northern Baptist Theological Seminary in Chicago, 1950, and a Master of Arts degree from Northwestern University in Evanston, IL, 1951.

He is an ordained Baptist Minister from the American Baptist Churches and served as pastor in Michigan Baptist Churches in Okemos, Millington and Three Rivers for over 24 years. In 1975 he founded the interdenominational church in Three Rivers, now called Riverside Church, where his son, Paul, is now the senior pastor since his father turned it over to him in 1992.

John has resided in Three Rivers, MI, since Aug. 1963. He has four children, fifteen grandchildren and three great grandchildren.

For ten years (1964-1974), he maintained a daily community telephone call service called "Dial-A-Meditation," receiving over 200,000 calls and delivering over 3,500 different meditations over the years. He also gave for many years, on our local radio station, WLKM, devotional messages.

John is the author of three books: "Assyria-The Forgotten Nation In Prophecy," "The Assyrian Revelation," and "No Prayer Power." He has had numerous speaking engagements throughout America and many foreign countries. He has met with the Israeli Prime Minister in Jerusalem and with Egyptian president Hosni Mubarak in Cairo where he prayed with him.

Rev. Booko also has three weekly short wave radio broadcasts out of WINB in Red Lion, PA. Sundays noon, 4:30 pm and Tuesdays 7 pm. They can also be heard on the internet of WINB.com

He also has a website @ www.Assyria.freeservers.com

On the internet, he has a daily prayer on youtube.com, type 'rev-johnbooko' and click on his picture and scroll to the prayer. Also an youtube is his daily Bible verse called "bibledig."

How to contact Rev. John Booko Ministries: 200 S. Hooker Ave, Three Rivers, MI 49093
Ph. 269-279-2672, e-mail: revbooko@hotmail.com He is also on Facebook.

BOOK DEDICATION

To Burnell, my dear, sweet, darling wife of 62 years, whom God used to make me what I am today.

Anna Burnell Booko's life began on a cold winter day, January 12, 1924 in Wakefield, MI where she was born at her parent's farm home, the first daughter of Elmer an Lillian Hanson. She was raised in Wakefield, where she enjoyed ice skating, roller skating, had a deep passion for music and drama, and played oboe in the school band. She was confirmed at the age of 13 in the Emmanuel Lutheran Church where she also taught Sunday School and played the piano.

Upon graduating from Wakefield High School in 1942, Burnell moved to Chicago to pursue her nursing career. She graduated from Augustina Hospital School of Nursing in 1945. It was there she was introduced through mutual friends to her future husband, John, at Moody Memorial Church, during a Halloween Party. They had their first date at a mid-week prayer meeting and shared their first kiss on John's birthday, November 29th 1946. They would unite in marriage on June 12, 1948 in Wakefield.

Burnell worked at Augustina Hospital (now Lutheran General) and later as a visiting nurse, while John was finishing seminary. In 1951 John and Burnell were blessed with their first child, a daughter, Joy. They moved a short time after to Okemos, MI where John would pastor his first church, Okemos Baptist, where Burnell played the piano and organ. It was there that Burnell gave birth to three boys, John, Paul, and David to complete their loving family.

In 1958 the family moved to Millington where John and Burnell pastored the Baptist Church for four years. John and Burnell were called to Three Rivers, in 1963 where they pastored First Baptist Church for twelve years. On July 6, 1975 they formed a new church, Three Rivers Christian Fellowship, which is now Riverside Church.

Burnell was very active as the wife of a pastor and leading various ministries like Singles Group, Flying Solo, and Blended Families. She also ministered to the families of her community by playing the organ at Hohner Funeral Home and Halverson Chapel for many years. She looked forward to Tuesday evenings when she would volunteer at the free Riverside Health Clinic.

Burnell loved to knit and sew. She often blessed family and friends with beautiful items as well as home made candy. She and John also loved to take bike rides during the warmer Michigan days. They traveled through John's ministry to many countries including Austria, Canada, Germany, Holland, India Japan, Mexico, and Sweden. Burnell and John also vacationed several times to Israel and spent many happy winters in Florida.

John and Burnell spent sixty-two wonderful years together. Their union gave birth to four loving children, Joy John, Paul, and David, who in turn blessed Burnell and John with fifteen wonderful grandchildren, Hannah, Matthew, Jonathon, Grace, John III, Daniel, Chrystal, Gloria, Jordan, David, Joseph, Luke, Ben, Abbey, and Brenin.

Burnell was the consummate nurse, wide counselor, mother to the motherless and servant of all. She brought happiness to every gathering as her child-like innocence brought laughter and grace to everyone wearied by the world. She was the ultimate Proverbs 31 women, equipped with the full armor of God. She demonstrated the fruits of the Spirit. And best of all, she loved without ceasing. We find it difficult to release her, flooded by the memories of her smile, beautiful spirit, words of wisdom and winsome personality. She willingly adopted us all, being our Spiritual Mom, which was an honor and blessing beyond words. She represented the consummate loving mother, supportive wife, coveted friend and sold-out follower of Jesus Christ.

She went to be with the Lord on April 30, 2010, and she is going to be at heaven's gate to greet me when I arrive. See you later sweetheart!

CHAPTER ONE

THIS IS MY LIFE: For me to live is Christ and to die is gain, Phil. 1:21

MY PURPOSE IN LIFE: To know the Scriptures, to know God's will and to have God's will done in my life and through me for His glory.

"Only one life, 'twill soon be past, only what's done for Christ will last."

SURELY GOODNESS AND MERCY SHALL (HAVE) FOLLOW(ED) ME ALL THE DAYS OF MY LIFE, AND I WILL DWELL IN THE HOUSE OF THE LORD FOREVER. (From Psalm 23:6)

THIS IS MY LIFE

November 29, 1922 was my entrance date into this world via Chicago, Illinois, the first child of Abraham and Phoebe Booko. My parents were born in south east Turkey which later became part of northern Iraq. Their nationality was Assyrian and their language is the Aramaic language. My father came to America in 1912 and my mother in 1920 where they met in Chicago and were married in 1921. Three brothers, Benjamin, George, Joseph and sister Bertha were added to the family between 1924-1931.

I grew up on the near north side of Chicago, near Lincoln Park on Ohio Street in an upstairs apartment with my bedroom window a few feet from the elevated train that roared past my window day and night. I remember sitting in my mother's lap and being taught Bible stories. My mother was an educated teacher in Iraq but my father was uneducated and too proud to have my mother help him learn English.

The earliest recollection of Christmas was when my mother told me that she met Santa Claus in the hallway of our apartment and got into an argument with him because she said he was not bringing me any presents. She said she pulled his beard and knocked him down. I was disappointed and said now for sure he won't be coming here again.

In 1926 I began kindergarten a year early to help mother with her other children. I was put on a streetcar alone and got off at the school and rode back home. I was in that grade for two years and graduated to the first grade when I could walk up the school stairs. I remember getting pennies from my classmates by pretending to swallow them. I learned to speak the Assyrian language before English because my father could not speak English and sometimes I would get the two languages mixed together when speaking.

We moved to 2032 Burling Street around 1928 and I attended the Arnold School across from our house. I used to have nightmares dreaming that I was falling off the Chicago River Bridge when it was raised to let the boats through.

I used to wait at the corner of Armitage Street for the streetcar to bring home my father from his job at a department store downtown where he worked as a cook. He was laid off during the depression of 1929 and later could not work because of arthritis in his knees. We had to go on relief (welfare).

I attended the Carter Memorial Assyrian Presbyterian Church sometimes with my mother, but mostly attended the Christ Presbyterian Church in our neighborhood until I was twelve years old.

I would go out on Sunday mornings and sell newspapers and also collected junk to sell at the junk yard to earn money in 1931. I had an ambition to be a comedian as I could imitate a Greek Ambassador on stage. I had a radio a crystal set that could pick up radio programs with my earphones. I used to enjoy listening to a scary program, "Lights Out" at midnight.

In 1932, I went with some of my friends to the bullet-riddled telephone pole by the Biograph Theatre that I used to attend, where John Dillinger, public enemy number one was shot and killed by the police coming out of the theater and running into the alley.

In 1933, I attended the Chicago's World Fair with the Kirkle family with whom I spent a lot of time, and their daughter Grace was my friend. I did not relate much with my siblings.

I began smoking at the age of 13 and did exciting exploits like climbing inside of a tall factory chimney and standing on the edge of the top and hanging over the side. We would hang on the outside of the streetcars for rides. At this time I stopped going to Sunday School.

After graduating from the elementary school in 1937, we moved to 1909 Sedgwick Street, a couple of blocks from Lincoln Park. From there I began attending the boys' Lane Tech High School until 1939. I would ride my bicycle most of the time to the high school which was a long distance away and would grab a hold of a street car to be pulled along. Much of the time I cut school and hung out in the back room of a candy store with friends. Because of missing 48 days of classes I failed my junior year and I transferred to our nearby Waller High School for the last two years, doing my junior year over. I learned German there for two years.

During my high school years, I worked for a dentist, Dr. Stearns. I did everything from taking X-rays, mixed silver in a mortar for fillings, sterilized instruments, ran errands especially to the "Bookie Joints" to place bets on horse racing. Also I worked later in a small machine shop on Hallsted Street.

I graduated from Waller High School in 1941 and got a job at Signode Steel Strapping Company as a drill press operator earning 50 cents an hour and worked there for 18 months. During this time I had an operation on my nose to remove a lump I had gotten in a roller skating accident. I also purchased an old Oldsmobile car for $80 and learned to drive it on my own.

When our country was attacked by the Japanese at Pearl Harbor, December 7, 1941, I learned of it as I came home from the neighborhood movie theater. I was angry about it and I went to the Navy recruiting center and tried to enlist as a Navy pilot. The officer asked me why I wanted to join and I told him I wanted to kill them. I was not accepted at that time, but the officer seemed pleased with my answer.

During this time (1942), I worked hard at the machine shop as a drill press operator on "piece" time, which meant I could earn more than my hourly rate of pay if I produced more pieces than was required on the job. I took advantage of the opportunity and became the top producer in the company. I came to be known as the "bonus kid."

I was still not a Christian and my mother had stopped speaking to me about the Lord because I would get angry when she would start. My social life consisted of being with my buddies, either playing cards or drinking at bars.

My mother respected my wishes and stopped sharing about the Lord to me, but she prayed to God about me. She would go into her prayer closet and sometimes I would hear her praying for me. My other siblings were believers.

When I would come home late at night (we were now living on 920 Hudson Avenue in the Mother Cabrini Green Housing) after living a rowdy life, I would come to bed and sometimes be awakened by my mother at my bedside praying for me.

As World War II was raging, I started to think "what if I died in this war; what is going to happen to me?" I knew from my mother's teaching that I would go to hell if I died, so I reasoned, "Now, is it worth it to live my life the way I am living it and die and go to hell for all eternity?" Fortunately, I said "No." I loved to gamble, and God used that gambling instinct in me to bring me to my conversion. No one talked to me specifically about the Lord; it was just through my mother's teachings and prayers that I came to the Lord.

When I went into the war, I was not thinking at the time that there was a heaven or a hell. Instead, I was trying to believe that "There is no God" so I would not be convicted. But in the face of war, my thoughts went another direction. I reasoned, "If I live to be seventy, and suppose there is a heaven and hell, if I keep living the way I am living now, I will be in hell forever. But, if I accept the Lord and live a good life, and if there is no leaven or hell, I have not lost anything; I have just lived a good life." So, I concluded, "What is keeping me from accepting the Lord?"

I thought deeply about the junk I was doing, and I said to myself, "I am throwing away eternity for this junk? No, I do not want to die and go to hell." As a gambler, I did not like the odds: Seventy years of dubious fun verses eternity.

I remember my mom teaching about accepting Christ, so I prayed, "Lord, I want to accept You as my personal Savior, I want to be saved. Please enter into my heart today. I ask Your forgiveness for my sins, and ask You to accept me into Your spiritual family and change my life. Amen."

When I said that simple prayer, a huge, invisible weight seemed to be removed from my heart! Immediately I shouted, "Praise God, this is just the peaceful feeling I have been looking for in the world." An unexplainable joy came to me.

I started reading the New Testament (the Gideon organization had given each of us servicemen a New Testament). I started reading about how Jesus died for my sins, and my heart was broken. I had originally accepted Jesus Christ because I was afraid of hell. But now, as I read about Jesus dying for me, I fell in love with Him and my heart just broke. I wept, "Oh Jesus, You did all of this for me? You gave up Your life so that I might spend eternity with You in heaven? Thank You, Lord Jesus. Now, I am going to live the rest of my life for You."

Then, I started witnessing to my Navy buddies. I would say, "Hey, you know, this being a Christian is great! I used to think if you became a Christian, you would not have any fun; I was all prepared when I accepted Christ not to have any fun. I was among some people who said 'You cannot do this, you cannot do that.' And I thought 'Man, it is no fun being a Christian.'" But I was wrong. "Hey, this is the greatest joy; there is nothing in the world so empty as when I go to the taverns, laugh with the boys, and then go home and feel so lonesome, so empty." It seemed as though my worldly life in the Navy had given me nothing.

I was so excited about the changes God was doing in my life that I called up mother and told her, "I just accepted Jesus Christ as my Lord and Savior."

You can well imagine how my mother rejoiced when she heard the news! **Her consistent and persistent prayers had been answered!**

During the six months at the Navy Pier in Chicago, I could go on liberty each week and visit my family. I had the privilege of leading my seventeen year old brother George to receive Christ as his Savior.

At the Navy Pier, I joined the Navy Choir so I could get an extra day leave each week. A fellow sailor started needling me a lot and I lost my temper and punched him in the head and drew blood. That stopped him but I injured my knuckle. I felt guilty that as a Christian I got into a fight.

About six months after I got saved in April I quit smoking as I asked God to help me quit.

After the six months of training at Navy Pier, I was awarded the rank of 3rd Class Petty Officer with one stripe on my uniform (this would be equivalent to a sergeant in the army).

I was sent to Pensacola, Florida, for two weeks of gunnery training so I could learn to shoot the twin turret 50 caliber machine guns on a Navy plane. I had volunteered for gunnery training thinking that in the dangerous war situation I could witness more effectively and lead those who feared death to the Lord. Later, I thought that was not too smart for my safety.

During this time, I got introduced to the Navigators organization through a buddy of mine who challenged me to memorize Bible verses. That began my discipline of memorizing and reviewing the Scriptures. At the same time I was devouring the reading of the Bible. I loved to study and know the Word of God. I witnessed for Christ a lot and tried to lead my buddies to Christ and always looked for other Christian sailors to study the Bible with.

During the year of 1944, I attended training in Memphis, Tennessee for radar instruction, Hutchinson, Kansas and Jacksonville, Florida for automatic pilot training. My main base of station was San Diego, California at the Naval Air Station outside of San Diego. I worked on instrument maintenance on the PB4Y Naval Bombers. I also was trained and flew as an instrument technician, known as a plane captain.

I was always airsick in the airplanes but I would go up anyhow since I could get extra flight pay. I had about 58 hours in the air. God protected me in some dangerous situations. One time a bomber airplane crashed near where I was standing and as I fell to the ground, pieces of plane were falling all around me. Another time, a propeller of the airplane got turned on just as I was walking beside the body of the plane and it missed me by inches.

I got transferred from a squadron to another for some unknown reason and a few weeks later, that squadron airplane with its crew perished in the Pacific Ocean.

I studied for a higher rank and became a 2nd Class Petty Officer which got me a little more pay and another stripe on my uniform. I was stationed in San Diego for eight months.

A memorable experience I had in the Navy was when I was in the States and had a short liberty leave and came on a train to Chicago and went directly on that Sunday to the Assyrian Church my mother was attending. I slipped in next to her as the congregation was singing and when she saw me next to her she almost screamed.

In the early spring on 1945, I was assigned to a ship that would be sailing to the Asiatic Waters as we were closing in on the Japanese. This ship was a Sea Plane Tender loaded with gasoline, oil, and other supplies for the seaplanes. I was in charge of all the instrument supplies.

This ship, the USS Gardener's Bay, sailed from the West Coast and I was very seasick for all the six days that it took to get to the Hawaiian Islands. For some unexpected reason I was dropped off in Hawaii instead of staying on the ship. The commanding officer of the ship had learned about my condition and had mercifully dropped me off on land. They probably did not think I would function too well in that condition in the war zone.

I was stationed at Kaneoe Bay Naval Air Station on the island of Oahu from April through December of 1945. The war with Japan ended in August when they surrendered. I had a wonderful fellowship time with the Navigators that met in Honolulu for Bible studies.

I was shipped back to the West Coast and was very blessed to see the Golden Gate Bridge in San Francisco and was honorably discharged from the Navy after 33 months of service on December 28, 1945.

During the months before my discharge from the Navy, I was asking the Lord what He wanted me to do in my civilian life. I was willing to try to get a job at any airport to work as an aviation mechanic. But the Lord wanted me to be in full time service for Him. God indicated to me that I was to continue witnessing and teaching His Word as I had been doing all along in the Navy. I told the Lord that I was willing to do this if He would help me get trained.

I began the new year of 1946 living with my parents and siblings on Hudson Avenue. While applying to go to a bible college, I enrolled in the night school classes at Moody Bible Institute. At the same time I joined the Moody Memorial Church where Dr. Ironside was the pastor and I got baptized.

I became active in the Moody Church, serving as a Sunday School teacher in the Junior Department, assisting the Youth Pastor, president of the Christian Companionship Club, announcer for the Sunday Youth on the March radio broadcast, as well as other responsibilities such as ministering at the Cook County Jail and the Pacific Garden Mission.

I chose to be enrolled as a student at the Northern Baptist Theological Seminary in Chicago and began my studies for the 5 year course in September 1946.

Two months later, at the C.C.C. Halloween party, I met the girl I was to marry. Burnell Hanson was a nurse at the Augustana Hospital and had seen me at the Moody Church. I learned that she had gotten saved about the same time as I did. I was impressed by her willingness to attend the Wednesday night prayer meeting at the church.

On my birthday, November 29, 1946, I told Burnell for the first time that I loved her and I kissed her. She told me that she loved me too.

I visited her parents, Elmer and Lillian Hanson, in her home town of Wakefield, Michigan in the Upper Peninsula for Christmas. Later, I asked her parents if I could get engaged to their daughter and they said "yes." Burnell also said "yes" and I gave her an engagement ring on March 5, 1947.

We set the date for our wedding for June 12, 1948. Burnell continued working as a Registered Nurse as Supervisor of a floor at Augustana Hospital and I continued my theological studies.

Our wedding took place as planned in Wakefield in her parent's church, Immanuel Lutheran. My mother, brother Ben (best man) and sister Bertha attended the wedding.

We went on a ten day honeymoon to mid-western Canada after stopping for our first night in Ante's Cabins in Ashland, Wisconsin.

I had ordered a new Chevrolet car from Burnell's father who had a Chevrolet garage dealership, but the car did not arrive for our trip. So, her dad let us use his car as we traveled to Winnipeg, Manitoba, Red River Valley and stops in Minnesota, Duluth and Bemidji. When we got back to Wakefield, our brand new green Chevrolet was waiting for us for $1200.

Dr. Ironside gave me some of his books as a wedding gift. I found a hard-to-get apartment for us with a newspaper ad when Burnell was in the U.P. getting ready for the wedding. It was on the north side of Chicago, 2151 Windsor Avenue (near Montrose and Lincoln Avenue). We were on the second floor of the apartment overlooking a nice alley. I don't remember how we furnished it, but I remember buying a few things.

Burnell got a job in 1949 as a visiting nurse as I continued my studies. By my taking extra courses and going to summer school, I was able to graduate in four years instead of five with a Bachelor of Theology Degree (Th.B) in May of 1950.

As the cost of my education was covered by the G.I. Bill, I enrolled at Northwestern University in Evanston, Illinois Graduate School to work on my Master's Degree in Speech. During that summer of 1950, I was called through the Moody Bible Institute placement to help in the youth work and assist the pastor in the Baptist Church in Okemos, Michigan. It was a blessed experience for us working with Pastor Holman Johnson. We lived with Mr. & Mrs. Cook.

We went back to Chicago to begin my studies at Northwestern University, which was a tremendous challenge for me to get my Master's Degree in the one year that I could attend. This was in the fall of 1950 and also when we learned that Burnell was pregnant.

As I was studying and commuting to N.U. in Evanston, Burnell continued her nursing job until the end of March and Burnell Joy was born on April 7, 1951 in the Augustana Hospital.

While I was a student in Seminary and in the Graduate School, I learned to be a Gospel Magician. I learned from one of my seminary professors, Dr. Warren Filkin from whom I purchased some of the magic tricks. I was asked to do my Gospel magic programs in churches, youth banquets and community programs.

While living in Chicago, we would have our invited guests talk on our tape recorder which was a brand new thing then.

Every summer we would visit Burnell's parents in Wakefield, 400 miles from Chicago.

As I was nearing the end of my graduate studies, I received a call from the Okemos Baptist Church to come as the Assistant Pastor of the church. After praying about it, we accepted the call.

I graduated from Northwestern University at the end of May 1951 with a grateful heart for receiving my M.A. degree in one year. I asked to be excused from the graduation exercise so we could move to Okemos the first week in June.

Some of the Okemos church members came with a truck and moved us to Okemos in an upstairs apartment on Hamilton Road. We began our ministry working with the young people with a salary of $25.00 per week.

We joined the Baptist Church and three months later I was ordained on September 20, 1951. Franklin Logsdon, pastor of Moody Church came to be the speaker at my ordination service. My mother and sister also attended.

That fall, Pastor Johnson resigned to work in Barakel Christian Camp and I was called to be the pastor of the church. We moved into the parsonage and I had my office in the parsonage.

During these years in Okemos, God gave us three sons: John Hanson, November 1, 1952, Paul Robert, June 6, 1954, and David James, May 7, 1956. We have historical tapes of our lives from 1948-1950. I began a written journal of my life and experiences in 1981 and have kept it current. We also have video tapes of our family life beginning in 1984.

My mother went to be with the Lord on October 9, 1956. She died of leukemia at the age of 60. I thank God for a Christian mother who first showed me the way of salvation.

We resigned as pastor of the Okemos church in August 1957 and entered into the work of helping other churches raise funds for their new church buildings through the Chase Associates, a Fund Raising Organization with headquarters in Kirkwood, New Jersey. A year and a half later we were called to the First Baptist Church of Millington in February of 1959.

In Millington, we labored for 4 ½ years in the Church and Community, seeking to win souls to Christ and to strengthen the Christians in their faith; at the same time having our own souls strengthened and our lives enriched.

I joined Rotary on January of 1963 and enjoyed the fellowship of the fine men along with the fun, food, and faith we could share together.

Early in 1963, we felt that God was indicating to us that we had completed the work we were to do in Millington and when the pulpit committee from the First Baptist Church of Three Rivers dropped in on us one Sunday in April, we saw that God was opening another area of service for us.

We were invited to visit in Three Rivers where I was the guest speaker on May 19th and after another meeting with the pulpit committee, we consented to have our name presented to the Church for consideration as candidate for the pastorate there.

The Church voted unanimously on June 7th to call us as the pastor and we accepted the call on the 9th, and with a heavy heart presented our resignation to our Millington congregation.

We moved to Three Rivers into a beautifully remodeled parsonage on August 6th and began our new ministry on the Sunday of August 11th.

On January 9, 1964, I was received as a member of the Three Rivers Rotary Club to again enjoy the fun, food, and faith with my fellow Rotarians.

My father passed away July 22, 1967 at the age of approximately 83. Burnell's father died on April 17, 1969 at age 73. Earlier that month I had a heart attack and recovered miraculously.

I ministered as pastor of the First Baptist Church for almost 12 years and then resigned on June 30, 1975 to begin a new ministry, the newly formed Three Rivers Christian Fellowship.

Our children have all graduated from college and are married and living in Three Rivers. Paul to Bonnie Bowker of Chicago, November 22, 1974, Joy to Mark Kleczynski of Battle Creek, June 21, 1975. David to Cathy Green of Three Rivers, May 17, 1980, Johnny to Bobbye Hargis of Davison, June 14, 1980.

As of April 7, 1980, we have three grandchildren, Hannah Joy (6/9/78) & Jonathan David Booko (4/7/80), and Matthew Mark Kleczynski (3/8/79).

Our son, Paul, was ordained to the full time Gospel ministry on November 12, 1978 and serves as co-pastor with me.

After meeting in the Andrews Elementary School building for almost four years, we built a new building on 10 acres of land on 6th Avenue. It was completed in 5 months and our first service was held in it on October 28, 1979.

We also had purchased a new house (2 years old) in September 1975 on 200 S. Hooker Avenue.

Burnell and I were given a trip to Israel by the church for November 20-30, 1978. We went to Hawaii for a vacation in January 1980 (two beautiful weeks). While in Jerusalem, I prayed over an outstanding bible teacher, Derek Prince.

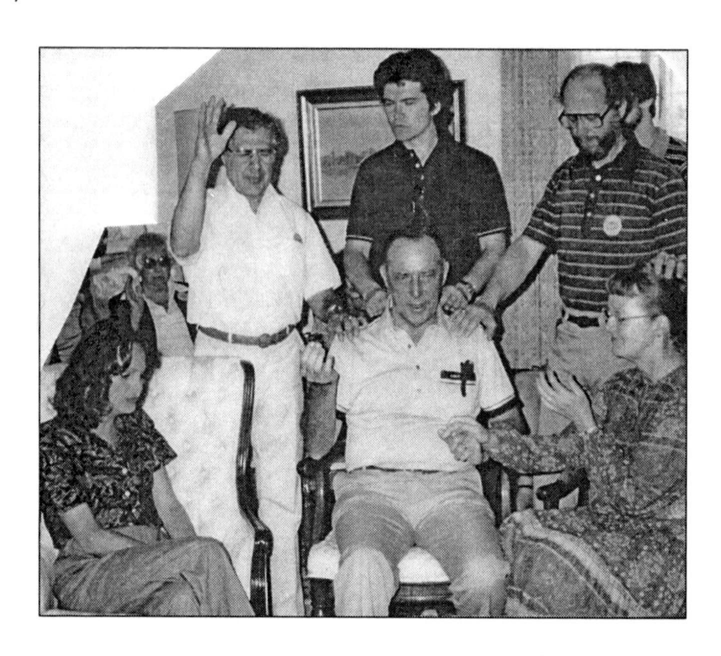

We are in a covenant relationship with other churches in our area (Marcellus, Kalamazoo, Agape, Kalamazoo New Covenant, Battle Creek). I look to Dan Wolfe for counsel and covering. He is the senior elder in the Agape Christian Fellowship.

On October 22, 1981, after prayer and counsel with Dan Wolfe, a change was made regarding Paul and my positions in the Three Rivers Christian Fellowship. Both of us got a promotion. Paul became the presiding elder of the Fellowship and I was considered the senior co-elder and godly advisor to Paul. My Fatherhood was to go beyond our local Fellowship as I would be available to share from my experience and teach in other churches.

On October 19, 1982, Dan Wolfe and I met with Erik Krueger and was given the ministry of building alliances of friendship with other Pastors, Churches, and Organizations. I am to be the Intercessors for America Representative in the North Central Region, also the Representative for the National Integrity Forum for the North Central Region and Paul became senior pastor.

As of October 12, 1982, two more grandchildren have been added, bringing the total to five. Grace Anna Kleczynski (5/18/82), and John Hargis Booko (10/12/82).

April 22 – May 15, 1982, Burnell and I visit Israel and Rome. Two weeks in Jerusalem.

Began learning to play the saxophone the church gave me for my birthday, January 1983.

Went to Israel with Mark Siljander in May 1983, and met Prime Minister Menachim Begin.

Burnell and I went to Northern Ireland to the International Intercessors Conference November 1984. From there we spent a week in London where I ministered to a group of Arabs and Assyrians.

Began meeting with other pastors in Three Rivers for monthly intercessory praying in January 1985.

Visited Egypt and South Africa with Mark Siljander. I prayed with President Hosni Mubarak April 1985.

On March 1, 1986 our 12th grandchild was born, Luke John Booko Kleczynski. (Daniel Booko 10/17/83, Chrystal Booko 10/24/83. Gloria Kleczynski 6/29/84, Jordan Booko 8/28/85, James David Booko 2/5/86, Joseph Booko 2/6/86) (8 boys and 4 girls).

The new church building addition construction began in December 1986. the church is debt free as we continue construction.

On July 13, 1987, our 13th grandchild was born, Benjamin Joseph Booko. (Now 9 grandsons).

Visited the United Nations in New York City as the guest of our U.S. Delegate, Mark Siljander, November 16-20 1987. I met a number of Ambassadors and delegates from many nations as I had lunch with them and attended receptions. Burnell attended the receptions with us.

In 1987, our granddaughter, Chrystal Booko set the world's record as the youngest barefoot water skier.

In January 1988, we began attending the Christian Retreat in Bradenton, Florida

With Gerald Derstine and to represent Intercessors for America there for about two weeks.

We began receiving our Social Security benefits in March 1988.

Dedication and Open House for our new TRCF Center addition of 3500 sq. ft. office and education wing, April 24, 1988. Debt free! Also have my office there for the first time with Paul.

April 29, 1988, attended Washington for Jesus at the Capitol with about 200,000 attendance.

June 30, 1988, our granddaughter, Grace Kleczynski, was struck by a car on N. Main Street as she was crossing the street. She was flown by helicopter to Bronson Hospital where she almost died three times. Intercessory prayer was made by many and God miraculously healed her after she was unconscious for 12 days. She came home from the hospital on July 9th with her leg and arm in casts.

Burnell's mother, Lillian Hanson, passed away to heaven on September 26, 1988.

On November 15-29, we led a group of 15 with Dan and Janice Wolfe to Jerusalem. Burnell and I remained there until December 11.

April 9, 1989 began two Sunday morning services, 9 and 11 am.

Record flooding in Three Rivers June 3, 1989. 11.8 ft.

On February 22, 1990, I spoke on the subject of Assyria and Assyrians for the first time at Christian Retreat.

Easter 1990, record church attendance: 472.

April 28, 1990, Pro-Life rally in Washington D.C. with Mark and Nancy Siljander, with over 350,000 in attendance.

Another grandchild born on May 21, 1990 to Johnny and Bobbye, Abigail Anna Sue Quita Booko. Now a total of 14 grandchildren: 9 boys, 5 girls.

Burnell's sister, Lorrie, passed away to heaven on November 25, 1990.

Presently my ministry has been devoted mostly to the local church (about 80%), and the rest to trans-local. I am doing a lot of administrative work in the church as I co-pastor with Paul and am a pastor to him. I also am the Moderator for our Southwest Michigan Presbytery. Burnell and I are Board Members for Blossoming Rose and we lead the intercessors prayer meeting at the annual symposium.

February 22, 1991, Mike Wourms encouraged me to have a book published about Assyria and he would help in the writing and printing of it.

March 18, 1991, Dave and Cathy Booko divorce papers signed.

March 31, 1991, Easter. Record attendance of 546 (235 at 9 am., 311 at 11 am.).

May 20, 1991, Bi-inguinal hernia surgery.

September 20, 1991, My 40th anniversary of my ordination to the ministry.

April 18, 1992, Three Easter services with record attendance of 654.

July 22, 1992, I announced to the church my change of ministry at the end of this year from local pastoral to full-time Trans-Local Ministry.

August 31, 1992 – My book, "Assyria – The Forgotten Nation in Prophecy" was published and the first printing of 2,000 copies arrived.

It is a remarkable miracle - To God be the Glory!

First read Isaiah 19:23-25

Israeli Prime Minister Menachem Begin

In that day there will be a highway from Egypt to Assyria, and the Assyrian will come into Egypt, and the Egyptian into Assyria, and the Egyptians will worship with the Assyrians. In that day Israel will be the third with Egypt and Assyria, a blessing in the midst of the earth, whom the Lord of hosts has blessed, saying, 'Blessed be Egypt my people, and Assyria the work of my hands, and Israel my heritage.'

ISAIAH 19:23-25 (RSV)

Egyptian President Hosni Mubarak

Rev. John Booko, an Assyrian American pastor from Three Rivers, Michigan, was invited and his trip was paid for by Israel and Egypt to come to their countries with his U.S. Congressman, Mark Siljander.

In Israel, he was asked by officials to pray at the Holocaust Museum, the Paratroopers Memorial, and by the U.S. and Israeli flags, after he had spoken to Menachem Begin.

In Egypt, he was permitted by President Mubarak to pray for him and his country, after which the president thanked him and gave him a hug.

In the light of Isaiah 19:23-25, when God prophesies that the three nations in the endtime will be Egypt, Assyria, and Israel, *a blessing in the midst of the earth,* God made John Booko, the Assyrian, a small sign of the future fulfillment of this prophecy, as he represented Assyria. Assyria will be *the work of God's hand* at the time of the second coming of our Lord Jesus Christ.

ASSYRIAN MINISTRY

Rev.John Booko, Assyrian/American author of *"Assyria-The Forgotten Nation* In Prophecy" and "The Assyrian Revelation"
200 S. Hooker Ave., Three Rivers, MI 49093; Ph.269/279-2672
e-mail: revbooko@hotmail.com web:www.assyria.freeservers.com

November 6, 1992 – Video taped five segments of my book for Assyrian TV broadcasts.

November 21, 1992 – My Retirement Honors Banquet with 180 in attendance. Hannah singing to me.

November 29, 1992 - Reception for my retirement from the local pastorate and my 70th birthday.

December 31, 1992 – Moved my church office into my home office to begin my Trans-local Ministry.

1993 – My book takes me all over the country on speaking engagements; especially Virginia in June and California in August. Spoke on 31 occasions and sold over 1,000 copies of book.

September 22, 1993 – Received a second printing of my book; 3,000 copies.

September 26, 1993 – Evangelist Jack Van Impe wants to order 5,000 copies of my book in 1994.

December 14, 1993 – Paid $960 for the translation and printing of my book into the Malayan language of India, Kerala Province to be given to the pastors and leaders under K.C. George.

1994

January 8 – Donated my library books to Indiana Christian University, South Bend, Indiana

May 10 – Dr. Jack Van Impe sent out a promotional letter for my book to 207,000 homes in U.S. and Canada.

December 26 – Departure from Chicago for overseas ministry in Kerala, India and Tokyo, Japan.

1995

January 1-10 - India ministry with Burnell in Triviadrum, Mallappally, Kottayam (spoke to 5,000), Chengannur.

January 11-19 – In Japan with Kenny and Lila Joseph. Spoke in their church. In Shizuoka (about 60 miles south of Tokyo) we felt the earthquake in Kobe and Osaka.

(Speaking all over the country on the subject of my book. See the enclosed itinerary to 8/96.) (Sold over 8,000 copies of my book).

June 24,25 – Celebration of TRCF 20th anniversary with a portrait of Burnell and me unveiled and placed in the Center.

July 22 - I was spared a serious injury when I dove off the trampoline into the swimming pool at Paul's place.

1996

February 27 – Spoke at the International Prophecy Conference in Tampa, Florida on Assyria.

August 3 – David and Kimberly were married in Saugatuck, Michigan.

September 19-22 – Representing Intercessors for America as missionaries to USA at the World Congress Missionary Conference at Fort Wayne, Indiana, Calvary Temple.

1997

April 1 – Begin Pastoral governing with Paul for one year in absence of the elders.

July 3- Received the Rotary Paul Harris award.

August 29 – Attended the Assyrian American National Federation Convention in Dearborn, Michigan and spoke to about 150 delegates.

September 7 – Brenin Ellyse Booko, born to David and Kim.

December 2 – Bradley Stuart prayer prophecies; Burnell a faithful servant and motherhood for younger women. John a father to Joshuas, Elishas and Timothys.

1998

May 26 – Took out a $500,000 life insurance policy on us to create a million dollar portfolio for our heirs. (Subtract the pre-inheritance monies already given, including $2,000 for each of the grandchildren's education at High School graduation.) ($166,000.)

June – Our Golden Wedding Anniversary banquet with relatives and friends outside of church. (See videos of the event) Saturday 6th.

July 13 – August 13 – Celebration of our 50th wedding anniversary with ministry on the 12th.

August 26 – Received the 4th edition of my book (2,128) for a total of 12,128 books.

September 7 – Breakfast at the Washington DC Congressional Dining Room

December 25 – Gave each of our children $25,000 in stocks as pre-inheritance gift.

1999

January 28 – Three weeks in Arizona visiting Ben and Sharon in Scottsdale,

January 28 Pastors/Leaders Conference in Phoenix, Dorene Falk in Sedona, Grand Canyon, Assyrian Church in Phoenix.

March 12 – Signed papers for the exchange of our TRCF building for the old High School. Paid $1.00 for the school and received $700,000 for our property.

Burnell and David continue to learn the Assyrian language on Wednesdays at lunch at David's office.

May 16 – Attended the Millington Baptist Church pastors and people's reunion.

June 12 – Began working on my second book "The Assyrian Revelation."

August 13 – Our high school building renovation begins.

November 22 – Paul and Bonnie's 25th wedding anniversary. Gave them 100 oz. of silver.

2000

January 22 – The carbon monoxide detector sounded at 11:30 pm. and saved our lives as the furnace vent was blocked.

March – Matthew and Grace rededicated and revived lives for the Lord.

March 17-19 – Midwest Prophecy Conference speaker in Omaha, Nebraska.

May 7- Last Sunday at TRCF Center on 6th Avenue.

May 14 – First service in our new building on 207 E. Michigan Avenue. Meeting in the gym. New name for the church "Riverside Church."

May 25 – Matthew tells us that he is called of God into full-time ministry.

July 3 – Finished writing my second book. It took 418 hours for about 400 pages.

October 17 – Spoke at Northern Baptist Seminary Chapel on Assyria.

2001

March 31 – Attended the Homecoming for the Three Rivers Baptist Church.

May 28 – Announcement of our giving to each of our grandchildren for their High School graduation a $2,000 scholarship gift.

July 18 – Allendale, Michigan TCT TV interview about my book.

September 20 – My 50th anniversary of my ordination. The church presenting me with a plaque, money, cards and refreshments of October 10th service.

October 27 – Receiving the first shipment of my second book "The Assyrian Revelation" on the total of 1,948.

October 30 – In Washington DC, meeting with the Iraqi ambassador, Akram Al-Douri, with Mark Siljander and closing the meeting with a prayer.

December 1 – Received 50 copies of the Russian translation of my first book.

2002

January 26 – Boarded the cruise ship for a week with 20 other Bookos until February 2. I was the chaplain on the ship and conducted the Sunday morning service.

April 2- Met with Mar Dinka IV in Morton Grove, Illinois for over an hour and gave him my two books.

April 14 – Began video taping the reading of my 2nd book for Assyrian TV for a total of 7 and ½ hours. Finished on the 27th.

July 3-7 – Burnell's Wakefield High School reunion in Ironwood, Michigan.

August 30,31 – Attended the Assyrian National Convention in Detroit and gave a lecture.

September 7,8 – Missionary Conference at New Hope Christian Center in Waterloo, Indiana representing our Assyrian Ministry.

October 23 – Speaking in Herndon, Virginia at Beacon Hill Baptist Church and asking all to stand and life hands to pray for the capture of sniper. They were caught that night.

November 29 – My 80th birthday celebration by the family and the church on December 1.

2003

April 20 – Easter services at the new High School with attendance of 1153.

June 9 – My first book translated and printed in the Chichewa language of Malawi, Central Africa. 1000 books which can be read in five African countries.

June 12 – Celebrating our 55th wedding anniversary at Rotary Club at Scidmore park, Nottawa ice cream, library and movie.

June 26- 30 – New York City tour with seniors and staying at the Waldorf Astoria Hotel.

July 20 – Speaking at Central Church of the Nazarene with Johnny and Bobbye's family.

July 29 – Adjusted our life insurance to $250,000.

August 20 – Front page of the Three Rivers Commercial features our 40 years of ministry in Three Rivers.

October 12 – Began our first Sunday church monthly service at Bickford Adult Care with attendance of 12.

November 5 – Church celebration of Paul's 25th anniversary as pastor.

November 28 – Pontiac Silver Dome football game with Three Rivers High School winning the State Championship with David making 3 touchdowns.

December 21- 30 – Cancun, Mexico trip with the whole family of 25 for Christmas present. A beautiful Christmas service.

December 28 – Preaching in the Presbyterian Church in Cancun.

2004

January 10 – Chicago bus trip to see Lion King and dinner.

February 10 – Donated the portable baptistery to Riverside Church.

February 14 – My fall off my office chair and desk onto the floor on my side and back with no injury.

March 7 – Seeing Mel Gibson's "The Passion of the Christ" with church taking all of the theater seating.

March 22 – My three nieces, Amber, Lisa, and Britt meeting with their father, my brother George at his apartment.

June – Four of our grandsons graduating from high school.

June 12 – Celebrating our 56th wedding anniversary.

June 19 – My #1 book arrived, translated in the Malawi language of Chichewa.

July 30 – Church Family Camp at Oakhill, Angola, Indiana to August 1.

August 17 – Two of our grandchildren reciting the Lord's Prayer in the Assyrian language.

September 26 – One year anniversary of holding monthly Sunday services at the Bickford Adult Foster Care.

October 10 – Began my short wave radio broadcast on WINB, every Sunday evening, 7:45 – 8:15 pm with audio tapes.

October 13 – Began the Golden Agers Bible Study in our home on the second and fourth Wednesdays of each month.

October 31 – Lectured at the Congregation of Moses Synagogue in Kalamazoo.

November 4 – Tom Booko's Jewish wife, received Christ as her Savior.

November 29 – My 82nd birthday celebration.

December 17-24 – Travel to Maya Riviera, Mexico at Reef Coco Beach with David and his family and Johnny, Bobbye, and Abbye.

Passing our 200 booklets in Spanish and 6 New Testaments.

December 31 - New Year's Eve fellowship with Paul and Bonnie.

2005

January 12 – Burnell's birthday 81st celebration including going to Miller Auditorium in Kalamazoo to see the musical "42nd Street."

January 15 – Speaking at the Sabbath Church of God in Mishawaka, Indiana.

February 13 – Our friend Pansy Lam got baptized today.

March 3 – At Rotary Club, I won the raffle twice and again on 17th.

April 4 – Received my first letter from my short wave radio broadcast from Nigeria.

April 9 – Began giving financial support to Henri Ologoudo of Benin, Africa for the founding of a new church named after us (The Church of Booko Africa).

April 10 – The Assyrian Social Club of Chicago had a banquet for my honor.

May 21 – Joy healed of her bone spur after 2 years.

May 27 – Sent 50 tapes of my Assyria messages to Assyrian Universal Alliance.

June 19-21 – Attended the Rotary International Convention in Chicago.

June 28 – Submitted my first article for the Three Rivers Commercial newspaper.

July 9-11 – Ministry in Kalkaska, Michigan.

August 27 – Baptized Samuel Turdo in Joe's swimming pool in Schaumburg, Illinois.

September 1 – Yacoub Yacoub, with wife Maria and cousin Narsi visiting us from Toronto.

September 7 – Began bowling on Seniors Bowling League every Wednesday.

September 30 – One year of broadcasting Assyrian Ministry every Sunday on short wave radio.

October 11-13 – Representing Intercessors for America at Mission America Coalition in Rosemont, Illinois.

November 29 – A great time of celebrating my 83rd birthday.

December 12 – Burnell's diagnosis by Dr. Mutnal of Kerotosis on her face and cancer mole.

December 16 – Meeting with Board of Elders of our church to have Denny and Jerry included on the Elder's Board with Paul.

December 22 – Burnell's MRI report of severe osteo-arthritis in her left hip.

December 24- Christmas Eve Service attended by my 3 bowling partners from Constantine.

December 29 – The bursting of the bursitis of my knee from my fall in bowling.

December 31 – Burnell and me looking over the outstanding events of 2005 and giving thanks and praises to our Lord and trusting Him in hope for the New Year.

2006

January 12 – We retired from Blossoming Rose Board after serving for 20 years.

January 21 – Burnell's cancer by her lip removed and was benign.

February 19 – Grandson Benjamin got baptized in church today.

February 20 – Dr. Hopkins, neuro-surgeon at Borgess said Burnell's hip is ok but her spine is sending pain to her hip. He prescribed physical therapy.

April 16 – A blessed Easter with all the family, except Grace, were together for dinner.

April 16 – Church attendance for the 3 services was about 1300.

April 27–29 – We attended the "Life Changers Conference in Mt. Pleasant, Michigan.

April 30 – Spoke at Central Michigan Christian Church in Mt. Pleasant.

May 3 – Burnell began chiropractic treatments with Dr. Dana Higley.

May 14 – Johnny gave a Mother's Day gift of painting our house.

June 5 – We bought 10 cemetery lots at Riverside Cemetery for our family.

June 10 – Booko families reunion at Twin Lakes, Palatine, Illinois. All of us except Daniel and Grace were there about 22 other Bookos from Illinois and Scottsdale, AR (Ben and Sharon). Mary David, Peter and Pat David were there. About 45 in attendance. We all got Booko reunion shirts.

June 26 – We sowed extra giving to Intercessors for America and World Missionary Press for spiritual warfare.

July 2 – Preached on "Heaven" in our church with Q & A time.

July 4 – Chrystal got engaged to Jeff.

July 5-7 – An attack of Gout on my left 4th toe was healed.

July 8 – Our house got painted.

July 24 – We got the idea to give each of our four children another pre-inheritance gift for Christmas of $50,000 and to give it to them on Thanksgiving Day. David will arrange for the distribution.

August 9 – David Jr. finished painting our garage in 24 hours.

August 26 – Jonathan and Karla wedding. I offered a patriarchal prayer.

September 1 – Gave a lecture at the Assyrian National Convention in Schaumberg, Illinois.

September 11 – At the Chamber of Commerce Get Together, I won the top prize of six Broadway plays at Miller Auditorium at WMU in Kalamazoo.

September 13 – At our son David's Ameriprise luncheon at the Black Swan Inn in Portage, I won the drawing for a Coach Ken Carter basketball.

September 15 – Dan Delaney in our Wednesday Bible Study had a heart attack and was healed with the laying on of hands and drove home.

October 7 – Our grandson, David, made 6 touchdowns for Hope College and won against Alma the favored school.

October 15 – At church, I did the message on a tic/tac and coke bottle. Also, for two Sundays answering written questions by the members hosted by Paul.

October 18 – William Mikhail in California finished translating my first book into the Arabic language.

October 20 – Met General Georges Sada, author of the book "Saddam's Secrets" in the Delta Plex in Grandville, Michigan. We exchanged books.

October 22 – Burnell got dizzy in the bathroom and fell backwards into the tub and slammed her head without breaking any bones or head concussion. A miracle.

October 24 – We decided on having a total knee replacement on Burnell's knee.

November 14 – Sending out letters to all the Booko families for donations to the "Booko Church of Africa" to give Christmas presents to orphans.

November 23 – Our children received their pre-inheritance money totaling $200,000. It went into their individual accounts with Ameriprise by David.

November 28 – I tripped and fell face first in the garage as I was holding three bags of clothes to give to the Free Store. The bags cushioned my face.

December 10 – I was made the co-president with Paul for the Christ Training Center (Bible College) at Riverside Church to begin in January 2007.

December 12 – The Bookos sent $1,000 to the orphans at the Booko Church in Benin, W. Africa, village of Denou.

December 13 – Burnell has her total knee surgery replacement on her left knee at Bronson Hospital by Dr. Bruce Rowe.

December 16 – Burnell came home to do her own physical therapy with my help.

December 21 – Burnell got out of bed and back in by herself at 7:30 am.

December 31 – Burnell walking some without her walker or wheel chair. Taking less pain pills and swollen leg reducing. Praise the Lord!

2007

January 1 – Burnell and I going over the outstanding experiences of 2006 and giving praise to our Lord.

January 6 – Received a letter from a pastor in Nigeria, Africa who heard my short wave radio broadcast and commended me for it.

January 23 – Spoke at the Immaculate Conception Catholic Church to the Daughters of Mary about Assyria and Assyrians.

February 1 – Dr. Mutnal said Burnell is in depression and should not sleep so much, but to exercise more.

February 17 – Finished arranging 13 thirty minute audio tapes for the WINB short wave station and signed up for another weekly broadcast on the 21st to be heard on Sunday mornings 6:30 am. Called "Booko Bible Teaching."

February 22 – Began writing and assembling materials for my new book on "No Prayer Power." Doing this to war against Satan's attacks on us.

March 7 – Took Burnell to the Three Rivers Hospital. Her tests showed she had pneumonia, potassium deficiency and bladder infection. Out in a week.

April 7 – Henri of Benin, W. Africa had me speak to his church congregation on the phone for five minutes as he translated it in French.

April 25 – Began typing on the computer the pages for my book.

May 4 – At the church banquet, Burnell choked on a piece of steak and had to have Heimlich Maneuver to get it to come out in about 5 minutes just before the paramedics from the fire department came. She had sore ribs for about a week.

May 11 – Burnell tripped and fell forward on the left side of her face in the back yard on the cement walk. She was bleeding, bent her glasses, big bump on her eyebrow and a very black eye.

June 3 – My website was upgraded to 16 pages by Mark Kleczynski.

June 12 – For our 59th wedding anniversary we bought a 42 inch plasma TV.

June 13 – Burnell had her cataract surgery on her right eye. Left eye July 11.

June 16 – Hannah and Allen Clark got engaged today with an engagement ring.

July 1 – I preached at Riverside Church on Noah and the Ark and some people came into the ark of salvation at the invitation. A love offering was taken for us.

July 26 – Mailed the pages of my prayer messages for my book to Mike Wourms of Christian Services Network for him to put it together for print.

August 4 – Matthew wants to be in ministry full time as a healing evangelist.

August 18 – Mark, Joy, and Matthew took me to Binder Park Zoo in Battle Creek and I fed the giraffes.

September 16 – We are counter attacking Satan again for trying to harm us in the accident of us slipping and falling in the bath tub. We gave an extra $1,000 for the work of the Lord.

September 24 – Received analysis of my book from Mike Wourms saying my book on prayer could be a powerful blessing to the body of Christ. It could be about 200 pages and cost about $8100 for 500 copies.

November 29 – On my 85th birthday I am having Caleb in the Bible as my hero

December 2 – The church Imagine campaign raised $1.5 million for 3 years. Our pledge was $34,500.

December 5 – The physician's assistant for Dr. Green thinks Burnell's fatigue problem is due to her lung disorder in not getting enough oxygen. She was put on oxygen 24/7 on December 26.

December 24 – Gloria received her engagement ring from Scott Lammon.

December 31 – Burnell and I went over the 2007 outstanding experiences in my journal and together we thanked the Lord and praised Him for bringing us through victoriously. We toasted the New Year with champagne.

2008

January 9 – I purchased a tenor sax to play along with my alto sax.

January 16 – Mark Siljander was all over the news about being indicted for his association with a Muslim group that was being investigated by the CIA.

February 16 – Dr. Sargon Dadesho promoted my Assyrian Revelation book on his satellite TV that brought me a lot of calls to buy my book.

March 4 – Dr. Glendora Greene (family physician) asked what the secret of our happy marriage was. I said our praying together and doing I Corinthians 13 Love Chapter.

March 9 – Grandson David fell through the ice in Lake Michigan at Holland into 20 feet of icy water and pulled himself up safely.

March 18- Sold my Assyrian library of 8 boxes to the Ashurbanipal Library in Chicago for $1,000.

March 29 – Received a DVD of the Booko Church in Benin, West Africa.

April 18 – Felt the earthquake at 5:30 am.

May 4 – Went to Hope College to see David graduate.

May 15 – Being a caretaker for Burnell has made me a better man.

May 27 – Our last Golden Agers Bible study.

June 12 – Our 60th wedding anniversary! Praise God!

June 24 – Mailed a Gospel letter to Sezin Sengil in Ankara, Turkey.

June 29 – Riverside Bible Institute first graduation of 19 students.

July 5 – At 11 pm., I fell downstairs in the dark into the family room from the kitchen. I slammed on my right side and head on the floor. I was dazed as Burnell came to me but no broken bones. The next day I preached on "Hell, No."

July 7 – Dr. Ed Griffin x-rayed my left knee and said it was osteoarthritis.

July 8 – Rick Cordes, staff writer for the Three Rivers Commercial, interviewed us and did a Community Profile page on us for the 11th.

August 18 – Recorded another ½ hour of jokes on the other side of 7/85 audio tape.

August 29 – Went to be with brother Joe to attend Bet-Nahrain Assyrian Convention in Rosemont, Illinois. I set up a table with my books and literature and spoke at a Seminar on the 30th.

September 3 – Burnell got back on Zoloft for her depression.

September 5 – Sent my brother George a letter with my "Hell" tract with a warning along my tract on "Heaven" with the note "Happy Birthday."

September 6 – Gloria and Scott Lammon wedding in Mendon. I prayed a blessing over them in the ceremony.

September 19 – I asked God about Burnell this morning. He told me she is under His care and she will come through victoriously.

September 29 – My book manuscript arrived today.

October 3 – Received $1,000,000 Iraqi Diners for $949 US.

October 4 – We began attending our Saturday night church services 6:00 pm.

October 11 – Burnell told Paul and Bonnie her depression is gone on 100 mg Zoloft.

October 20 – Began recording the Psalms from the Message translation.

October 26 – A remarkable experience as I woke up to go to the bathroom and said it was 2:12 am. in my mind and it was.

November 3 – Church attendance for the three services was over 1,000.

November 4 – I bought a new laptop computer for $424 and sold the old one for $150.

November 11 – Burnell had her tooth extracted by Dr. Tom Slack in Kalamazoo and someone from the church paid the cost of $375.

November 20 – Finished the audio tape recording of the Psalms.

December 2 – Sent $1,000 to Booko Church in Benin, West Africa with money collected from the Booko families.

December 5 – Signed us up for Hospice care.

December 17 – Shipment of my 1,000 "No Prayer Power" books arrived today.

December 29 – I signed up with Healthtrac.

December 31 – New Year's Eve. We went over the year's outstanding events in our lives and gave thanks and praised our Lord together. Then toasted the New Year with a glass of wine.

2009

January 3 – Had a book signing at Lowry's book store on my prayer book.
January 5 – Began exercising at Healthtrac each Monday morning.
January 29 – Finished recording "The Bible In Verse" with four 90 minutes tapes.
February 20 – I have a third weekly short wave radio broadcast on Mondays, 8:00-8:30 pm. on WINB.
February 25 – Writing "gleanings" in my little black book (308 to date)
March 6 – Bonnie's mother, Ollie, passed on to heaven.
March 16 – I was featured in the April Intercessors for America newsletter with a portion of my book printed. Also was listed on their internet site to hear my message on Prayer and speaking the Lord's Prayer in Aramaic.
April 12 – Record church attendance of 1610 in three services.
April 27 – Cataract surgery on my right eye
June 13 – Burnell fell in the dining room as she was walking with her cane. I took her the next day to the hospital emergency where the x-ray showed she had fractured her right pelvic bone. She remained in the hospital for 3 weeks coming home on July 3.
July 7 – Christina Koscis volunteered to get Burnell ready for bed and to put her to bed every night of the week to help me out.
August 11 – David said we made 2100% gain on a stock we bought in March.
August 13 – Diane Stauffer said Burnell is in her last days of life on earth.
August 14 – Paul and Bonnie came to videotape Burnell's interview.
August 16 – Booko reunion at Paul and Bonnie's house with Bertha, Joe, Tom and Alyssa, Joy, Johnny, David families.
August 23 – In two months, our Riverside Church baptized 108 believers in the St. Joseph River.
September 5 – Matthew and Lauren wedding in Long Island, New York.

September 22 – We decided to bequeath our life insurance policy to Riverside Church.

October 12 – Scott and Gloria announced her pregnancy. Our first great grandchild to be born in June 2010.

November 23 – Finished mounting about 400 foreign stamps in my stamp albums.

December 4 – Made pre-need funeral arrangements with Hohner Funeral Home with Lee Hohner for Burnell and me.

December 13 – Burnell still sings to me every morning when I come to her "Good morning to you. . .dear sweetheart, I really love you."

December 31 – Got Burnell up and went over our outstanding experiences of 2009, praising the Lord; ate pizza rolls, watched the New Year ball come down and had communion of wine and cracker.

2010

January 7 – Paid Hohner Funeral Home for our Pre-paid funeral contract $12,152.

January 12 – Burnell's 86th birthday (not knowing it would be her last).

January 18 – Sent my stopping terrorists idea to President Barack Obama, editors of Kalamazoo and Three Rivers papers, and e-mail to my list of friends to send it on to others.

January 18 – Baked my first pie in my life; a delicious rhubarb pie.

February 22 – Gave Dan Wolfe copies of my Prayer Book to give to all of the pastors and elders at the Council meeting at Gull Lake.

March 1 – I began to organize my 2350 memory verses into easily remembered and hard.

March 20,21 – Answering Bible questions on the church platform with Paul.

April 4 – Easter church services record attendance of 1730.

April 30 – Burnell, my darling wife, mother, and grandmother, passed on to heaven on Friday night, 11:30 pm. at 86 years of age.

May 7 – Visitation for Burnell at Hohner's. Family gathering 1:00 pm.; public 2-4 and 6-8.

May 8 – Burnell's funeral at Riverside Church, 11:00 am. The family gathered at 10:15 am. with Bertha, Joe, Mary, Grace, Tina. Wonderful sharing at the service by many. Wonderful cemetery committal. Wonderful food and fellowship afterward at the Riverside Concourse.

May 9 – I asked Jesus on Mother's Day to say "Happy Mother's Day" to Burnell and to my mother Phoebe for me.

May 10 – I was blessed by Luke 6:21 "Blessed are you who weep now, for you shall laugh."

May 12 – Organized Burnell's clothes, shoes, purses, jewelry, etc. to give away. Gave the diamond jewelry to Joy, Bonnie, Bobbye and Kim. Received about $2600 for Burnell's memorials to the church besides flowers. I mailed "thank you" notes to all the donors.

June 1 – At 5:30 am. I gave my singleness to God to do whatever He wants.

June 8 – Norah Ruth Lammon, born to Scott and Gloria, my first great grandchild.

June 12 – On our 62nd wedding anniversary, I spoke in Mishawaka, Indiana at the River Valley Community Church prayer meeting.

June 18 – Received the Blossoming Rose Israel Tour brochures for our Israel Tour, February 14-25, 2011.

June 20 – Wonderful Father's Day blessing with many cards and one wrote I was "a father in the likeness of God the Father."

July 7 – Conducted wedding ceremony for Chrystal and Jeff Goes in the Stratosphere's 108th floor in Las Vegas.

July 7 – I sky jumped 855 feet from the Stratosphere along with Chrystal, Jeff, Jordan and Ben. I was featured as the oldest man who ever jumped at 87 years of age.

July 17 – The Three Rivers Commercial newspaper printed the story of my sky jump.

Ready to leap

Rev. John Booko, Founding Pastor of Riverside Church in Three Rivers, before doing the Sky Jump at the Stratosphere Las Vegas. He is the oldest man to have made this leap.

July 23 – My eyes have turned blue after being brown all my life.

July 24,25 – When I preached at our church on Christ's Second Coming, my introduction was the DVD of my sky jump in Las Vegas.

August 12 – Began mentoring men on the 2nd and 4th Thursdays of the month.

August 19-22 – Father and Sons gathering at Michindo.

August 28 – Signed up to serve in Awana children's ministry.

September 7 – Preached at Resurrection Life Church to the 55+ group in Grandville, Michigan.

October 4 – Began serving in Awana each Monday 5:45 – 8:00 pm.

October 19 – Took a five hour driver improvement course.

November 13 – I dreamed that Burnell and I ran into our bedroom and embraced and kissed.

November 22 – Paid $3433 for our cemetery monument in Riverside Cemetery.

November 23 – I joined the Three Rivers Area Faith Community (TRAFC) to represent our church.

December 11 – Turned in my $10,000 cash offering to our church Imagine 2 campaign on my pledge of $100,000 in three years.

December 16 – The couple that asked me to pray for them to have a baby is now going to have one.

December 25 – Christmas Day with Paul, Bonnie, and their family, 10 am.-8pm. with exchanging of gifts.

December 28 – Went with Paul, Bonnie, Hannah, and Daniel to Niles to see Karla's baby, Jack in her womb. Jonathan and her family were there.

December 31 – New Year's Eve party at Paul and Bonnie's, put on by Hannah and Abbye, Johnny, Bobbye and I. Went from 7:30 pm. to 1:30 am. Lots of people were there. I offered prayer and told of the morning miracle at Healthtrac. Later in the evening I sang the Swedish song "Barna Tru" and danced with Bobbye, Bonnie, Hannah and Abbye. Paul prayed us into the New Year.

2011

January 12 – Burnell's 87th birthday in heaven.

January 30 – Record Riverside Church attendance on a non-holiday of 1518.

February 14- Began the 12 day tour of Israel.

February 23 – I baptized my son, Johnny, in the Jordan River, and he and I baptized Bobbye. I was baptized by Johnny.

March 15 – Began the daily one sentence prayer on the Internet You Tube.

March 17 – My great grandson, Jack Frederick, was born.

April 24 – Easter service record attendance of 1791 with 86 decisions for Christ + 20 children.

April 28 – Paul and Bonnie bought the house on Thompson Lane on Portage River.

April 30 – Burnell's one year anniversary in heaven printed in the newspaper.

May 1 – Preached at Cedar Creek Community Church in Sparta, Michigan.

June 7 – Preached at Resurrection Life Church Seniors luncheon.

June 16 – Spoke at the Rotary Club with pictures of my Israel Tour.

June 30 – Founded a Nursing Scholarship Fund in memory of Burnell with the Three Rivers Area Community Foundation.

July 3 – I preached at our church on Psalms 23 and the need to get out of debt.

July 17 – A miracle of my grandson Ben having his lost wallet found on the street and brought to me at church.

July 29-31- Michindo retreat with my sons and grandsons.

August 13 – III John and Nicole wedding in Flint.

August 20 – Luke and Alyssa got engaged and asked me to perform the wedding ceremony in Canada.

August 26 – I wrote up "What I have learned in 60 years of ministry" and "Some of my greatest experiences."

September 30 – My 60th anniversary of my ordination and my church celebrating it on 25th with a love offering and refreshments.

October 1 – Healing meeting with Matthew at our church Saturday prayer meeting.

October 13 – Typed my 700 things I have learned in 60 years of ministry on 37 pages to give to my children.

October 21 – Jonathan and Karla gave me their Parrotlet and cage.

November 13 – Preached in Benton Harbor at the Twin Cities Covenant Community Church.

November 29 – On my 89th birthday, at midnight I sang "Happy Birthday to me" and thanked God for His goodness to me.

November 29 – Miracle avoidance of head-on car crash on snowy highway going to Fisher Lake Inn for birthday dinner with David, Kim and Brenin.

December 25- Christmas Sunday blessings with my family at Paul and Bonnie's new home.

December 31 – New Year's Eve at Jonathan and Karla's home with Paul, Bonnie and Hannah with supper, Jack, movie and midnight love and prayer.

2012

January 16 – I marched in the Martin Luther King Day march from City Hall to our Riverside Church building where we hosted about 75 people.

January 17 – David and I went to the gun shop in Kalamazoo where I purchased a 38 caliber pistol and bullets.

January 19 – My third great grandchild, Dayne Scott, born to Scott and Gloria Lammon.

January 26 – All twelve men that I am mentoring were present and six of them want to be in full-time ministry.

February 7 – The City Commission appointed me to the City Planning Commission.

February 24 – March 3 – Went to the Dominican Republic with forty of our church members as missionaries to help build a church building for a Haitian pastor, Jude. I had a few speaking opportunities.

March 6 – I finished adding to my list of what I have learned in 60 years of ministry for a total of 1001.

April 8 – Easter church attendance of 1800 with 66 salvation decisions.

April 18 – I got a special car parking sign for me to park by the church door.

April 30 – Burnell's second anniversary in heaven.

May 2 – At the Rotary Club high school seniors meeting, I presented Burnell's nursing scholarship of $500 to Lauren Masnari.

May 16 – I discovered the robbery of my silver coin collections while I was away in the Dominican Republic.

June 2 – At out Saturday morning prayer meeting, someone saw Jesus laying hands on each person's head and another saw angels behind us.

June 27 – My credit card was copied and fraudulently used to purchase shoes in Kalamazoo, Corey Bootery totaling $246.56. the thief was caught July 2 and made restitution.

July 1 – On the 37th anniversary of our church, I preached on "What I have learned in over 60 years of ministry."

July 7-13 – Went to Las Vegas with Jonathan and Johnny for Jonathan to enter the Word Series Poker Tournament. He lasted into the second day of play. I had a lot of opportunities for ministry, passing out Gospel tracts and talking to people about the Lord. Especially the cab driver who said he did not want to go to heaven.

August 3 – Began putting "Bibledig" on Youtube with a key Bible verse every day.

August 9 – I had my physical examination by Dr. Curtis Buchheis who told me that I had the body of a 65 year old and my blood was perfect as a 30 year old.

August 15 – I fell down a flight of six stairs from the upstairs bedroom to the kitchen hard floor at 5:00 am. and did not break any bones.

August 17-19- Went to Michindo Christian Camp with all my sons and their sons.

August 30 – At 2:24 am., I guessed the exact time it was when I woke up without looking at the clock.

September 28 – Visited my brother George at the Nursing Center in Glenview, Illinois with my brother Joe. We played cards together and I tried to tell George that Jesus and I love him. He did not want to hear anymore at this time. We keep praying for him.

October 8 – I signed up with Xulon Publishers to publish my 4th book entitled "Be Blessed by My 60 Years of Ministry."

October 20 – Conducted the marriage ceremony for my grandson Luke, marrying Alyssa Demers in Windsor, Canada in MacKenzie Hall.

November 24 – My 90th birthday celebration by my family at Riverside Church. About 300 people attended.

BIG HOUSE

November 28 – Rev. Ron Susek flew from Gettysburg, Pennsylvania to the Three Rivers airport to meet with me to interview me about my Assyrian ministry as he wants to write a book on Assyria and Assyrians and to preach on the prophecy of Isaiah 19:23-25 on Assyria becoming the work of God's hand.

November 29 – My 90th birthday. At the Rotary Club meeting, the club members sang "Happy Birthday, dear John" to me and applauded.

December 1 – My saxophone sleeve for the mouthpiece fell out of my hand and disappeared. I searched for it for three days until David and Jordan came and found it lodged inside the horn.

December 4 – Mailed 25 of my Assyrian Revelation books to Y. Mirza in Australia.

December 7 – Gave up all my stocks to be divided among my four children and paid off my church pledge of $100,001 to the Riverside Church Building Fund.

December 10 – Began taking piano lessons to be able to play by ear.

December 13 – Gave my mentoring men Christmas presents of Bibles, Concordance and Commentary on the Bible.

December 31 – Posted my top twelve predictions for 2013 on Facebook.

2013 NEW YEAR OF:

Publishing of my 4th book

50 years residing in the city of Three Rivers

50 years member of Three Rivers Rotary Club

38 years since starting the Riverside Church

62 years in the ministry

3 years of Burnell in heaven

My grandson, David, marriage to Sally

Candidate for citizen of the year

Year of my 91st birthday

One year closer to heaven

WHAT I HAVE LEARNED IN OVER 60 YEARS OF MINISTRY

SINCE ORDAINED, September 20, 1951 as a Baptist Minister. (Born 11/29/22)

1. Being saved is all by God's grace Eph. 2:8,9
   1) You can't work for your salvation nor work to keep it.
   2) All our sins have been paid by Christ on the cross.
   3) Our relationship is unchangeable with God.
   4) Our fellowship with God depends upon obedience to Him.
   5) The works we do for Christ will bring us rewards Mt. 16:27

2. There is another baptism beside water baptism called the baptism in the Holy Spirit done by Christ Mt. 3:11
   1) The Holy Spirit baptism empowers your Christian life Acts 1:8
   2) The Holy Spirit baptism brings you into the gifts of the Holy Spirit I Cor. 12:7-11

3. Greater is God in me than the devil and demons I Jn. 4:4
   1) We can cast out demons in the Name of Jesus Mk. 16:17
   2) Counter attack the devil James 4:7,8

4. You can't out give God Lk. 6:38; Mal., 3:10

5. The closer you get to Jesus and His leaders, the happier you are and blessed, III Jn. 2

6. Pray with praise, faith and thanksgiving Phil. 4:5,6 I Jn. 5:14,15
   1) Why worry when you can pray?
   2) Be an intercessor by praying for others

7. Live by faith, II Cor.5:7, Heb.11:6
   1) Act on the word of God.
   2) Saved by faith and healed by faith

8. Love never fails, I Cor. 13:8
   1) Faith works by love Gal. 5:6
   2) Love gives to God and others
   3) Love forgives
   4) We can have differences but still be in unity in the Body of Christ which is the church.

9. The joy of the Lord is our strength.
   1) Jesus gives it Jn. 15:11
   2) Happiness is knowing the Word of God and doing it Lk. 11:28
   3) Joy is the fruit of the Holy Spirit Gal.5:22

10. Live with eternity's values in view Mt. 6:19-21, Mt. 16:27

11. Put God and His Word first in your life Mt. 6:32,33

12. Saving one soul is worth more than all the money in the world to God, Mt. 8:36

Conclusion:

1. I give all the glory for what God has done in my life and through my life and His love.
2. I am thankful for all your love and I love you.

SOME OF THE GREATEST EXPERIENCES OF MY LIFE

1. Salvation in the U.S. Navy, April 1943 and spiritual growth to December 1945.
2. Baptized in Moody Church in Chicago.
3. Call of God into full time ministry: Training at Moody Bible Institute, Northern Baptist Seminary, Northwestern University (1946-1951).
4. Finding a good wife at Moody Church, October 31, 1946; engaged March 5, 1947; married June 12, 1948. (The most beautiful scene I have ever seen in all the world is my wife, Burnell, married for almost 62 years).
5. Births of our children, grandchildren, and great grandchildren.
6. Pastoring three Baptist churches (ordained in Okemos Baptist Church, September 20, 1951), Millington Baptist, Three Rivers Baptist. (Being voted out of this church) and started the Riverside Church in 1975 (formerly known as Three Rivers Christian Fellowship) and pastoring with son, Paul.
7. Putting our four children through college.
8. Leading many people to Christ.
9. My children and their spouses and the grandchildren being followers of Christ and serving in the church.
10. Prayer life with miracles of answered prayer.
11. Weekly three half hour short wave radio broadcasts.
12. Authoring three books.
13. Meeting with Israel Prime Minister and praying with the Egyptian president. (These meetings became a little sign of the prophecy in Isaiah 19:23-25).
14. Traveling all over the USA and the world with Burnell, speaking on the subject of Assyria in the Bible.
15. Memorizing over 2400 Bible verses.
16. Leaning to play the saxophone.
17. Performing weddings for our four children and grandchildren.
18. Giving pre-inheritance money to our children.

19. The Baptism in the Holy Spirit with the speaking of tongues.
20. Living and serving in Three Rivers since 1963.
21. Substitute teaching for 14 years.
22. Recording "Dial A Meditation" daily for 10 years with about 3500 meditations and 200,000 calls.
23. Member of the Rotary Club.
24. Caretaker for my wife Burnell during her three year illness and preparation for her departure to heaven 4/30/10.
25. Living to 90 years of age and more with good health.

CHAPTER TWO

A Father's Instructions For A Blessed Life

Listen, my sons, to father 's instruction; pay attention and gain understanding. I give you sound learning, so do not forsake my teaching. Get wisdom, get understanding; do not forget my words or swerve from them. Listen, my son, accept what I say, and the years of your life will be many. My son, pay attention to what I say, and the years of your life will be many. My son, pay attention to what I say; listen closely to my words. Do not let them out of your sight, keep them within your heart; for they are life to those who find them and health to a man's whole body. Above all else, guard your heart, for it is the wellspring of life. Put away perversity from your mouth; keep corrupt talk far from your lips.

Proverbs 4:1,2,5,10,20-24

A FATHER'S INSTRUCTIONS FOR A BLESSED LIFE FOR MY CHILDREN

Be bold and courageous. When you look back on your life, you'll regret the things you didn't do more than the ones you did.

When faced with a serious health problem, get at least three medical opinions.

Save one tenth of your income and invest it with a financial planner.

Bless a lot.

It is better to love than to be right.

Don't be afraid to say "I don't know."

Don't be afraid to say "I'm sorry."

Make a list of things you want to experience before you die.

Get your priorities straight. (No one ever said on his deathbed, “If I'd only spent more time at the office”)

GOD- FAMILY- CHURCH-WORK

Call your mother. Honor your father. Appreciate your siblings.

Instead of worrying about the problems, pray them out!

Pay your tithes and give your offerings faithfully as seed in the Kingdom of God.

Find a faithful pastor make him happy.

Expect miracles. . .they happen every day.

Keep your photo album up to date.

Pray with your spouse in your house daily, every night - bedtime.

Record outstanding experiences in your life.

Heaven is a real and wonderful place to look forward to.

It's fun being a devoted follower of Christ.

Look for good used, before buying new.

Give yourself a year and read the Bible cover to cover. Specialize on the New Testament, Psalms, and Proverbs.

Treat the Bible as food for your spirit.

Memorize key Bible verses and review them regularly.

Live by faith through Jesus Christ.

Faith works best with love.

Exercise and take vitamins 5 days a week.

Never deprive someone of hope; it might be all he or she has.

Pray for wisdom and courage.

Never take action when you're angry.

Have good posture. Enter a room with purpose and confidence.

Be willing to lose a battle in order to win the war.

Don't gossip.

Be a servant for God's sake.

Beware of the person who has nothing to lose.

When facing a difficult task, act as though it is impossible to fail.

If you are going after the big fish — take along the tartar sauce.

Don t spread yourself too thin. Learn to say no politely and quickly.

Never underestimate the power of forgiveness.

Instead of using the word problem, try substituting the word opportunity.

Never walk out on a quarrel with your spouse. You only will come back.
Wage war against littering. . .pick it up!
Don't procrastinate. Do what needs doing when it needs to be done.
Be creative and make deals.

There is power in prayer when you believe.

Have fun, but stay pure.

Remember — Jesus Christ is coming back to earth again soon.

Assyria will rise again and be the work of God's hand.

Always put God first.

Fasting is good for the soul and body.

Compliment people. . .especially children.

Watch a sunrise at least once a year.

Look people in the eye.

Say "Thank you" a lot. . .especially to God.

Treat everyone you meet as you want to be treated.

Read a book a month.

Make new friends, but love the old ones.

Keep secrets.

Admit your mistakes.

Be brave. Even if you're not, pretend to be.

Choose a charity and support it.

Praise God often and others, too.

Use credit cards only for convenience, never for credit.

Don't waste bricks building walls, but build bridges.

"Only one life, 'twill soon be past, only what's done for Christ will last."

Humility and obedience = favor and blessing.

When someone hurts you, be like Jesus Christ.

Trust God for big things.

Intercessory prayer works the power of God.

Work comes before reward. Serve the Lord.

For a good healthy life: Faith, Food Supplements, and Physical Exercise.

Think positively. Be enthusiastic!

It is more blessed to give than to receive.

Remember who is your real enemy — the Devil.

Laugh a lot and tell jokes.

Greater is God in you than the evil one in the World
Trust and obey to be happy in Jesus.

CHAPTER THREE

1001 words of wisdom that I have learned over 60 years of ministry

The multitude of years should teach wisdom, Job 32:7

"WHAT I HAVE LEARNED IN 60 YEARS OF MINISTRY" REV. JOHN BOOKO

1. Hug Jesus in the believer.
2. It is Himpossible.
3. Make God happy.
4. Enjoy the Lord.
5. Believe and receive.
6. I am not better than the unsaved, but better off.
7. Humility plus obedience equals favor and blessing.
8. Know Father God John 17:3
9. People are our product.
10. What you expect is what you get.
11. Impress people with the Lord, not me.
12. If you don't think you can give a tenth, how about a fifth?
13. Service is love in work clothes.
14. A white lie is a snow job.
15. The 7 deadly sins WLAPEGS - (wrath, lust, avarice, pride, envy, greed, and sloth).
16. If you disagree with me I will forgive you.
17. The K. O. G. is in us as righteousness, peace and joy Romans. 14:17, Luke 17:21
18. The church should come together because they love one another.
19. Sing scripture.
20. Our secret weapon is love.
21. Some prayers are on deposit.
22. The biggest test of faith is waiting.
23. There is a miracle in your mouth - confess it.
24. Satan would like to join us in our sin.
25. Worship and praise brings deliverance.
26. Devil attacking? Plant seed and counterattack.
27. God could not love you anymore than He does right now.
28. God never says "oops".

29.God permits something He hates that He may accomplish something He loves out of it.
30. Music lesson: B-sharp, never B-flat, always B-natural.
31. Lord help me to get out of the shaker and into the soup.
32. The measure of man is not his duration, but his donation.
33. Impression without expression leads to depression.
34.Tests prove persons were 40% stronger when they believed they were.
35. Faith - invisible means of support.
36. Live in the light of eternity.
37. Are you a problem or a solution?
38. Can I have victory in the Lord for one hour? Then another?
39. You are important to the Lord.
40. Life is half "if".
41."I will prepare myself and someday my chance will come," Abe Lincoln
42. I am under new management.
43. Receive Christ then follow His example.
44. Say "I am what God says I am."
45. Be a God pleaser.
46. Faith is love in action.
47. Money may not bring happiness, but being broke doesn't make you cheerful.
48. Without God I cannot. Without me He will not.
49. Abbreviation for New Testament: TNT
50. Shortest verses in New Testament: John 11:35,1 Thess. 5:16, Luke 17:32,1 Thess. 5:25. (KJV) 1 Thess. 5:17. (NIV) John 11:35, 1 Thess. 5:17, 1 Thess. 5:16, Luke 17:32, 1 Thess. 5:25
51. Jesus attended church (synagogue).
52. Be your own severest critic. Beat your enemies to it.
53. When criticism is unjust - laugh.
54. Let's not be denominations, just be friends of Jesus.
55. While we sorrow at their funeral, they are rejoicing in heaven. Our loved ones welcome us.

56. The more we ask, the more will say yes. Ask: "What do you think about Christ?" "Do you know the way to heaven?"
57. God gives His best to those who leave the choice with Him.
58. The filling of the Holy Spirit produces fruit. This baptism equals power.
59. We stay filled with the Holy Spirit by continual obedience to the Word.
60. Where there is no thirst or interest for the sermon, it is dry.
61. Acts 11: 15 "As I began to speak, the Holy Spirit fell upon them."
62. Gods says "Yes", "No", "Later", or "I will if you will."
63. Shoot people with prayer.
64. A sin a day for 20 years is 7300 sins.
65. To make mistakes is human, to repeat old mistakes is stupid.
66. Give God an "offering" of praise. Be a praise-aholic.
67. Trouble or pain: it will pass - it won't last.
68. Faith honors the Lord. God honors faith.
69. I don't agree with you but I still love you.
70. Jesus loves me, don't you too?
71. If you want faith go where it is.
72. Ask "Have you prayed about it?"
73. God is not through His creating of you.
74. Cast out evil spirits in Jesus' name.
75. Happiness is hearing God's Word and obeying it. Luke 11:28
76. Ask "What did you think I said?"
77. The Word of God is the will of God.
78. Everyone Christ healed is dead. There is a sickness unto death.
79. Even in sickness, thank God that healing is taking place.
80. Jesus sends out to preach the K.O.G. and heal the sick. Luke 9:1,2 It is by His power.
81. Make a picture of the things you want to remember.
82. Adopt the attitude you want the other person to express.
83. Leadership is leading people into their good.
84. INFORMAT10N- INSPIRATION- INVOLVEMENT
85. Cancel all consent you gave the devil in the past.
86. When someone asks "How are you?" say "Saved", "happy", "thankful", "praise God", or "blessed."

87. What do I do? I help people get saved and healed.
88. You will not get people to trust the Savior until they trust you.
89. I take vitamins so I will look nice when I die.
90. 0ver 30 billion people since Adam and Eve.
91. 40% of the new church are lost in 7 years.
92. Show the "how" in preaching.
93. God's order: character, experience, position.
94. Christians should love their neighbors as their cars.
95. It takes about 100 hours to read the whole Bible (about 4 days).
96. Shortest book in Bible: 3 John
97. Scripture: memorize, visualize, personalize.
98. Memorization does not depend on ability, but on interest.
99. The Word of God is like seed: plant it and reap it.
100. Proverbs 4:22 says having God's word in our hearts is healthy for the body (as well as soul).
101. NT refers to Jesus as Savior 17 times, as Lord about 470.
102. A church has personality.
103. The church - you have to be bad enough to get in.
104. On the dollar back on right side on seal - "E pluribus unum" = "one from many" (above eagle's wings). Good motto for the church.
105. Many are cold and a few are frozen in churches.
106. He who laughs lasts. He who lasts, laughs.
107. Ecclesiastes 12 - Signs of old age.
108. Nahum 6:2 The plain of ONO.
109. God loves me just as much as He loves you.
110. One can hide in a large church.
111. Bible study: exegisis (out of), isegisis (into)
112. Are you happiest person you know?
113. The greatest in K.O.H. - Matthew 18:4 humble; Mark 10:43 servant.
114. God works in us. That's His job. Phil. 2:13
115. Don't react, respond in the Spirit.
116. You are Christ in His branch form John 15:5
117. I misunderheard.
118. Relying on an unfaithful person is a pain. Proverbs 25: 19

119. You can't have Abraham faith with Thomas' sight.
120. Did you misunderhear?
121. Catch people doing right.
122. Difficult people help you grow.
123. Better to be a "goody goody" than a "bady bady" (Ern Baxter)
124. God is working for my good. . . Yes, He really is.
125. A nation reaps what it sows.
126. The Great Commission has become the great omission.
127. The church was formed in a prayer meeting. Acts 1
128. So much is accomplished in so little time by prayer.
129. Bum out is not due to hard work but to frustration.
130. People don't care how much you know 'til they know how much you care.
131. Join the Prayer Force.
132. According to Romans 3:23, we all have 'come short' no matter how tall you are.
133. Greatness through gratefulness.
134. Faith is like a muscle.
135. Negaholics need deliverance.
136. Hosanna means "save, we pray".
137. Death is a gift that gives us the gift of heaven.
138. God gave me my personality.
139. Under pressure? Plant seed.
140. Prayer has no power; God's power is released through prayer.
141. Prayer is the rail on which God's train runs on.
142. Assyrian New Year April 1, 2000 = 6750
143. Manna is an Aramaic word which means "what is it?"
144. I work for Jesus; He is my boss.
145. It is one thing to believe, it is another to receive.
146. When born, you cried and those around you smiled. When you die, you smile and those around you cry.
147. God could not love you any more than He does now.
148. Support what God supports.
149. To be happy in Jesus: Pray and obey.

150. Matthew 7: 7,8 is conditional prayer.
151. Moses was 120 years old when he died, yet strong. Deut. 34:7
152. Let the government of your tongue be made manifest by your silence.
153. Jesus' brothers and sisters Matthew 13:55,56; Mark 6:3
Grandparents: Mary-Heli Luke 3:23, Joseph Matthew 1:16
154. A woman named Noah: Num. 26:33, 27:1, 36:11: Joshua 17:3
155. Do I want to be right or do I want a relationship?
156. Speak with tongues of love.
157. Little girl and Lord's prayer: "Deliver us from e-mail."
158. Simplified prayer: "Help" then "Thank you".
159. God can use our weaknesses.
160. "Seasoned" rather than senior.
161. People listen to people who listen.
162. "Good morning Jesus, good morning love."
163. If an impulse remains it may be God's guidance. If it is sudden, it may not be. (Don Basham)
164. I am an ambassador for Christ 2 Corinthians 5: 19-21.
165. Lester Sumrall said God told him not to ask Him for money, but ask God's people.
166. Hope is desire with expectation.
167. Faith will get you going. Love will keep you going.
168. Be willing to be different. Jesus was. (Charles Simpson)
169. Christ's greatest commandment is LOVE.
170. Faith creates - fear destroys.
171. One another is fellowship.
172. Mother's advice (Mary) "Whatever He tells you to do, do it."
173. "I'll be saying you".
174. 'HOW GREAT YOU ARE!"
175. Don't try to believe, but believe to try (Ken Hagin)
176. Prayer to Jesus. Revelation 22:20
177. Character and experiences will give you position.
178. "If you don't feed the demons they will want to leave" (Mumford)
179. Works of the flesh (Gal. 5:19-21) let demons in.
180. If you can control it, it is flesh, if it controls you it is demons.

181. Learn to act instead of react.
182. We need Satan in order to learn how to fight.
183. More blessed than the mother of Jesus Luke 11:27,28
184. As Jesus was praying heaven was opened. Luke 3:21
185. Jonah 3:5a "The Ninevites believed God."
186. Proverbs 10:22 I am blessed. How are you? BLESSED
187. I am the clay, God is the potter Isaiah 64:8
188. When the church is seen, do they see Jesus?
189. John 6:2-15 Jesus left them burping on a miracle.
190. God said His name is "I Am" Exodus 3:14. That means "He Is" Jesus also is the "I Am" John 4:26; 8:58
191. The mind of Christ in us takes effect when we obey Him.
192. What pleases God?
193. The storm that sends the chicken to the hen house sends the eagle soaring (Charles Simpson)
194. God will entrust us with big things when we obey Him in little things.
195. God is working in all our circumstances.
196. Christ will make gooder what we give Him.
197. Christ is the great exchanger.
198. Gifts (given) fruit (grown) prizes (won)
199. A woman who is intensely spiritual is more sexual (LaHaye)
200. God has His own timetable.
201. The highway to your city runs through my heart.
202. Exercise your gifts to perfect them.
203. Prayer is hanging out with God.
204. Father knows best.
205. The Gospel is "come". Matthew 11:28 and "GO" 28:19
206. Friendship costs.
207. My degree SLDC- short legged demon chaser.
208. Two kinds of church members: burdens or burden bearers.
209. Decide to be what God wants you to be.
210. There is always time to do what God wants us to do.
211. The believer has been bought with a price 1 Peter 1: 18
212. EL SHADDAI - the all Bountiful One

213. The joy of the Lord is our strength, so make Him happy.
214. "Built on the foundation of the apostles and prophets, with Christ Ephesians 2:20
215. The healing of memories may be necessary.
216. The dream speaks about ourselves symbolically.
217. Demons are like germs that get in where it is not clean.
218. If one says a gift is coming, you say "thanks".
219. PBPGINTWMY (Please be patient, God is not through with me yet)
220. We grow in grace or disgrace.
221. We go to church because we love one another.
222. On my tombstone, "See you later".
223. I think. . . . . . . I believe
224. I am too blessed to be stressed.
225. God created things that were not as though they were. Romans 4:17
226. Overcome evil with good. Romans 12:21
227. Jesus was four days late for Lazarus but on time.
228. Jesus said to Thomas "Stop doubting and believe."
229. I'd like to be a smile merchant.
230. Give and it shall be given to you. It is more blessed to give than to receive.
231. Lay down carpets of love.
232. Instead of criticizing - pray.
233. Conversing with Jesus is sweet prayer.
234. Expect miracles every day in your life.
235. Say "good morning Lord", when awakened as though you were arriving in heaven.
236. God loves me short.
237. Jesus broke the bread and used it; so He will use us broken.
238. Your test can become your testimony.
239. "Turn pain into purpose." Fran Dresher
240. Rock and Roll: My feet on the Rock and Name on the Roll.
241. Ask if the person believes there is a heaven. (to witness)
242. You are either a son or a daughter of God or of the devil.
243. God said He would never leave me or forsake me. Hebrews 13:5

244. ENJOY GOD.
245. Love your appearance as God gave it to you.
246. Crucifixion is the prelude to resurrection.
247. Repent means to change one's mind and to think differently.
248. Men - 1 Samuel 10:26; 1 Corinthians 16:13
249. Religiousness is saying religious words and not really meaning them. It is believing but not obeying. A form but no power.
250. Leviticus 26:8 - Deuteronomy 32:30 a few chasing many
251. Ask "What three things am I thankful for today?"
252. What a great welcome home awaits us when we leave this world and go to our heavenly home.
253. Jesus said "According to your faith will it be done to you." Matthew 9:29
254. Begin with the end in view.
255. The days ahead of me are fewer than those behind.
256. The lavishness of God's love.
257. Our brokenness releases a fragrance to God.
258. I am blessed because someone prayed for me.
259. Living in sin pushes the Holy Spirit out and lets the devil in.
260. Sing to the Lord and make Him happy.
261. Every day is a new life for me.
262. Christ saved us with much pain.
263. The love for God is made of the will.
264. Giving is the negations of the self life.
265. Do God's work cheerfully.
266. God makes the armor that fits me.
267. Jesus grabbed hold of Peter as he was sinking.
268. I want to be the little stone that loosens the avalanche.
269. Glory be to the Father, Son and Holy Spirit. Repeat!
270. God asks and waits. We also can ask and wait.
271. The smaller I make myself the bigger God is in me.
272. Religion is form without substance.
273. Ask people if they believe there is a heaven to go to after death.
274. The Jews had the Italians kill Christ; don't they owe God an apology?

275. It is one thing to believe, it is another to receive.
276. "Ask, seek, knock, and you shall receive' is conditional.
277. To be happy in Jesus, pray and obey.
278. The Bible has about 31,000 verses and 1189 chapters. Total words about 800,000. Takes about 56 hours to read it all.
279. Jesus said "Whoever practices and teaches these commands will be called great in the kingdom on heaven."
280. Do I want to be right or do I want a relationship?
281. When you were born you were crying; when you die you are smiling.
282. A generational blessing is more powerful than a generational curse.
283. Did the Apostle Paul know his letters would become Scripture?
284. When you can't go to someplace, your prayers can.
285. Clothe yourself with Jesus and be blessed. (Remember Jacob & Esau & Isaac)
286. Empty self to be filled with the Holy Spirit.
287. Believe in love.
288. I am on God's side.
289. Jesus is my brother.
290. What am I doing? Loving God.
291. God's love is more powerful than all others together.
292. Christ has feelings too.
293. My soul is smiling.
294. Be nice to all the brothers and sisters of Jesus.
295. Don't go a single day without pronouncing God's name to someone.
296. Smile at God.
297. Be like Jesus, act like Jesus.
298. Don't leave Jesus alone without you.
299. God is more beautiful than all His creation.
300. The heavens declare the glory of God. 100 billion stars in our galaxy and 100 billion galaxies.
301. Jesus said "Don't be afraid."
302. One act of love can make up for many flaws (wrongs).
303. God's grace is sufficient.
304. I am God's little boy.

305. This planet would be nothing to God without you.
306. Do all you can; then give it up to God.
307. I kiss God in you.
308. What you do perfectly adds to the value of the church.
309. I have the presence of Christ. I have His mind.
310. It's your move!
311. What was Jesus thinking on the cross for 6 hours?
312. I am who God says I am.
313. I have what God says I have.
314. Best prayers "Help" "Thanks."
315. ATONEMENT means AT-ONEMENT.
316. JUSTIFICATION = JUST-AS-IF-I-CAN'T-SIN.
317. "It is more blessed to give than to receive" Acts 20:32
318. Praise the Lord anyhow.
319. You are a joy to love.
320. SHMILY (see how much I love you)
321. PLEASE GOD
322. PRAYING AND SAYING
323. I am recovering.
324. How am I? Blessed!
325. I live by faith not by works, not by sight. 2 Corinthians 5:7
326. Praise has power.
327. God's name is "YAH" Psalms 68:4 (NJKV)
328. God is closer to you than anyone.
329. Savior brother is Jesus.
330. God never remembers out sins as His children.
331. Know the power of love, faith, and humility.
332. I intend to live forever - so far, so good.
333. Happy wife - happy life.
334. It is possible to love everybody if you don't know them too well.
335. A short pencil is better than a long memory.
336. Belittle yourself before others.
337. God is my Father and friend.
338. It is God who works in me to do His will.

339. Jesus gave His life for me.
340. God is not only near me but in me.
341. Please God.
342. Sin separates us from fellowship with God.
343. There is tough love.
344. Love is a treasure.
345. "A thousand shall flee at the rebuke of one" Isaiah 30: 17
346. Compared to eternity our life is a blink of an eye.
347. To understand heaven is like a baby in the womb understanding earth.
348. My hope and faith are built on God.
349. "His eye is on the sparrow and I know He cares for me."
350. "This world is not my home. I'm just passing through."
351. My body is His, so take good care of it.
352. God loves to be loved. I love you Lord.
353. I possess what I confess.
354. Try singing the Scripture.
355. Praise is the way to blessing and healing.
356. Jesus heals the broken.
357. Be a faith builder.
358. I am the righteousness of God in Christ.
359. I am a new creature.
360. I am what God says I am.
361. He has made me glad.
362. Doing God's will is having union with Him.
363. Lord, help me to love more.
364. Bless and not curse Romans 12:14
365. If you are short, you better be good at something.
366. Difficulties can make you strong.
367. I'll do my part and God will do His part.
368. Prayers are the messages to God and His power.
369. The Trinity in prayer.
370. Difficulties make me stronger.
371. Trials help us.

372.The time has come for me to be old.
373. With rain comes thunder.
374. If someone agrees with you, you have learned nothing.
375. Another good thing about an air conditioner is that the neighbors can't borrow it.
376. Why wait to do good?
377. My words will either praise the Lord or the devil.
378. The Lord has given me a sound mind.
379. Have a "never again" list.
380. You can do!
381. Why worry when you can pray?
382. Cast out the evil spirit in the name of Jesus Christ.
383. Let God's will be done.
384. I want to be a praiser, lover, and giver.
385. I am sure of somethings.
386. What do I want echoed back to me?
387. I want to be used of God.
388. What I confess I will possess.
389. Have an attitude of gratitude.
390. Isn't it enough that God saw the good you did?
391. God loves me and I love Him.
392.Practicing praising.
393.Please God.
394.If you want peace prepare for a war.
395.What you desire you will believe.
396.Write your hurts in the sand, your blessings in concrete.
397.A great many blessings are free.
398.I'd rather wear out than rust out.
399.Your Word have I hid in my heart that I sin not.
400. Expect the impossible.
401. Bring others with me to Jesus.
402. God is my happiness.
403. God cares for me.
404. "He was there all the time."

405. Serve the Lord with joy!
406. Remember all that God has done for me.
407. It is more blessed to give than to receive.
408. God loves a cheerful giver.
409. Cast all my cares on Christ.
410. Faith and works are the oars of life.
411. Faith and love go together like a horse and carriage.
412. I am a seed!
413. I want to be more generous in my giving (5/09)
414. Breathe in "YAH, exhale WEH. The breath of God. His name.
415. Judge actions not motives.
416. All the trials, troubles and sufferings for Jesus will be repaid.
417. I am so happy I chose to follow Jesus.
418. Hebrews 2:10 says Jesus was made perfect through suffering. Same with me.
419. This troubled world is not my final home.
420. I want to be PRAY-PARED.
421. Pray the Scriptures.
422. Pray with KUMBY-YAH.
423. LAL Laugh a lot
424. LAL Love a lot
425. Have fun but stay pure.
426. Always remember Jesus is coming for you.
427. Fasting is good for the souls as well as the body.
428. Believing prayer is when you don't ask again.
429. Beside asking - thanking.
430. God is working on me. I am His masterpiece.
431. Worry about nothing. Pray about everything.
432. Be filled with the Holy Spirit so when you are pushed around the fruit spills.
433. When you can't sleep, pray for people.
434. Keep your eye on the Healer rather than the disease.
435. Do what you love.
436. You will be remembered for how you made people feel.

437. Fight the good fight of faith.
438. Satan is a loser.
439. Cast out the demons in the Name of Jesus.
440. Make God feel good.
441. Sow your seed, don't eat it.
442. Your struggle will make you stronger.
443. Forgiveness is expected of a believer.
444. Treat the Bible as food for your spirit.
445. Four F sounds for health: Faith, Food supplements, Physical exercise, Fun.
446. 11th Commandment: Love
447. 12th Commandment: "Thou shall not sweat it."
448. The kingdom of God is in me Luke 17:21.
449. Have the be-attitudes Matthew 5
450. Imagine what the world would be like if everyone loved Christ and did His will.
451. Praise gives God glory.
452. Our love gives joy to God's love.
453. What is my purpose in life? God's purpose!
454. To have love, joy, peace, you have to have the other six.
455. Why can't pastors in a town gather together around Jesus Christ the Son of God and our Savior and Lord?
456. Come to God with joy; it will make Him smile.
457. God is in the blessing business, so are His children.
458. I am never alone. God is with me and in me.
459. Give love to get love.
460. Trust works not words.
461. The best defense is offense.
462. Am I going to sink or swim?
463. No matter how crumbled a $20 bill is, it is still valuable.
464. A piece of coal becomes a diamond under pressure.
465. Acts of obedience hurries the miracle.
466. Giving is God-like.
467. Go where you are appreciated.

468. Be a gentle giant.
469. I am immortal till my work is done.
470. If you can't memorize Scripture, then meditate on it.
471. God is pleased to see us happy.
472. Smile at God and He smiles back.
473. I am a son of dust.
474. We gain with pain.
475. Decisiveness make a good manager (Lee Iacocca)
476. Speak to the problem like Jesus did.
477. It is not who I am but whose I am.
478. Grandchildren are a crown to the aged. Proverbs 17:6
479. Sometimes it is better not to know some people.
480. Watch your thoughts, they control your actions.
481. Remember what Christ did on earth and imitate.
482. Prayer Ministry is a great ministry.
483. My work is believing.
484. There is a good reason for unanswered prayer.
485. "Only to be what He wants me to be, every moment of everyday."
486. Even Christ was criticized and condemned.
487. God heals but the doctor gets the money. Even if the patient dies, the doctor gets paid.
488. Can I make God happy and laugh?
489. I have been bought with a great price.
490. Do something you don't like to get something you like.
491. Consider the needs of others rather than your own.
492. I pray you enough (of everything).
493. Pray for the persecuted believers in the world.
494. Nothing is going to happen today that God and I cannot handle.
495. Peace starts with a smile.
496. Prefer fruit of the Spirit rather than a religious nut.
497. Better to look forward than back.
498. Remember we are dealing with people and their emotions.
499. When criticizing - smile.
500. Do good deeds in remembrance of Jesus.

501. 1 Corinthians 3:6 I planted the seed, Paul watered it, and God gave the increase to Riverside Church.
502. Every step I take brings me closer to heaven.
503. If you don't take time to exercise you will find time to be sick.
504. As I am on my way to heaven, the sight of this world grows smaller.
505. When I close my eyes in death I open them in heaven.
506. Wise living gets honor, stupid living gets the booby prize.
507. Some family trees produce nuts.
508. We can choose our friends but not our relatives.
509. People are nicer to you when you are in your eighties.
510. Circumcision of the heart Romans 2:29
511. Our church is God's Kingdom. Christ said He will build His church.
512. MUSICIONARIES
513. Heaven is where God is.
514. SHOOT PRAYERS at others.
515. Focus on the Provider and not the problem.
516. God is not mad at me. He is mad about me.
517. Three people die every second in this world.
518. On Christs' second coming don't concentrate on the how and when but on the Who.
519. Speak to the mountain!
520. Jesus said He is preparing a place for us and He is a carpenter.
521. I wish you enough. I wish yuu more than enough.
522. What we believe separates us; whom we believe unites us.
523. HL - Humility and Love
524. In heaven will you have your mansion near me?
525. I am an ambassador for someone's miracle.
526. My life is an offering to God.
527. "Your children I will save" Isaiah 49:25
528. OH, OH, OH, how good is the Lord. . .
529. Communication problems
530. Thank you for the honor you give me in accepting my gift.
531. You have to be brave to forgive.
532. Don't carry a grudge. It is too heavy.

533. Don't talk about the Lord as though He is not in the room.
534. Trust is an aspect of love.
535. Faith, hope (trust), love with humility - God loves.
536. Serve the Lord for the joy of serving.
537. God anoints with the oil of joy Hebrews 1:8
538. John the Baptist was filled with the Holy Spirit while in his mother's womb (Lamsa) (TLB)
539. Disagree without being disagreeable.
540. Give to the poor and you will have treasure in heaven - Jesus Matthew 19:21
541. Not my will but YHWH
542. If I don't tithe and give offerings I am a thief.
543. Serve the Lord with all your heart remembering all He has done for you.
544. Don't waste bricks building walls - build bridges.
545. Only one life 'twill soon be past. Only what's done for Christ will last.
546. Humility and obedience equals favor and blessing.
547. When someone hurts you, be like Jesus.
548. Have fun but stay pure.
549. Remember your real enemy is the devil.
550. Remember Jesus Christ is coming back.
551. Assyria will rise again and be the work of God's hand.
552. Be enthusiastic.
553. Trust God for big things.
554. Always put God first.
555. Fasting is good for the soul.
556. Compliment children.
557. Memorize key Bible verses and review them daily.
558. It is better to love than be right.
559. Bless a lot.
560. Expect miracles.
561. Write down outstanding experiences in your life.
562. Give honor where honor is due.
563. Did God take her because He had something for her to do in heaven?

564. 10 billion trillion stars in the 13.7 billion year universe.
565. Thank the Lord that He made you different.
566. Because He lives I can face tomorrow.
567. I serve a risen Savior.
568. Jesus could be singing with me.
569. There is going to be a prize-giving day in heaven.
570. Death is a gift that gives us the gift of heaven.
571. The greatest thing in all my life is knowing God, loving God, and serving God.
572. Obedience to God is our greatest protection in life. The second is our spouse.
573. Our greatest faith words are "Thank you, Jesus."
574. Jesus loves me, won't you too?
575. IS THIS HELPING ANYBODY?
576. . . . the multitude of years should teach wisdom. Job 32:7
577. Focus on God and not on the problem.
578. Make me like Jesus.
579. God rewards those who earnestly seek Him", Heb. 11:6
580. Knowing God's Word gives us wisdom.
581. Approved workmen are not ashamed equals AWANA
582. Give - Serve - Love
583. "An ounce of prevention is worth a pound of cure."
584. The joy of the Lord is my strength.
585. Love is an action not words.
586. Healing is a kingdom of God mystery.
587. Christianity does not offer crutches but wings.
588. If you could only see me now in heaven.
589. Love grows by loving.
590. God wants our attention.
591. To be wise know God's word in the Bible.
592. I want Jesus to love through me.
593. Another F to the four: Friends with Faith, Food, Fitness, Fun
594. More than enough blessings, less than enough troubles.
595. Conformed to the image of Christ Romans 8:29

596. Faithfulness is full of faith.
597. Focus on what you are giving to.
598. Keeping God's commands is what counts 1 Corinthians 7:19b
599. Smile when you talk to God.
600. Think of God smiling at you.
601. Think of how much God loves you.
602. Tell God how much you love Him.
603. Love grows by loving.
604. I have had hundreds of thousands of blessings.
605. Jesus loves me, this I know!
606. Remember to speak the heavenly language.
607. I'd rather have Jesus than anything. . .
608. I'm on my way to heaven shouting victory!
609. Shoot prayers at people.
610. Make me a blessing.
611. To God be the glory!
612. Think about God more during the day.
613. Love lifted me!
614. Faith is like a muscle.
615. God is a sensor. He responds.
616. I want to be in a place where signs and wonders will follow me.
617. Do you want to see a miracle? Look at me!
618. You withdraw from your old age bank account what you have put in.
619. 1 Corinthians 16:14 (4 words) "DO EVERYTHING IN LOVE"
620. I want God's will in: MY WILL, MY WORDS, MY WORKS, MY WORSHIP, MY WEALTH, MY WORKOUTS.
621. Think of the good things you have said and done Phil. 4:8
622. Life isn't always fair but it is still good.
623. Today is your special occasion.
624. A bad situation will not last.
625. The best is yet to come.
626. The fulfillment of the commandment is love.
627. Share your joy and double it.
628. Anointing is the power of God giving us the enablement.

629. Prayers are only messages to God. God has the power.
630. I wouldn't trade my life for anyone else's.
631. God has also given me what I want and desire.
632. Think deeply, speak gently, love much, laugh often, work hard, give freely, pray and be kind.
633. Love makes all things beautiful.
634. Agree to disagree in love.
635. Have someone to love, something to do; something to look forward to = happiness.
636. It came to pass.
637. When the Lord blesses, bless Him back and others.
638. I want to be Christ's ambassador of love.
639. Love can do miracles.
640. Know the power of speaking in tongues.
641. Jesus is the baptizer in the Holy Spirit.
642. I just want to be where you are.
643. It is great to have the favor of God.
644. ASAP -Always say a prayer
645. "God, my Father, walk through my house and take away all my worries and illnesses and watch over my family, Amen."
646. Do you love yourself? Matthew 22:29
647. Have you thanked God for making you beautiful?
648. Presence equals Passion.
649. Dying for the believer is moving to heaven to see Jesus and other loved ones.
650. People who went to heaven with my help will thank me.
651. Love is creative.
652. Joy is power.
653. Loving the church is loving Christ's body.
654. I not only love God, but I am in love with Him.
655. My Father God is in heaven and in me.
656. Don't believe a liar even if he is telling the truth.
657. A liar steals your trust.
658. Live as though this was your last day on earth.

659. Be child-like not childish.
660. What a Friend we have in Jesus.
661. The way you say what you say has the power.
662. I'm in like with you.
663. Be good at listening.
664. We are all born crazy and do crazy things.
665. Me and God are a majority.
666. How to bring joy to a joyous heaven? Get someone saved.
667. A little thing done in love adds up to a big thing.
668. What shall I say when I arrive in heaven?
669. What will the Lord say to me at my arrival in heaven?
670. I hope I get a mansion of ivory in heaven for Burnell and me.
671. Give God praise offerings.
672. Be a doctor of diving healing.
673. Let not the past dictate to what I believe now.
674. When someone doesn't pay what they owe you, give it to God.
675. There is a law of honor. Who do you honor?
676. There is a law of place. You need to be in the fight place to prosper.
677. The law of the seed is what you sow, you reap.
678. Lord Jesus, live your life through me.
679. I want to be a blessing wherever I go.
680. Give God a smile and receive His smile.
681. Why pray? Because we love Him. Same for church and other endeavors.
682. You see what you want to see.
683. The greatest is love.
684. God wants us to work with Him. He provides the nuts, we have to crack.
685. Consequences!
686. Believe and then you understand.
687. She was my miracle that made me strong.
688. "You are the wind beneath my wings."
689. I'm blessed, how are you doing?
690. One of the sweetest things I've ever known is loving you.
691. I'm God's heir Gal. 4:7
692. Before you ask God "Why" ask yourself "Why".

693. Look at others with eyes of love.
694. What do you have that money can't buy?
695. Watch + pray + trust + obey to be happy.
696. You can't run away from prayers.
697. Love loves to love.
698. Also say "thanks" to God when He says "no" to my prayer.
699. Preach like you are in a boxing ring.
700. The door of my heart is open and you are welcome to come in.
701. Have you ever broken the sound barriers? (Pray & Witness)
702. Let God's creative work continue.
703. The wages of sin is more sin.
704. A white lie is still a lie.
705. Temptation: if you don't like the TV program you turn the channel.
706. Honesty is not the way to grace; grace is the way.
707. Love lets the other person walk over you.
708. If you disagree with me I will forgive you.
709. Head faith fluctuates with the symptoms; heart faith is constant like the Bible.
710. The local church should be a miniature picture of heaven.
711. Fellowship is two fellows in a ship going in the same direction.
712. We will have a N.T. Church when we have a N.T. people.
713. Body Ministry: People, Program, Powers.
714. The Church should come together because they love one another.
715. A smile is something that adds to your face value.
716. Feet accustomed in the way to God find it in the dark.
717. What have you done that only a Christian would do?
718. We cannot feed the flesh and grow in the spirit.
719. The quickest way to correct the other fellows attitude is to correct your own.
720. Tests proved persons were 40% stronger when they believed they were.
721. "Nothing great was ever achieved without enthusiasm." (Emerson)
722. Are you part of the problem or the solution?
723. Be patient with the faults of others, they have to be patient with yours.

724. Prejudice is being down on what you are not up on.
725. Unless you try to do something bigger, how can you prove you're growing?
726. Can I have victory in the Lord for one minute? Then another?
727. See everything, overlook a great deal, correct a little (Pope John)
728. "Under new management"
729. Receive Christ, obey Christ's words, follow Christ's example.
730. Promise, principle, problem, provision.
731. I am what God says I am.
732. Most are self-pleasers, others man-pleasers, the fruitful person is a God-pleaser.
733. PBPGINTWMY (Please be patient, God is not through with me yet)
734. Abbreviation of "The New Testament" TNT
735. What does Christ have in heaven that is man-made? His nail prints.
736. Christ is referred to as Savior about 16 times; As lord about 600 times in the N.T.
737. The sheep that stay close to the Shepherd are the best fed.
738. Christ's second coming: "RE-ENTRY"
739. Remember, the banana: when it left the bunch it got skinned.
740. What we owe our children the church helps to pay.
741. Don't find fault, find a remedy.
742. He who provides for this life but takes no care for eternity is wise for a moment but a fool forever.
743. The key to personal revival is "confession".
744. Talk to the Lord about sinners, and talk to sinners about the Lord.
745. Some of us tell the Good News as though it were a rumor.
746. Declare bankruptcy before the Lord
747. What may be impossible is Him-possible.
748. Enjoy the Lord and bless the Lord.
749. Sit-walk-stand (Eph.; Plii. 2:13, Ps. 1)
750. We are a patchwork quilt - a body of people sewn together.
751. Nothing will stop God, but He can be slowed down by our limiting Him.
752. Believe and receive, or doubt and do without.

753. "Occupy 'till I come."
754. I Cor. 10:31, Whatever we do, do all to the glory of God. God empowers us.
755. Living in the presence of God!
756. Don't settle for less in God.
757. Take your limits off God.
758. Humility & obedience = favor & blessing
759. Presumption is believing for something God never said for us.
760. Change! Have you got any?
761. Spiritual maturity is knowing the will of God and doing it.
762. Say a creative word. One that produces life.
763. Command by the spirit to reprogram the mind to accept the healing.
764. Christ seed is in us (I In. 3:9); it will bring forth His likeness if we will nurture it. (THE ETERNAL SEED)
765. "Being" is obeying God's Word.
766. Be hungry, be drawn, desire, apprehend.
767. Faith that works by love, Gal. 5:6
768. Love is not only a good feeling, but commitment and responsibility.
769. In Christ all is legally ours, but faith walks it out.
770. "I'm blessed, how are you?"
771. Don't act like a man, but like God.
772. Don't waste time in the flesh, but go against the spiritual root source through authoritative prayer. Eph. 6: 12.
773. Motives issue in conduct, conduct issues in character, character into destiny.
774. It is better to love than to be right.
775. Spiritual maturity is to act redemptively in every situation.
776. If we decide "why" we can learn "how".
777. "A token for good" Ps. 86: 17 KJV
778. Knowledge + discipline equals maturity
779. The vastness of the power of Jesus Name - use it frequently.
780. Walking in the light of Your presence Ps. 89:15
781. The character of God in my life: love & holiness.

782. The attitude of Christ in my life: humility and servanthood.
783. The peace and joy of the Holy Spirit.
784. "Lord, show me myself as you see me. Show me your priorities & views."
785. Truth in its first appearance seems negative; like light coming in darkness.
786. Strength to serve is greater than strength to rule.
787. The reason Christians fight so much is because they are brothers and sisters.
788. Let God's people say (Ps. 118:1-3) "His love endures forever"
789. Life is relationships: God, marriage, family, church, etc.
790. The law of RECIPROCITY - "for every action there is an equal opposite action.
791. Change means pain - don't focus on the pain but the transformation.
792. "Trends are bottom-up; fads are top-down"
793. Take the bitter with the better.
794. Vision is necessary for purposeful labor.
795. Where is your thinking coming from?
796. Jesus promised to answer believing prayer.
797. Prayer is asking - answered prayer is receiving (Mt. 7:7, 21,22)
798. Repentance is changing one's mind and agreeing with all God says and doing them.
799. In Christ I will not sin, out of Christ I will.
800. I don't have to serve sin anymore In. 8:32
801. A man is really humble when he can take humiliation.
802. Head faith fluctuates with the symptoms, heart faith is constant like the Bible.
803. The church people should come together not only because they love the Lord, but that they love one another.
804. Paul boasted of his weaknesses II Cor. 12:9
805. The Spirit-filled life is a Spirit-controlled life.
806. The biggest test of faith is waiting.
807. Be Jesus possessed.
808. There's a miracle in your mouth - confess it.

809. Repentance and submission vs. rebellion and stubbornness
810. Christian is "I" following in Christ
811. We cannot feed the flesh and grow in the Spirit.
812. Still water and still religion freeze quickest.
813. Impression without expression leads to depression.
814. Are you a problem or a solution?
815. Can I have victory in the Lord for one minute? Then another?
816. "Good" may be the enemy of the "best".
817. Under new management.
818. Take people as they are and where they are and patiently expect them to be better than they used to be.
819. Don't try to make your people drink, make them thirsty.
820. Get people to love Christ so much that they will want to please Him.
821. The pastor is to assist the people in their ministry.
822. Lord fill my mouth with worthwhile stuff and nudge me when I've said enough.
823. How are things going? Eternity will tell.
824. Love the people and brag on the Lord.
825. God says, "Yes", "No", "Later", or "I will if you will."
826. Are we making it possible for God to answer our prayer?
827. Lots of unbelievers will be saved - when they believe in Christ.
828. Bring our surrender (etc. . .) up to date.
829. "Unsaved believers" (Alan Redpath)
830. We don't dare defy God's law of gravity, but many break His moral law.
831. We may get accustomed to living with our sin, God doesn't.
832. Sin is not always bad but it is always wrong.
833. It is better to say a good thing about a bad fellow than a bad thing about a good fellow.
834. Head off the temptation.
835. Service is love in work clothes.
836. If you had more time what would you do with it?
837. Give God a praise offering.
838. Praise takes away our self-consciousness.

839. Jesus loves me, won't you too?
840. Forgiveness: "I've come to realize how wrong I've been in ______; will you forgive me?
841. Love is surrender to God's Will.
842. If you want faith, go where it's at.
843. Marriage insurance: appreciation, praise, thanks and security (PATS)
844. Biggest problem in a family is a lack of purpose.
845. Husbands ask your wife what she really wants in her husband.
846. Sex is God's wedding present to the man and wife. Any other use of it is stolen.
847. Wanting to want to quit a bad habit is not wanting to quit.
848. Let us not limit God.
849. We don't pray about the revealed Word of God, we obey it!
850. God will not love you anymore a thousand years from now.
851. God's divine resistance when we have not the right motives.
852. Remember that everyone Christ healed is dead.
853. We do not know why all men are not healed; as we do not know why all men are not saved.
854. I will believe I am healed like I believed I am saved.
855. Pray for the healing of the inner man.
856. Be a faith, hope, love healer.
857. Give as a love offering to God our desire of smoking.
858. No matter how important you think you are, let someone else tell you.
859. "E pluribus unum" = one from many.
860. We all build up walls about us that hinder fellowship.
861. Many are cold but a few are frozen.
862 Sign on a London church bombed during war - "It is dangerous to enter this church."
863. Has your life truly been changed? If so, in what way?
864 For deliverance: Humility-honesty-confession-renunciation-forgive others-call on the Lord.
865. Belief in Christ is shown by obedience to His commands.
866. God loves me just as much as He loves you.
867. See a person as God seems him.

868. Knowledge + discipline = maturity
869. I belong to the body of Jesus.
870. The Lord has put His Word above His Name Ps. 138:2
871. Paul had disciples too (Acts 9:25 TCNT)
872. How to be the greatest Mt. 18: 14
873. Our spirit is released according to the degree of our brokenness.
874. Our rest lies in looking to the Lord, not ourselves.
875. Unless we actively cooperate, God will not undertake anything for us.
876. We must give God our will then act.
877. Let Jesus be big in me.
878. Faith springing out of Christ is right.
879. Knowing God (Jer. 9:23,24) (to be His friend)
880. There are some promises of God we don't want. Mt. 18:35
881. Concern for God's will must far exceed concern for self.
882. The Spirit glorifies the Son, the Son glorifies the Father.
883. What God will bless as a supplement He will curse as a substitute.
884. Incline me-draw me PS.119:36
885. The God-head abides in the obedient behavior Jn.14:16,21,23
886. "Fill my cup, Lord", I clean it up, Lord!
887. Ready for the baptism in H.S.? Repent-expect-ask-yield-drink
888. The baptism of the H.S. is having the fullness of Jesus.
889. The fruit of the H.S. is Christ's love in us.
890. The evidence of the baptism of the Holy Spirit is the manifestation of the character of Christ in the believer.
891. Have God-centered prayers.
892. The prayer of faith is agreeing with God's Word.
893. "Deactivated prayer."
894. He is all I need for salvation.
895. The blood of Christ does not cleanse excuses but confessed sin.
896. Christ did not try to do, He did it. So with our union with Him.
897. He is our life.

898. We cannot know Christ's life in us unless we know His Lordship over us.
899. The blood of Christ is the legal power by which the H.S. manifests His power.
900. Worship is "worth-ship" of God.
901. Praise is the fruit of our life that moves us into worship.
902. Worship literally means "kiss the hand".
903. While we are beholding Him, we are becoming Him.
904. Occupying 'till He comes (with prayer, praise, teaching, etc..) Luke 19:13
905. Ministering to the Lord first.
906. Love is not only a good feeling, but commitment and responsibility.
907. I'm blessed, how are you?
908. Fear that initiates action is wholesome.
909. That which you can do nothing about it, take hold of it and get rid of it by faith.
910. Glory is the character of Christ in activity.
911. Mk. 11: 24 causes us to have thank prayers and laughing meetings.
912. What may be impossible is Himpossible.
913. Bless the Lord - make Him happy.
914. Enjoy the Lord.
915. Nothing can stop God, but He can be slowed down by our limiting Him.
916. Believe and receive or doubt and do without.
917. Relate together around the person of Christ.
918. A kingdom principle: What you do not use, you lose Lk. 19:26
919. I Cor. 10:31 Whatever we do do all to the glory of God.
920. I do it as God empowers and leads me.
921. Living in the presence of God.
922. Our secret weapon is Agape love (ex. God loves you and I do too)
923. More things are done in the Bible through saying than praying Mk.11:23
924. Before we can say nothing happened, wait for the story to be finished.
925. Temptation is the point at which man decides whether or not to obey God.
926. Be Jesus possessed.

927. Be conscious of the Lord's presence and be considerate of the feelings of others.
928. Abhor selfish motives as sin.
929. Say a creative word- one that produces life.
930. Command the spirit to reprogram the mind to accept the healing.
931. Christ's seed in us will produce His likeness (I In. 3:9), but we must nurture it.
932. Being is obeying God's Word.
933. Occupy 'till He comes Lk. 19:13 ("put this money to work until I come" NIV)
934. Don't settle for less in God.
935. Take the limits off God.
936. Humility and obedience = favor and blessing
937. Death is helplessness and suffering
938. We come to Jesus, but the end is the Father In. 14:6
939. Knowing the Father is maturity In.17:3
940. In Christ all is legally ours, but faith walks it out.
941. 1'm blessed, how are you?
942. The character of God in my life: Love & Holiness
943. The attitude of Christ in my life: Humility & Servanthood
944. Trusting God is not a feeling but a decision.
945. Lord, show me your priorities.
946. Strength to serve is greater than to rule.
947. Truth will be vindicated.
948. Life is relationships.
949. For every action there is a equal opposite reaction.
950. Take the bitter with the better.
951. The secret of our strength is remembering our purpose.
952. Is what I am doing pleasing to God?
953. Our greatest faith works are "Thank you Jesus".
954. Trouble is the breeding ground for miracles.
955. Pain is often a bridge to success.
956. No one has been a loser longer than Satan.
957. Reducing to love, 1\:1t. 22:37-40

958. Loving Christ's body is loving the church.
959. Love is just a compliment away.
960. Visualize the help coming to your need.
961. The knowledge of God and Christ brings us power II Peter 1:2
962. God is responsible to keep His promises.
963. What did the disciples ask Jesus to teach them? PRAY
964. God believes in you.
965. "And it came to pass" the sickness, hardships and pain
966. We are someone's miracle.
967. "The day of death is better than the day of birth" Eph. 7: 1
968. When Christ returns, He will reward according to our works, Mt.16:27
969. Why dwell on what God didn't do for you, but on all God has done for you.
970. One lost being saved is worth more than all the money in the world.
971. What would you rather have? One person saved or 10,000 people healed of disease?
972. "Tis so sweet to trust in Jesus"
973. I'm so happy and here's the reason why; Jesus took my burdens all away.
974. "I'm so glad God brought you into my life."
975. His eyes are always watching over me.
976. The opposite of fear is love. Love casts out fear.
977. Sometimes we have to give up the good to get God's best.
978. "You make my heart smile everytime I see you."
979. Prayer is intimacy with God.
980. Want what God wants.
981. Present suffering is not worthy to be compared with our future glory. Rom.8:18
982. A sinners wealth is stored up for the righteous. Provo 13:22
983. God rules in realms to which He is admitted.
984. I sinless.
985. Some get healed immediately, some later, some not.
986. We need to grow up and be potty trained.
987. Jesus didn't live up to all people's expectations.

988. We will hear from God if we are willing to obey.
989. I am child-like but not childish.
990. Give God a smile.
991. Enjoy God's daily miracles.
992. What we don't hate, we permit.
993. Direct your anger against the real enemy.
994. To God be the glory for all the good said and done by me.
995. It is great to be a prayer warrior.
996. What is greater that faith? Love!
997. Remember to love yourself and to forgive yourself.
998. Miracles are happening every day.
999. Leave love notes behind as you go through life.
1000. Feed on the Word of God daily.
1001. The greatest thing in all my life is loving you.

CHAPTER FOUR

From my daily one line prayer on the Internet WWW.YOUTUBE.COM Type "revjohnbooko" and click on my photo to read my one line prayer every day.

A DAILY PRAYER FOR YOU!

THANK YOU, LORD, THAT I AM TOO BLESSED TO BE STRESSED

Grow my faith, Lord, when I cannot see.

Thank You, Lord, for the great gift of your love that is mine at all times

Dear Lord, give me faith to see behind all the dark clouds of my life where the sun always shines.

Thank you, Lord, for your peace in a time of storm

Thank you, Lord, that I need not fear because you are with me

Dear Lord, help me to bring a smile to someone's face today

THANK YOU, LORD, THAT YOU HAVE PLANS TO PROSPER ME AND TO GIVE ME HOPE FOR THE FUTURE.

LORD, AS WINTER VANISHES AND SPRINGTIME TAKES ITS PLACE, MAKE SORROW ALSO DISSIPATE AND MAKE JOY COME BY YOUR GRACE.

DEAR LORD, HELP ME TO STOP IN MY BUSINESS TO LISTEN TO YOUR VOICE INSIDE ME, TO GUIDE ME.

DEAR LORD, I NEED YOU TO GUIDE ME IN THE DECISION I HAVE TO MAKE

DEAR LORD, I BRING ALL MY CARES TO YOU BECAUSE YOU CARE FOR ME.

DEAR LORD, WHEN OTHERS FAIL ME, PLEASE STAND BY ME

THANK YOU, LORD, THAT YOU ARE SAVIOR, HEALER AND HELPER

DEAR LORD, TURN MY PAIN INTO SOME GOOD PURPOSE

DEAR LORD, MY HOPE IS IN YOU AND I KNOW YOU WILL NOT LET ME DOWN. . .

DEAR LORD, BECAUSE YOU HAVE FORGIVEN ME, I WILL FORGIVE OTHERS. . .
LORD, GIVE ME COURAGE TO STAND FIRMLY FOR WHAT I BELIEVE. . .

DEAR LORD, THANK YOU FOR SAVING ME THROUGH FAITH IN JESUS CHRIST BY YOUR GRACE WITHOUT ANY OF MY GOOD WORKS. . .

DEAR LORD, INSTEAD OF WORRYING ABOUT ANYTHING LEAD ME TO PRAY ABOUT EVERYTHING. . .

DEAR LORD, PLEASE TAKE AWAY ALL MY WORRIES AND ILLNESSES AND BLESS MY FAMILY

DEAR LORD, I WANT TO TRUST YOU WITH ALL MY HEART

DEAR LORD, GIVE ME THE STRENGTH TO DO EVERYTHING I NEED TO DO NOW

DEAR GOD, PLEASE WORK OUT THIS SITUATION FOR SOME GOOD PURPOSE.

LORD, I NEED A MIRACLE NOW!

DEAR LORD, I WANT THAT POWER THAT RAISED CHRIST FROM THE DEAD TO RAISE ME OUT OF MY WEAKNESS. . .

LORD JESUS, AS YOU HAVE FORGIVEN ME AS YOU SUFFERED ON THE CROSS, HELP ME TO FORGIVE THAT ONE WHO DID ME SUCH WRONG. . .

THANK YOU, LORD JESUS, FOR TAKING MY PLACE ON YOUR CROSS FOR THE FORGIVENESS OF ALL MY SINS. . .

THANK YOU, LORD, FOR LOVING ME UNCONDITIONALLY

LORD, SHOW ME SOMEONE WHO IS POOR THAT I MAY HELP

LORD, HELP ME TO ALWAYS PLEASE YOU

DEAR LORD, GIVE ME STRENGTH TO DO WHAT I NEED TO DO

LORD, TAKE ANY HATE OUT OF MY HEART AND SET ME FREE

THANK YOU, JESUS, FOR INVITING US TO COME TO YOU WHEN WE ARE WEARY AND BURDENED, AND YOU WILL GIVE US REST. . .

DEAR LORD, LET NO WORRY OR FEAR HAVE ANY PLACE IN MY HEART. . .

THANK YOU, LORD, THAT YOU WILL PROVIDE A WAY OUT FOR THE TROUBLE THAT HAS COME MY WAY

DEAR LORD, I CAST ALL MY WORRIES ON YOU BECAUSE YOU CARE FOR ME..

THANK YOU, LORD, THAT YOU LOOK FORWARD TO HEARING FROM ME. . .

DEAR LORD, I WANT YOUR PEACE IN MY HEART AND MIND

DEAR LORD, HELP ME TO THINK OF WHATEVER IS TRUE, RIGHT AND LOVELY. . .

DEAR LORD, THANK YOU FOR YOUR PROMISE TO BE WITH ME ALWAYS AS I BELIEVE IN YOU. . .

Dear God, Let my day be full of love!

DEAR GOD, WITH YOUR HELP I CAN FACE TOMORROW'S PROBLEM

Dear Lord, Help me make the right words to a friend who doesn't know your love.

DEAR LORD, GIVE ME STRENGTH TO MEET THE CHALLENGES OF THE DAY. . .

THANK YOU, LORD, THAT AS I TRUST YOU, YOU WILL PROVIDE FOR WHAT I NEED. . .

DEAR LORD, I ASK FOR YOUR GUIDANCE IN THE DECISIONS I HAVE TO MAKE. . .

DEAR GOD, THANK YOU FOR LOVING ME AND GIVING ME HOPE FOR A GOOD FUTURE. . .

O GOD, WITH YOUR HELP I BELIEVE THE IMPOSSIBLE CAN BE POSSIBLE. . .

PRAISE BE TO YOU MY GOD, FOR THE PROMISE THAT WHOEVER CALLS ON THE NAME OF THE LORD IS SAVED. . . .

THANK YOU, GOD, I AM TRUSTING IN YOU AND I AM NOT AFRAID OF THE DARK. . .

DEAR GOD, I KNOW THAT YOU CAN ENABLE ME TO RIDE OUT OF THE WAVES OF NEGATIVITY. . .

DEAR GOD, GUIDE MY WAYS AND THOUGHTS AND USE ME TO HELP OTHERS.

DEAR GOD, I WILL NOT FEAR OR BE DISCOURAGED BECAUSE YOU HAVE SAID YOU WOULD BE WITH ME AND HELP ME. . .

DEAR GOD, I PRAISE YOU FOR ALL YOUR BLESSINGS IN MY LIFE

THANK YOU, LORD, FOR YOUR UNCONDITIONAL AND UNDYING LOVE FOR ME. . .

DEAR LORD, THANK YOU FOR YOUR WORDS IN THE BIBLE THAT TEACH ME ABOUT YOU WONDERFUL WAYS. . .

DEAR LORD, THANK YOU FOR YOUR PROMISE THAT BELIEVING IN YOU ASSURES ME THAT I HAVE ALL MY SINS FORGIVEN AND THAT ONE DAY I WILL BE IN HEAVEN WITH YOU AND WITH ALL MY BELIEVING LOVED ONES. . .

DEAR GOD, AS I TRUST IN YOU, HELP ME TO OVERFLOW IN HOPE

DEAR GOD, TAKE AWAY THE FEAR THAT IS HAUNTING ME

DEAR LORD, YOU HAVE SAID I SHOULD NOT WORRY, SO I WON'T WITH YOUR HELP. . .

THANK YOU, LORD, FOR ACCEPTING ME JUST AS I AM AND HELPING ME TO BE A BETTER FOLLOWER OF YOURS. . .

DEAR LORD, AS YOU HAVE FORGIVEN ME OF ALL MY FAULTS, HELP ME TO FORGIVE THE ONES WHO HAVE HURT AND OFFENDED ME. . .

DEAR LORD, GIVE ME YOUR PEACE DURING THIS TIME OF TROUBLE. . .

O GOD, WITH YOUR HELP I BELIEVE THE IMPOSSIBLE CAN BE POSSIBLE. . .

PRAISE BE TO YOU MY GOD, FOR THE PROMISE THAT WHOEVER CALLS ON THE NAME OF THE LORD IS SAVED. . .

DEAR LORD, I WANT YOUR PEACE TO FILL MY SOUL

DEAR LORD, I GIVE YOU MY AVAILABILITY TO WORK IN AND THROUGH ME TO DO YOUR WILL. . .

THANK YOU, LORD, THAT YOU LOVE ME AND HAVE A WONDERFUL PLAN FOR MY LIFE. . .

LORD JESUS, LIVE YOUR LIFE THROUGH ME

THANK YOU, LORD, FOR THE PEACE I HAVE IN CHRIST

DEAR GOD, FILL ME WITH YOUR LOVE SO I CAN PASS IT ON TO OTHERS. . .

THANK YOU, LORD, THAT YOUR EYE IS ON THE SPARROW AND I KNOW YOU ARE WATCHING OVER ME. . .

DEAR LORD, MEET ALL MY NEEDS ACCORDING TO YOUR WILL

THANK YOU, LORD, FOR DOING IMMEASURABLY MORE THAN WHAT I ASK OR EVEN IMAGINE

DEAR LORD, I PRAISE YOU FOR THE WONDERFUL LIFE THAT YOU HAVE MADE FOR ME. . .

DEAR LORD, HELP ME TO TEAR DOWN THE WALLS I HAVE BUILT UP THAT HINDER FELLOWSHIP. . .

THANK YOU, LORD, FOR THE WONDERFUL WORDS OF LIFE IN THE BIBLE. . .

DEAR LORD, GIVE ME THE UNDERSTANDING AND THE COURAGE IT TAKES TO FORGIVE. . .

DEAR LORD, MAY WHAT I SAY AND DO SHOW THAT I AM A DEVOTED FOLLOWER OF CHRIST. . .

DEAR LORD, OPEN MY EYES THAT I MAY SEE AND ENCOURAGE THE FINEST AND BEST IN OTHERS. . .

DEAR GOD, HELP ME TO HAVE RIGHT THOUGHTS ABOUT OTHERS

DEAR LORD, HELP ME TO SPEAK ENCOURAGING WORDS TO PEOPLE WHEN THEY ARE HURTING. . .

DEAR LORD, HELP ME TO LOVE MERCY AND TO BE HUMBLE BEFORE

DEAR LORD, HELP ME TO COMFORT THE BROKEN-HEARTED WITH YOUR COMFORTING WORDS. . .

DEAR GOD, TAKE SORROW AND MOURNING AWAY AND GIVE ME GLADNESS AND JOY. . .

DEAR LORD, YOU ARE MY SAVIOR, MY STRENGTH AND MY SONG

DEAR LORD, YOU ARE MY SALVATION, I WILL TRUST AND NOT BE AFRAID. . .

THANK YOU, LORD, FOR YOUR HOLY SPIRIT THAT IS MY COMFORTER AND GUIDE. . .

THANK YOU, LORD, FOR MAKING SOMETHING BEAUTIFUL OF MY LIFE. . .

DEAR GOD, I WANT YOUR WILL TO ALWAYS BE DONE IN MY LIFE

THANK YOU, LORD, THAT YOU LOVE ME JUST AS MUCH AS ANYONE ELSE IN THE WORLD. . .

LORD, HELP ME TO START EACH DAY WITH A NEW ATTITUDE AND PLENTY OF GRATITUDE. . .

LORD, I THANK YOU THAT YOU ARE FORGIVING AND AN UNDERSTANDING GOD. . .

THANK YOU LORD, THAT YOUR WORD SAYS I CAN DO ALL THINGS THROUGH CHRIST WHO GIVES ME STRENGTH. . .

DEAR LORD, RENEW MY HEALTH AND STRENGTH TO SERVE OTHERS. . .

DEAR LORD, AS I TRUST IN YOU, YOU SUSTAIN ME IN MY PAIN

THANK YOU LORD, FOR WHEN I AM DISCOURAGED AND THINK I AM NOTHING, YOU REVIVE MY SOUL. . .

DEAR LORD, HAVE YOUR WAY IN MY LIFE THAT YOU LOVE WILL SHINE THROUGH ME. . .

THANK YOU, LORD, YOU HAVE SAID YOU WILL NEVER LEAVE ME OR FORSAKE ME..

DEAR LORD, MAKE A WAY FOR ME OUT OF THE WILDERNESS I AM IN. . .

DEAR LORD, TAKE CARE OF MY ENEMIES AS I PRAY FOR THEM

BREATHE ON ME BREATH OF GOD AND MAKE MY LIFE NEW

DEAR GOD, KEEP ME FROM FALLING

THANK YOU LORD, FOR GIVING ME THE POWER TO LOVE AND HAVE A SOUND MIND. . .

THANK YOU, LORD, THAT YOU WILL NOT LET ME BE TEMPTED BEYOND WHAT I CAN BEAR. . .

DEAR GOD, HELP ME TO BE PATIENT AS I AWAIT MY ANSWERS TO PRAYER. . .

DEAR LORD, HELP ME TO BE CONSCIOUS OF YOUR PRESENCE IN MY LIFE. . .

DEAR GOD, WHEN THE STORMS OF DOUBT AND FEAR HIT ME, HELP ME TO STAND FIRM ON YOUR PROMISES. . .

DEAR GOD, HELP ME TO BELIEVE SO THAT I MAY UNDERSTAND

DEAR GOD, IN TIMES OF TROUBLE HELP ME TO BE BETTER AND NOT BITTER. . .

DEAR GOD, WHEN I FEEL DEPRESSED, HELP ME TO PRAISE YOU

DEAR LORD, THANK YOU FOR ANSWERED PRAYER

THANK YOU, LORD, FOR HEALING AND HOPE WHEN I PRAY TO YOU

DEAR LORD, HELP ME TO BE A GOOD EXAMPLE TO OTHERS

DEAR GOD, TAKE THIS PAIN OUT OF MY LIFE TODAY LORD, GIVE ME A CHEERFUL FRAME OF MIND

DEAR GOD, GIVE ME A BIG BLESSING TODAY

DEAR LORD, HELP ME NOT TO BE A LOSER

DEAR LORD, GIVE ME VICTORY OVER MY BAD HABIT

DEAR GOD, PROTECT ME AND ALL OF MY FAMILY FROM DANGER, HARM AND SIN..

DEAR LORD, LOVE THROUGH ME WHEN I AM UNABLE TO DO IT ON MY OWN. . .

DEAR LORD, WIPE ALL MY SORROWS AWAY AND TURN MY NIGHT INTO DAY. . .

LORD, HELP ME TO BE FORGIVING EVEN THOUGH I DON'T FEEL LIKE IT. . .

LORD, HELP ME TO HAVE JOY IN MY STRUGGLES

LORD, PLEASE BE MY STRENGTH WHERE I AM INSECURE

DEAR GOD, GIVE ME GOOD HEALTH

LORD, HELP ME TO BELIEVE THE BEST ABOUT OTHERS

PRECIOUS LORD, I LOVE YOU BECAUSE YOU FIRST LOVED ME

DEAR LORD, HELP ME TO LIVE BY FAITH IN YOUR WORD MORE THAN BY WHAT I FEEL. . .

DEAR GOD, I DON'T UNDERSTAND EVERYTHING ABOUT YOUR WAYS BUT I WILL TRUST YOU IN EVERYTHING. . .

DEAR GOD, I LOVE YOU WITH ALL MY HEART AND I THANK YOU FOR YOUR LOVE TO ME. . .

DEAR LORD, FILL MY HEART AND MIND WITH HOPE

DEAR GOD, TAKE ALL MY GUILT AWAY

THANK YOU GOD, FOR WHAT YOU HAVE DONE AND FOR EVERYTHING YOU WILL DO FOR ME. . .

DEAR LORD, GIVE ME WISDOM AND COUNSEL IN THE DECISIONS I MAKE. . .

DEAR GOD, HELP. . . . . AND THANK YOU

DEAR GOD, I PRAY THAT ME AND OUR CHURCH WILL BE OUT OF DEBT WITHIN TWO YEARS. . .

DEAR LORD, MAY THOSE YOU HAVE GIVEN ME TO LEAD BECOME MORE LIKE YOU. . .

DEAR LORD, HELP ME NOT TO BE AFRAID TO SAY "I LOVE YOU" TO OTHERS. . .

DEAR GOD, TEACH ME HOW TO REALLY LOVE MY FAMILY, FRIENDS, AND EVEN STRANGERS. . .

DEAR LORD, I AM HAPPY BECAUSE YOU HAVE ACCEPTED ME

DEAR GOD, I WANT TO PRAISE YOU WITH ALL MY HEART

DEAR LORD, I JUST WANT TO THANK YOU FOR ALL YOUR BLESSINGS. . .

DEAR LORD, I JUST WANT TO SAY I LOVE YOU

DEAR LORD, HELP ME TO MAKE OTHERS HAPPY

DEAR LORD, GIVE ME STRENGTH FOR TODAY AND BRIGHT HOPE FOR TOMORROW. . .

DEAR LORD, I NEED YOUR PRESENCE TO GUIDE AND PROTECT ME

DEAR GOD, EMPOWER ME BY YOUR HOLY SPIRIT TO DO WHAT I COULD NEVER DO IN MY OWN POWER. . .

DEAR LORD, I AM TRUSTING YOU TO PROVIDE FOR ALL MY NEEDS

DEAR GOD, REMIND ME THAT I NEED NOT BE FEARFUL SINCE I AM TRUSTING IN YOU. . .

DEAR LORD, I LOVE YOU AND I LOVE THE LIFE YOU HAVE GIVEN ME

DEAR LORD, I WILL WORRY ABOUT NOTHING BECAUSE I CAN PRAY ABOUT EVERYTHING. . .

DEAR GOD, AS YOU HAVE FORGIVEN ME, I ALSO FORGIVE

DEAR LORD, I WANT YOUR WILL TO BE DONE IN MY LIFE ALWAYS

DEAR LORD, REMIND ME THAT I DO NOT WALK ALONE FOR YOU ARE ALWAYS WITH ME. . .

DEAR LORD, EVEN IF MY TALENTS ARE SMALL, HELP ME TO USE THEM AS YOU WANT. . .

DEAR LORD, GIVE ME YOUR PEACE AS I TRUST IN YOU

DEAR LORD, WHATEVER I ASK YOU IN PRAYER, I ALWAYS WANT YOUR WILL TO BE DONE. . .

DEAR GOD, I LOVE YOU AND I WANT MY HEART TO REPEAT THAT TO YOU AS OFTEN AS I DRAW BREATH. . .

DEAR LORD, FILL MY CUP WITH YOUR LOVE SO WHEN I AM BUMPED ONLY LOVE WILL SPILL OUT. . .

DEAR LORD, YOU ARE MY RESTING PLACE

DEAR LORD, I WANT TO SHOW MY LOVE TO YOU BY BEING SURRENDERED TO YOUR WILL. . .

TO HELP WITH YOUR HELP. . .

DEAR LORD, SHOW ME HOW TO USE MY MISTAKES AS STEPPING STONES TO GREATER HEIGHTS. . .

THANK YOU, LORD, FOR HELPING ME USE THE GIFTS YOU HAVE GIVEN ME. . .

DEAR GOD, THANK YOU FOR BEING MY DEPENDABLE FATHER, TO LOVE, TO GUIDE AND TO HELP ME EACH DAY. . .

DEAR LORD, I AM AMAZED THAT YOU WOULD HAVE SUCH MERCY ON ME TO FORGIVE ME TIME AND TIME AGAIN. . .

DEAR GOD, HELP ME TO EXPERIENCE THE JOY THAT COMES WITH BEING ACCEPTED JUST AS I AM. . .

DEAR LORD, HELP ME TO REMEMBER "HE THAT IS GREATEST AMONG YOU SHALL BE YOUR SERVANT" . . .

DEAR GOD, HELP ME TO MEET THE CHALLENGES THAT I FACE TODAY. . .

DEAR LORD, THANK YOU THAT YOU NEVER REMEMBER A CONFESSED WRONG THAT I HAVE MADE. . .

DEAR GOD, I WANT YOU TO BE MY FIRST CHOICE AND NOT MY LAST RESORT.

DEAR GOD, THANK YOU THAT THE NAME OF JESUS CHRIST IS THE PASSWORD TO A BETTER LIFE. . .

DEAR LORD, THANK YOU FOR CLEANSING AWAY ALL MY SIN BY YOUR PRECIOUS BLOOD SHED ON THE CROSS. . .

DEAR LORD, HELP ME TO ACT IN FAITH UPON YOUR WORD RATHER THAN JUST BELIEVE. . .

DEAR LORD, THANK YOU FOR BEING A CARING FATHER

THANK YOU, LORD, FOR YOUR WORD THAT SAYS YOU ARE MY LIGHT AND SALVATION, WHOM SHALL I FEAR?

DEAR GOD, CHASE AWAY THE DREAM MONSTERS FROM THE DARK PLACES OF MY LIFE. . .

DEAR LORD, KEEP MY MIND AND HEART OPEN TO SEE NEEDS AND RESPOND WITH LOVE AND PRAYER. . .

DEAR GOD, I WANT YOUR WILL TO BE DONE ON EARTH AS IT IS IN HEAVEN. . .

DEAR LORD, HELP ME NOT TO DOUBT YOUR WRITTEN WORDS

DEAR LORD, THANK YOU THAT YOU ARE GREATER IN ME THAN THE EVIL ONE. . .

DEAR GOD, THANK YOU THAT YOU LOVE ME AND HAVE A WONDERFUL PLAN FOR MY LIVE. . .

DEAR GOD, HELP ME TO LOVE WHAT YOU LOVE AND TO HATE WHAT YOU HATE. . .

DEAR GOD, THANK YOU FOR THE MIRACLES YOU PERFORM FOR ME EACH DAY. . .

DEAR GOD, HELP ME TO LISTEN TO YOUR WHISPER

DEAR LORD, SPEAK TO ME THROUGH YOUR WRITTEN WORD

DEAR LORD, HELP ME TO BE GENEROUS WITH KIND WORDS AND MONEY. . .

DEAR GOD, THANK YOU THAT YOU HAVE SAID YOU WILL NEVER LEAVE ME OR FORSAKE ME. . .

DEAR GOD, AS I SEEK TO BUILD A STRONG BODY, HELP ME TO BUILD A STRONG SPIRIT. . .

DEAR LORD, IN YOUR NAME I CAST OUT ALL SICKNESS AND DISEASES. . .

DEAR LORD, HELP ME TO LEAVE ALL MY WORRIES IN YOUR MIGHTY HANDS. . .

DEAR GOD, THANK YOU FOR YOUR PROMISE THAT YOU WILL GIVE SUPPLY FOR ALL OF MY NEEDS. . .

DEAR LORD, WHEN I AM CRITICIZED UNJUSTLY, HELP ME TO LAUGH. . .

DEAR LORD, HELP ME TO OVERLOOK UNKINDNESS'S AND TO SHOW A FRIENDLY, FORGIVING SPIRIT. . .

DEAR GOD, IN THE QUIET OF THIS MOMENT, SPEAK TO ME IN MY HEART. . .

DEAR LORD, KEEP ME FROM CONCENTRATING ONLY ON THE MATERIAL TO THE NEGLECT OF THE SPIRITUAL. . .

DEAR GOD, HELP ME TO GROW IN WISDOM AND TO BE DEPENDABLE. . .

DEAR GOD, THANK YOU FOR YOUR PROMISE THAT WHOEVER CALLS ON THE NAME OF THE LORD JESUS CHRIST WELL BE SAVED FOR HEAVEN. . .

DEAR LORD, GUARD ME AGAINST LOSING MY TEMPER WHEN THE GOING IS ROUGH. . .

DEAR LORD, HELP ME TO REMEMBER THAT I AM NEVER ALONE

DEAR LORD, THANK YOU FOR MY CHURCH FAMILY

DEAR LORD, HELP ME TO BE FAITHFUL TOWARD YOU AND OTHERS

DEAR LORD, I WILL TAKE TIME TO PRAY THAT CALM WILL REMAIN WITH ME DURING STRESS AND TRIALS. . .

DEAR LORD, KEEP ME FROM GIVING UP BECAUSE OF WHAT SEEMS TOO HARD TO OVERCOME.

DEAR LORD, HELP ME TO REMEMBER THAT EVERY ACT OF KINDNESS TO OTHERS IS AN ACT OF KINDNESS TO YOU. . .

DEAR LORD, HELP ME TO DO TO OTHERS AS I WOULD HAVE THEM DO TO ME. . .

DEAR LORD, HELP ME TO FIND IN ALL CRITICISM A MEANS BY WHICH TO GROW

DEAR GOD, THANK YOU THAT I CAN DO ALL THINGS THROUGH CHRIST WHO STRENGTHENS ME. . .

DEAR GOD, THANK YOU FOR ALL THE PEOPLE THAT LOVE ME. . .

DEAR LORD, HELP ME TO SHARE WITH OTHERS HOW THEY CAN BE SURE OF GOING TO HEAVEN WHEN THEY DIE BY RECEIVING CHRIST AS SAVIOR. . .

LORD, RAISE UP THE RIGHTEOUS AND PUT DOWN THE DISHONEST. . .

DEAR GOD, GIVE ME THE COURAGE AND THE STRENGTH TO DO THE DIFFICULT THING. . .

DEAR GOD, HELP ME TO PUT MY GOOD THOUGHTS INTO ACTIONS. . .

DEAR LORD, MAY I LEARN TO SAY WITH APOSTLE PAUL, "FOR ME TO LIVE IS CHRIST. . .

DEAR LORD, THANK YOU FOR THE FELLOWSHIP MY CHURCH GIVES ME. . .

DEAR LORD, MAY I SHOW CHRIST'S SPIRIT IN MY DAILY LIVING

DEAR GOD, THANK YOU FOR THE BIBLE AS MY TRUE GUIDE FOR LIVING. . .

DEAR LORD, HELP ME TO SEE MY OWN FAULTS THAT I MAY LOOK MORE KINDLY ON THE FAULTS OF OTHERS. . .

DEAR GOD, GIVE ME THE PATIENCE, FAITH AND COURAGE THAT GROW OUT OF TROUBLES AND DISAPPOINTMENTS. . .

DEAR GOD, I WANT YOUR HOLY SPIRIT TO FILL MY LIFE. . .

DEAR GOD, TOUCH ME AND HEAL ME

DEAR LORD, I WANT YOU TO HAVE YOUR WAY IN MY LIFE

DEAR LORD, I WILL SERVE YOU BECAUSE I LOVE YOU

DEAR LORD, I GIVE YOU PRAISE FOR ALL THE THINGS YOU HAVE DONE FOR ME.

DEAR LORD, I GIVE YOU ALL THE GLORY FOR EVERYTHING GOOD IN MY LIFE.

DEAR GOD, HELP ME TO FREE MYSELF OF FEELINGS THAT BRING DOUBTS TO MY FAITH IN YOUR WORD. . .

DEAR GOD, IN GOVERNMENT LEADERSHIP, RAISE UP THE RIGHTEOUS. . .

DEAR LORD, I WANT TO HAVE AN ATTITUDE OF GRATITUDE. . .

DEAR GOD, IN EVERYTHING I GIVE YOU THANKS. . .

DEAR LORD, I PRAY FOR A SAFE AND HAPPY THANKSGIVING DAY FOR EVERYONE. . .

DEAR GOD, HELP ME TO FIND A REMEDY RATHER THAN A FAULT. . .

DEAR LORD, HELP ME TO LISTEN TO YOU SPEAKING TO ME. . .

DEAR LORD, I SURRENDER ALL TO YOU. . .

DEAR LORD, BRING PEOPLE TO ME WHO NEED HELP. . .

DEAR GOD, I THANK YOU THAT THE BEST IS YET TO COME INTO MY LIFE. . .

DEAR LORD, I PRAY THAT ALL OF MY FAMILY WILL BE DEVOTED TO YOU. . .

DEAR LORD, THANK YOU FOR YOUR AMAZING GRACE THAT SAVES SOMEONE LIKE ME

DEAR GOD, I WANT TO SMILE AT YOU AND OTHERS MORE. . .

DEAR GOD, HELP ME TO BE ALWAYS FILLED WITH YOUR HOLY SPIRIT. . .

DEAR LORD, I WANT TO PLEASE YOU ALWAYS. . .

DEAR LORD, USE ME FOR YOUR GLORY. . .

DEAR GOD, IN THE CHOICES OF LIFE I CHOOSE FAITHFULNESS, MERCY, COMPASSION AND CHARACTER. . .

DEAR GOD, IN THE CHOICES OF LIFE I CHOOSE PATIENCE, KINDNESS, AND JOY..

DEAR GOD, IN THE CHOICES OF LIFE I CHOOSE LOVE. . .

GRACIOUS GOD, I AM THANKFUL THAT I AM WHAT YOU SAY I AM. . .

THANK YOU, LORD, THAT PEACE IS THE PERSON OF CHRIST IN MY LIFE. . .

DEAR LORD, WHAT I NEEDED THE MOST AND DESERVED IT THE LEAST, I GOT FROM YOU. . .

SPIRIT OF THE LIVING GOD, FALL AFRESH ON ME. . .

DEAR LORD, I KNOW THIS WORLD IS NOT MY HOME, I'M JUST PASSING THROUGH. . .

THANK YOU, LORD, FOR YOUR INFINITE GRACE GIVEN TO ME. . .

LOVING LORD, I PRAISE YOU THAT AS YOU SAVED MY SOUL YOU ALSO HEALED MY BODY. . .

DEAR LORD, INSTRUCT ME AND TEACH ME THE WAY I SHOULD GO

DEAR LORD, I PRAISE YOU FOR YOUR GOODNESS, GRACE AND GENEROSITY TO ME. . .

DEAR LORD, HELP ME TO PLANT YOUR WORD IN MY HEART AND TO REAP ITS BENEFITS. . .

DEAR LORD, I WANT TO PLEASE YOU IN ALL I DO. . .

THANK YOU LORD, THAT FAITH IS MY INVISIBLE MEANS OF SUPPORT. . .

DEAR LORD, THANK YOU THAT YOU COULD NOT LOVE ME ANY MORE THAN YOU DO NOW. . .

DEAR GOD, I WANT TO BELIEVE AND RECEIVE RATHER DOUBT AND BE WITHOUT. . .

DEAR LORD, I WANT TO MAKE YOU HAPPY. . .

DEAR GOD, YOUR GREAT LOVE TO ME IS AMAZING. . .

DEAR LORD, THANK YOU FOR GIVING JESUS CHRIST TO BE MY SAVIOR. . .

THANK YOU LORD THAT OLD THINGS ARE PASSED AWAY AND ALL THINGS ARE MADE NEW IN CHRIST. . .

DEAR LORD, I AM SO HAPPY THAT YOU ARE COMING BACK AS YOU PROMISED. . .

DEAR GOD, HELP ME TO LOOK FORWARD RATHER THAN LOOKING BACK. . .

DEAR GOD, I LOVE YOU WITH ALL MY HEART. . .

DEAR GOD, PUT A CONTINUAL HUNGER IN MY HEART FOR INTIMACY WITH YOU. . .

DEAR GOD, INSTEAD OF ME CRITICIZING, I WANT TO PRAY. . .

MY DEAR GOD, THANK YOU FOR LOVING ME SO MUCH THAT YOU SENT YOUR ONLY BEGOTTEN SON, THAT I MIGHT BELIEVE IN HIM AND HAVE EVERLASTING LIFE. . .

DEAR GOD, I WANT TO BE WHAT YOU WANT ME TO BE. . .

DEAR GOD, HELP ME TO BE FAITHFUL IN LITTLE THINGS. . .

DEAR LORD, HELP ME TO LOVE MORE. . .

DEAR GOD, WORK ON ME TO DO YOUR WILL. . .

DEAR LORD, HELP ME TO DO MY WORK CHEERFULLY. . .

DEAR LORD, I AM THANKFUL FOR THE ONE WHO PRAYED FOR ME. . .

THE GREATEST THING IN ALL MY LIFE IS KNOWING YOU. . .

DEAR GOD, I THANK YOU THAT YOU HAVE MADE ME DIFFERENT. . .

DEAR LORD, HELP ME TO BE AWARE OF YOUR PRESENCE IN MY DAILY LIFE. . .

DEAR GOD, I THANK YOU FOR THE GLAD REUNION I WILL HAVE WITH MY LOVED ONES IN HEAVEN. . .

DEAR GOD, YOU BEGAN A GOOD WORK IN ME AND I TRUST YOU TO CONTINUE IT. . .

DEAR LORD, I THANK YOU FOR YOUR WORD THAT SAYS OLD THINGS ARE PASSED AWAY AND ALL THINGS HAVE BECOME NEW. . .

DEAR GOD, I WANT TO GIVE YOU GLORY BY MY PRAISING YOU. . .

I WANT TO DO PHYSICAL AND SPIRITUAL WORKOUTS. . .

DEAR LORD, WHEN I CAN'T SLEEP, I'LL PRAY FOR PEOPLE. . .

DEAR LORD, I CAST ALL MY WORRIES UPON YOU AS YOU SAID IN YOUR WORD. . .

HELP ME TO REMEMBER IT IS MORE BLESSED TO GIVE THAN TO RECEIVE. . .

DEAR GOD, YOU ARE MY HAPPINESS. . .

I WANT TO WRITE MY HURTS IN THE SAND AND MY BLESSINGS IN CONCRETE. . .

DEAR GOD, I WANT TO HAVE AN ATTITUDE OF GRATITUDE. . .

DEAR GOD, I TAKE MY WORRIES TO YOU AND LEAVE THEM THERE.

DEAR GOD, THE VERY THOUGHT OF YOU FILLS ME WITH JOY AND HOPE. . .

DEAR LORD, I WANT TO CONTINUALLY BE FILLED WITH YOUR HOLY SPIRIT. . .

DEAR GOD, I WILL PRAISE YOU AS LONG AS YOU GIVE ME BREATH.

DEAR GOD, I LOVE YOU BECAUSE YOU FIRST LOVED ME. . .

DEAR GOD, I WANT TO FOCUS ON YOU AND NOT THE PROBLEM. . .

BREATHE ON ME BREATH OF GOD, UNTIL MY HEART IS PURE. . .

BREATHE ON ME, BREATH OF GOD, FILL ME WITH LIFE ANEW. . .

THANK YOU, LORD, FOR THE ASSURANCE THAT WHEN I CLOSE MY EYES IN DEATH, I OPEN THEM IN HEAVEN. . .

DEAR LORD, I WANT MY PURPOSE IN LIFE TO BE YOUR PURPOSE

DEAR LORD, WHEN I CAN'T FALL ASLEEP AT NIGHT I WILL PRAY. . .

YOU ARE MY STRENGTH WHEN I AM WEAK; YOU ARE MY ALL IN ALL. . .

"AMAZING LOVE. . . I KNOW IT'S TRUE . . . . .AND IT'S MY JOY TO HONOR YOU."

"AMAZING LOVE HOW CAN IT BE THAT YOU MY KING WOULD DIE FOR ME?'. . .

THANK YOU FOR THE PEACE YOU PUT IN MY HEART AS I TRUST IN YOU. . .

DEAR LORD, THANK YOU FOR FREEING MY SPIRIT TO BE ABLE TO LIFT MY HANDS TO PRAISE YOU. . .

DEAR LORD, OPEN MY EYES THAT I MAY SEE THE TRUTHS AND PLANS YOU HAVE FOR ME. . .

THANK YOU FOR YOUR PROMISE THAT YOU WILL NEVER LEAVE ME OR FORSAKE ME. . .

O LORD, YOU ARE SO GOOD AND KIND, SO FULL OF MERCY FOR ALL WHO ASK YOUR AID.

I CALL UPON YOU, LORD, AND YOU HELP ME

I AM WAITING FOR YOU, DEAR LORD, PLEASE COME AND HELP ME. . .

I AM DELIGHTED TO KNOW YOU, LORD. . .

THANK YOU LORD, THAT YOU NEVER FORSAKE THOSE WHO TRUST IN YOU. . .

LORD, I WILL NOT WORRY WHEN I CAN PRAY. . .

DEAR LORD, DON'T ALLOW US TO ENTER TEMPTATION. . .

DEAR GOD, I WILL TRUST YOU EVEN WHEN I DO NOT UNDERSTAND. . .

DEAR LORD, BECAUSE YOU ARE MY SHEPHERD I WILL NOT FEAR OR LACK. . .

DEAR GOD, THANK YOU FOR THE SONG YOU HAVE PUT IN MY HEART

DEAR LORD, I LOOK FORWARD TO YOUR SECOND COMING TO EARTH. . .

DEAR LORD, THANK YOU FOR YOUR PROMISE THAT YOU WILL NEVER LEAVE ME OR FORSAKE ME. . .

THANK YOU, LORD, THAT YOU LOVE EACH OF US AS IF THERE WERE ONLY ONE OF US. . .

DEAR GOD, DRAW ME INTO DEEP PERSONAL INTIMACY WITH YOU. . .

DESPITE MY TROUBLING CIRCUMSTANCES, I WILL STILL PRAISE YOU. . .

LIVE YOUR LIFE THROUGH ME, LORD. . .

DEAR LORD, I NOT ONLY LOVE YOU, I AM IN LOVE WITH YOU. . .

THANK YOU, LORD, FOR WATCHING OVER MY FAMILY. . .

DEAR LORD, MAY OUR COUNTRY HAVE A SPIRITUAL REVIVAL TO SURVIVE.

THANK YOU LORD, THAT THE BAD SITUATION WILL NOT LAST. . .

DEAR LORD, I WANT TO ALWAYS GIVE YOU THE GLORY FOR THE COMPLIMENTS I GET. . .

DEAR LORD, I WANT YOU TO LOVE THROUGH ME. . .

THANK YOU, LORD, FOR THE PRIVILEGE OF BRINGING EVERYTHING TO YOU IN PRAYER. . .

THANK YOU LORD, THAT LITTLE IS MUCH WHEN YOU ARE IN IT. . .

DEAR GOD, I CONFESS MY SIN TO YOU AND YOU FORGIVE AND FORGET IT. . .

YOU HAVE MADE ME GLAD. . .

DEAR LORD, I THANK YOU FOR MY CHURCH THAT IS DOING YOUR WILL..

LORD, GIVE ME STRENGTH AND WISDOM TO ACCOMPLISH MY WORK. . .

DEAR GOD, MAKE ME A BLESSING TO SOMEONE TODAY. . .

DEAR GOD, MAKE SOMETHING BEAUTIFUL OUT OF MY LIFE. . .

DEAR LORD, YOU GAVE YOUR LIFE TO RANSOM MY SOUL, NOW I BELONG TO YOU. . .

WE CAN MAKE OUR PLANS, LORD, BUT THE OUTCOME IS IN YOUR HANDS. . .

DEAR LORD, DIRECT MY PATH. . .

DEAR LORD, I WANT TO TRUST AND OBEY YOU. . .

I PRAISE YOU, LORD, FOR ALL THAT YOU HAVE DONE TO ANSWER MY PRAYER. . .

THANK YOU, LORD, THAT YOU ARE WITH ME IN MY TROUBLE AND WILL RESCUE ME.

LORD, YOU DIED FOR ME AND I WILL LIVE FOR YOU..

OH WHAT LOVE THAT YOU WOULD DIE FOR ME. . .

THANK YOU, JESUS, FOR PAYING THE DEBT FOR ALL MY SINS. . .

DEAR LORD, NO MATTER WHAT REJECTION I HAVE FACED, YOU HAVE ACCEPTED ME. . .

DEAR GOD, DON'T LET ME GRIEVE OVER PAST MISTAKES. . .

LORD, I WANT TO BE POSITIVE AND ENTHUSIASTIC. . .

DEAR LORD, I WANT TO BE HOOKED ON HELPING. . .

I PRAISE YOU FROM WHOM ALL BLESSINGS FLOW. . .

THANK YOU, LORD, FOR THE FRIENDS I HAVE THAT STAND UP FOR ME. . .

LORD, HELP ME TO BE OF GOOD COURAGE. . .

DEAR LORD, TURN THINGS AROUND FOR MY GOOD. . .

THANK YOU LORD, FOR GOOD HEALTH. . .

LORD, I WANT A LARGE SUM OF MONEY TO GIVE AWAY. . .

LORD, EVEN THOUGH I DON'T UNDERSTAND WHY YOU DO OR DON'T DO, I WILL TRUST YOU. . .

THANK YOU LORD, THAT THE BEST IS YET TO COME. . .

I GIVE YOU THANKS FOR ALL THAT YOU BRING INTO MY LIFE. . .

LOVE THROUGH ME, LORD. . .

LORD, I WANT TO HELP ANSWER YOUR PRAYER THAT WE WOULD BE ONE. . .

DEAR GOD, YOUR LOVE LIFTED ME. . .

LORD, HELP ME TO SHOW LOVE TO MY NEIGHBORS. . .

HELP ME TO HANDLE MY FINANCES WISELY. . .

THE GREATEST THING IN ALL THE WORLD IS LOVING YOU. . .

THANK YOU, LORD, FOR THE MIRACLES IN MY LIFE. . .

LORD, GIVE ME A HUNGER TO READ YOUR WORD DAILY. . .

DEAR LORD, DO NOT LET ME ENTER TEMPTATIONS. . .

THOUGH I WALK THROUGH THE VALLEY OF THE SHADOW OF DEBT, I WILL FEAR NO EVIL FOR YOU ARE WITH ME. . .

DEAR GOD, GIVE ME A LOT OF WISDOM..

LORD, I WANT TO BELIEVE, HELP MY UNBELIEF. . .

DEAR GOD, SHOW ME WHAT YOU WANT ME TO DO TODAY. . .

LORD, THANK YOU FOR THE MIRACLES IN MY LIFE. . .

DEAR LORD, HELP ME TO UNDERSTAND THE BIBLE BETTER. . .

I DON'T WANT TO BE A FAULTFINDER. . .

I FORGIVE EVERYONE WHO HAS EVER OFFENDED OR HURT ME. . .

I WANT TO BE MORE LIKE JESUS. . .

IN HOURS OF LONELINESS, WEARINESS AND TRIALS, JESUS, HELP ME. . .

DEAR LORD, WHEN WE ALL GET TO HEAVEN, WHAT A DAY OF REJOICING THAT WILL BE. . .

DEAR GOD, I AM SO GLAD YOU BROUGHT HER INTO MY LIFE. . .

LORD JESUS, COME BACK TO EARTH SOON. . .

THANK YOU, GOD, THE BEST IS YET TO COME AND WON'T IT BE FINE. . .

THANK YOU FOR YOUR GOODNESS AND FAITHFULNESS IN MY LIFE. . .

LORD, HELP ME TO DISAGREE WITHOUT BEING DISAGREEABLE. . .

AMAZING LOVE, LORD JESUS, THAT YOU DIED FOR MY SINS. . .

LORD, TELL MOTHER I'LL BE THERE IN ANSWER TO HER PRAYER. . .

LORD, GUIDE ME TO EAT PROPERLY. . .

DEAR LORD, GIVE ME A HUNGER TO KNOW YOU BETTER. . .

DEAR GOD, I SMILE BECAUSE YOU LOVE ME. . .

LORD, HELP TO HELP PEOPLE GET SAVED. . .

DEAR GOD, HELP ME TO RESIST THE DEVIL'S TEMPTATIONS. . .

DEAR LORD, I WANT TO TAKE TIME TO MEDITATE ON YOU AND YOUR LOVE TO ME. . .

YOU DO RIGHT NOW. . .

LORD, I WANT TO MAKE YOU HAPPY WITH ME. . .

DEAR LORD, HELP ME TO MAKE THE RIGHT CHOICE. . .

DEAR GOD, I THANK YOU FOR MY SWEET PET. . .

STRENGTHEN ME WITH YOUR STRENGTH, LORD. . .

HOLY SPIRIT, TAKE CONTROL OF MY THOUGHTS, SPEECH AND ACTIONS. . .

DEAR GOD, SET ME FREE FROM ALL GUILT, SHAME AND FEAR. . .

DEAR GOD, THE MONEY I HAVE LOST IN LOANING, I GIVE TO YOU. . .

LORD, I WANT TO BE LIKE A LITTLE CHILD IN TRUSTING YOU. . .

LORD, HELP ME TO BE SENSITIVE TO THE FEELINGS OF OTHERS..

I THANK YOU, LORD, THAT YOUR WILL IS BEING DONE ON EARTH AS IT IS IN HEAVEN IN MANY PLACES AND WITH MANY PERSONS. . .

MARANATHA, COME LORD JESUS. . .

YAHWEH, YOU HAVE CREATED ME AND I AM YOURS. . .

DEAR GOD, HELP ME TO LIVE A HOLY LIFE FOR YOU. . .

LORD, SPARK A NEW HOPE IN MY HEART. . .

THANK YOU, LORD, THAT I HAVE A RELATIONSHIP WITH YOU. . .

DEAR LORD, INCREASE MY THIRST FOR THE FILLING OF YOUR HOLY SPIRIT. . .

THANK YOU, LORD, THAT MY PRAYERS ARE ON DEPOSIT AND YOU WON'T FORGET THEM. . . .

DEAR LORD, THANK YOU FOR THE GREAT IDEAS YOU GIVE ME. . .

THANK YOU, LORD, THAT YOU CANNOT LOVE ME ANY MORE THAN YOU DO RIGHT NOW. . . .

DEAR GOD, I LOVE YOU SOOOOOO MUCH. . .

THANK YOU LORD, THAT NOTHING IS GOING TO HAPPEN TO ME THAT YOU AND I TOGETHER CAN'T HANDLE..

DEAR LORD, HELP ME TO SERVE OTHERS. . .

THANKS, LORD, FOR BEAUTIFUL MEMORIES. . .

WHAT A PRIVILEGE TO SERVE A MIGHTY GOD. . .

LORD, SAVE MY LOVED ONE TODAY. . .

HEAL MY PET, LORD. . .

HELP ME ALWAYS TO SPEAK THE TRUTH. . .

THANKS, LORD, FOR THE DAILY MIRACLES IN MY LIFE. . .

LORD, HELP ME TO RESIST THE DEMON. . .

I THANK YOU, LORD, FOR ALL OF THE MIRACLES YOU ARE DOING IN OUR CHURCH. . .

DEAR LORD, I ALWAYS WANT TO BLESS YOU. . .

MY DEAR GOD, I WANT TO MAKE YOU SMILE. . .

I TRUST YOU THAT YOU ARE WORKING THINGS OUT FOR MY GOOD. . .

THANKS FOR BEING WITH ME THROUGH THE STORM. . .

Lord, make me useful. . .

DEAR GOD, HELP ME TO BE PATIENT FOR THE ANSWER TO MY PRAYER. . .

MY FATHER IN HEAVEN AND IN ME, HALLOWED BE YOUR NAME, YAHWEH. . .

IN THE LORD. . .

OTHERS MAY REJECT ME, BUT I AM ACCEPTED BY YOU, LORD. . .

GLORY BE TO YOU, LORD, FOR THE 1001 VIEWS SO FAR TODAY OF MY ONE LINER PRAYERS. . .

THANKS FOR YOUR PEACE WHEN I KEEP MY MIND ON YOU. . .

HELP ME TO LOVE THE UNLOVELY. . .

DEAR GOD, I THANK YOU FOR HEAVEN. . .

THANK YOU, LORD, FOR SAVING ALL THE MEMBERS OF MY FAMILY,

LORD, HELP THAT ONE WHO STOLE FROM ME TO REPENT AND BE SAVED. . .

I FORGIVE MY DAD WHO DID NOT KNOW HOW TO SHOW ME LOVE. . .

LET NO SICKNESS BE IN ME. . .

DEAR LORD, SHOW ME THE WAY I SHOULD GO. . .

DEAR LORD, I WANT EVERY PRAYER OF MINE TO MEAN I WANT YOUR WILL TO BE DONE. . .

THANK YOU, GOD, THAT YOU NOT ONLY FORGIVE MY SINS, BUT YOUALSO FORGET THEM. . .

THANK YOU, LORD, FOR PREPARING A PLACE IN HEAVEN FOR ME AND MY FAMILY. . .

DEAR LORD, WHEN FEAR COMES, HELP ME TO SING IT AWAY. . .

DEAR GOD, DO NOT LET FEARFUL NIGHTMARES COME INTO MY SLEEP. . .

USE ME, LORD. . .

DEAR LORD, I WANT TO KNOW YOU MORE INTIMATELY. . .

HELP ME TO BLESS MY ENEMIES. . .

I PRAY FOR ALL OF OUR GOVERNMENT LEADERS TO BE TRUSTING

I LOVE YOU, LORD, WITH ALL MY HEART. . .

DEAR LORD, HELP ME TO SHOW MERCY TO OTHERS. . .

USE ME, LORD, TO DO WHATEVER YOU WANT ME TO DO. . .

DEAR LORD, MY LOVED ONES HAVE LOST THEIR WAY, BRING THEM BACK TO YOU. . .

THANK YOU, LORD, YOU WILL NOT LET ME CARRY BURDENS THAT ARE MORE THAN I CAN BEAR. . .

THANKS FOR THE LOVE, JOY AND PEACE YOU BRING MY WAY. . .

I APPRECIATE YOUR PRESENCE IN MY TROUBLE. . .

LORD, I CAST MY BURDENS ON YOU. . .

DEAR LORD, HELP ME TO SLEEP IN PEACE. . .

DEAR LORD, HELP ME TO BLESS MY ENEMIES. . .

THANK YOU, HOLY SPIRIT, FOR HELPING ME PRAY. . .

I PRAY THAT ALL MY FAMILY WILL BE DEVOTED FOLLOWERS OF CHRIST. . .

LORD, I WANT TO BE WHAT YOU WANT ME TO BE. . .

DEAR GOD, KEEP THE LITTLE CHILDREN SAFE. . .

LORD, HELP ME TO SET ASIDE THAT HURT THAT WAS GIVEN ME. . .

DEAR LORD, I WANT TO SOAK IN YOUR FELT PRESENCE. . .

THANK YOU, LORD, FOR MY FAMILY. . .

DEAR LORD, I LOVE THAT YOU ARE COMING BACK TO EARTH TO RAISE THE BODIES OF THE BELIEVERS FROM THEIR GRAVES. . .

DEAR GOD, SEARCH MY HEART AND MIND AND REMOVE ANYTHING THAT DOES NOT PLEASE YOU. . .

LORD, I AM SO HAPPY THAT YOU LOVE ME. . .

DEAR GOD, I PRAISE YOU FOR YOUR BEAUTIFUL CREATION. . .

MAKE ME A BLESSING TO SOMEONE TODAY. . .

SHOW ME WHAT IS MY PURPOSE IN LIFE. . .

LORD, I WOULD LIKE THIS DAY TO BE THE GREATEST DAY OF MY LIFE. . .

GUIDE ME IN MY CHOICES THAT I MAY KNOW WHICH IS THE RIGHT THING TO DO. . .

LORD, KEEP ME FROM GIVING UP BECAUSE OF WHAT SEEMS TOO HARD TO OVERCOME. . .

LORD, HELP ME TO REMEMBER THAT EVERY ACT OF KINDNESS TO OTHERS IS AN ACT OF KINDNESS TO YOU.

LORD, HELP ME TO DO TO OTHERS WHAT I WOULD WANT THEM TO DO TO ME. . .

LORD, HELP ME TO SHARE MY SPIRITUAL RICHES WITH OTHERS. . .

HELP ME TO TRUST AND NOT BE AFRAID. . .

LORD, HELP ME TO GO THROUGH DAYS WITHOUT SINNING. . .

THANKS FOR THE BEAUTY OF YOUR CREATION. . .

DEAR LORD, HELP ME TO BE JOYFUL ALL DAY TODAY. . .

LORD, FILL MY HEART WITH JOY TO MAKE IT KNOWN TO OTHERS THE HAPPINESS OF FOLLOWING YOUR WAY OF LIFE. . .

THANK YOU FOR THE FELLOWSHIP MY CHURCH GIVES ME. . .

HELP ME TO LIVE IN SUCH A WAY AS TO BRING GLORY TO YOUR NAME. . .

LORD, GUIDE ME TO CHOOSE WISELY. . .

LORD, HELP ME TO SHOW OTHERS THAT THE LIFE CENTERED IN YOU IS THE RICHEST AND MOST REWARDING WAY TO LIVE. . .

THANK YOU LORD, FOR MY HAPPY TIMES. . .

LORD, HELP ME TO USE UNHAPPY TIMES AS TIMES FOR GROWTH. . .

LORD, REVEAL YOUR PURPOSE IN MY TRIALS. . .

THANK YOU FOR ALL MY FRIENDS. . .

DEAR GOD, RAISE UP YOUNG PEOPLE WHO LEAD OUR COUNTRY IN RIGHT WAYS. . .

DEAR LORD, GUIDE ME TO MAKE WISE CHOICES. . .

DEAR LORD, HELP ME TO OVERCOME OBSTACLES THAT TEND TO GET ME DOWN. . .

THANK YOU, THANK YOU, THANK YOU, THANK YOU, THANK YOU, LORD!

THANK YOU LORD, FOR MAKING ME A HAPPY CHRISTIAN. . .

THANK YOU, LORD, FOR ALL MY BLESSINGS. . .

HELP ME TO THINK THOUGHTS OF GOOD WILL, LOVE, UNDERSTANDING AND SYMPATHY TOWARD OTHERS. . .

LORD, I AM THANKFUL FOR YOUR LOVE FOR ME. . .

PRECIOUS LORD, THANK YOU FOR YOUR STRENGTH IN MY WEAKNESS. . .

THANK YOU, LORD, FOR ALL THOSE WHO HAVE BEEN USED BY YOU TO MAKE ME BETTER. . .

LORD, HELP ME TO LET GO OF THE PAST AND KEEP MY EYES ON THE FUTURE. . .

LORD, HELP ME TO PLUG INTO YOUR POWER. . .

LORD, HELP ME TO BE AN EXAMPLE OF YOUR LOVE.

THANK YOU, JESUS, FOR BEING MY SAVIOR. . .

THANK YOU, LORD, FOR GIVING ME A GIVING HEART. . .

LORD, HELP ME TO SEE THE WAYS I NEED TO CHANGE. . .

THANKS, LORD, FOR MAKING ME HAPPY. . .

GOD, HELP ME TO MAKE YOU SMILE. . .

HELP ME TO BE LIKE JESUS. . .

LORD, I WANT TO ALWAYS PLEASE YOU. . .

THANK YOU LORD, THAT YOU MAKE A WAY FOR ME TO GET OUR OF TROUBLES. . .

LORD THANK YOU, THAT YOU WONT LET ME CARRY A BURDEN TOO HEAVY FOR ME. . . .

DEAR LORD, I RELEASE ALL MY WORRIES TO YOU. . .

LORD, HELP ME TO REMEMBER YOUR PRESENCE IN MY LIFE. . .

DEAR GOD, THANK YOU FOR THE FRIENDS WHO LOVE ME. . .

GOD, HELP ME TO BE PATIENT WHILE WAITING FOR YOUR ANSWER TO MY PRAYER. . .

THANKS FOR THE HAPPINESS I HAVE AS YOUR CHILD. . .

DEAR LORD, I WAIT FOR YOUR GOOD TIMING IN GRANTING MY REQUESTS. . .

THANK YOU JESUS, YOU PAID THE DEBT FOR ALL MY SINS. . .

JESUS, HURRY BACK PLEASE. . .

THANK YOU, LORD, FOR THE ASSURANCE OF BEING SAVED FOR HEAVEN BY RECEIVING CHRIST AS MY SAVIOR. . .

LORD, I WILL TRUST AND NOT BE AFRAID. . .

I PRAISE YOU, MY GOD. . .

LORD, MAY THIS DAY BE GOOD. . .

HELP ME TO BE AN ENCOURAGER. . .

THANKS LORD, FOR THE GIFT OF LAUGHTER. . .

HELP ME TO LIVE BY FAITH AND NOT BY SIGHT. . .

I HAVE BEEN FORGIVEN, SO I FORGIVE OTHERS. . .

YOU STRENGTHEN ME FOR WHAT NEEDS TO BE DONE.

THANKS FOR THE SUPPLY OF ALL MY NEEDS. . .

THANKS FOR GIVING ME THE POWER OF LOVE AND A SOUND MIND. . .

THANK YOU FOR THE ANGELS THAT HAVE BEEN SENT TO HELP ME. . .

THANKS THAT YOU WILL NEVER DESERT ME OR FORSAKE ME.

I PRAISE YOU, THAT BY YOUR STRIPES, LORD JESUS, I AM HEALED. . .

LORD, SHOW ME THE WAY I SHOULD GO. . .

LORD, KEEP ME SAFE. . .

YOU ARE A VERY PRESENT HELP IN TROUBLE. . .

INSTRUCT ME AND TEACH ME THE WAY I SHOULD GO. . .

LORD, INCREASE MY FINANCES. . .

LORD, HELP ME TO PAY OFF THE LARGE FINANCIAL DEBT. . .

THANK YOU, LORD, FOR THE GIFT OF LAUGHTER.

GOD, MAKE ME ALERT TO YOU, SPEAKING TO ME.

LORD, HELP ME TO BE CHILD-LIKE.

LORD, HELP ME TO THINK RIGHT.

LORD, HELP ME TO GIVE AND RECEIVE JOYFULLY.

DEAR LORD, I KNOW YOU WILL PROVIDE FOR ME.

THANK YOU, LORD, THAT YOU ARE WITH ME WHEREVER I GO. . .

DEAR GOD, HELP ME OUT OF THE TROUBLE I AM IN. . .

LORD JESUS, THANKS FOR THE POWER IN YOUR NAME. . .

LORD, THANKS FOR MY FAITHFUL FRIENDS. . .

LORD, HELP ME TO TAKE CARE OF MY BODY. . .

HEAVENLY FATHER, ENABLE ME TO BE MORE CARING TO OTHERS. . .

LORD, HELP ME TO BE GENEROUS WITH THE BLESSINGS YOU GIVE ME. . .

LORD, FORGIVE MY WORRYING AND BRING ME PEACE. . .

GOD, HELP ME TO BRING JOY TO OTHERS. . .

THANK YOU LORD, FOR MY MOTHER WHO PRAYED FOR ME. . .

LORD, HELP ME TO COVER THE FAULTS OF OTHERS WITH LOVE. . .

GOD, HELP ME TO BE A GOOD EXAMPLE TO OTHERS. . .

HEAVENLY FATHER, THANK YOU FOR GIVING LOVING GRANDPARENTS.

DEAR GOD, HELP ME IN HELPING OTHERS. . .

HOLY SPIRIT, FILL ME TO OVERFLOWING. . .

GOD, YOUR PRESENCE DISPELS ALL FEARS. . .

THANK YOU LORD, FOR BRINGING SOMETHING GOOD OUT OF MY SUFFERING. . .

LORD, I WANT YOUR WILL TO BE DONE IN MY LIFE ALWAYS. . .

THANKS LORD, THAT WAITING UPON YOU RENEWS MY STRENGTH. . .

GOD, PREVENT ME FROM JUDGING OTHERS. . .

LORD, HELP ME TO PART WITH THE NEGATIVE PAST. . .

LORD, AS I READ YOUR WORD, SHOW ME HOW TO LIVE IT OUT. . .

THANK YOU LORD, FOR THE COMFORT I RECEIVE AS I COMFORT OTHERS. . .

GOD, I PRAISE YOU FOR YOUR MARVELOUS CREATION. . .

LORD, HELP ME TO RELAX. . .

LORD, HELP ME TO THINK ON THINGS THAT ARE GOOD. . .

DEAR GOD, IN MOMENTS OF FEAR HELP ME TO LISTEN TO YOUR DIRECTIONS. . .

I WANT TO COUNT MY BLESSING AND GO TO SLEEP. . .

I WANT TO TRUST IN YOU WITH ALL MY HEART. . .

THANKS, LORD, FOR YOUR PRECIOUS PROMISES TO ME. . .

THANK YOU, LORD, FOR YOUR HEALING POWER IN MY LIFE. . .

I LIVE BY GRACE AND NOT BY LAW. . .

THANK YOU LORD, FOR MAKING ME WHAT YOU WANT ME TO BE. . .

THANK YOU GOD, THAT YOU SAID "GOODNESS AND MERCY WILL FOLLOW ME. . ."

LORD, HELP ME TO FIND COUNSELORS TO HELP GUIDE ME. . .

EVEN THOUGH I GO THROUGH THE SHADOW OF DEATH, YOU ARE WITH ME. . .

LORD, I WANT TO BLESS YOU AT ALL TIMES. . .

FATHER, THANK YOU FOR THE DETOURS YOU HAVE MADE IN MY LIFE. . .

LORD, HELP ME TO OVERCOME THE FEAR OF REJECTION. . .

FATHER, HELP ME TO BE MERCIFUL AS YOU ARE MERCIFUL TO ME. . .

LORD, HELP ME TO REMEMBER THAT WHAT I DO FOR OTHERS, I AM DOING IT FOR YOU. . .

LORD, GUIDE ME HOW TO MAKE SOMEONE'S LIFE BETTER. . .

GOD, REMIND ME TO LOOK TO YOUR WORD FOR GUIDANCE. . .

DEAR LORD, THANK YOU FOR THOSE WHO PRAY FOR ME. . .

IN EVERYTHING I WANT TO GIVE THANKS. . .

GOD, THANK YOU FOR YOUR ARMOR THAT I CAN HAVE ON. . .

LORD, HELP ME TO HAVE A CLEAN CONSCIENCE. . .

LORD, LET THE WORDS OF MY MOUTH BE ACCEPTABLE IN YOUR HEARING. . .

USE ME, LORD, IN ANYWAY YOU WANT.

LORD JESUS, HELP ME TO SEE YOU IN OTHERS.

LORD, HELP ME TO REMEMBER THAT MY LIGHT IS SHINING WHEREVER I GO.

THANK YOU, LORD, FOR THE WISDOM THAT GIVE ME.

GOD, GIVE ME GOOD UNDERSTANDING.

I THANK YOU, LORD, THAT I AM WHAT YOU SAY I AM.

LORD, HELP THE LEADERS OF OUR COUNTRY TO FOLLOW YOUR WAYS.

GOD, BLESS OUR YOUTH TO FOLLOW YOU.

GOD, HELP ME TO APPRECIATE YOUR GREAT POWER.

LORD, MAY OUR CHURCH BE USED OF YOU TO MAKE DISCIPLES.

LORD, MAY THE RULERS OF THE NATIONS TRUST IN YOU.

LORD, HELP ME TO THINK OF YOU DURING THE DAY.

LORD, OVERRULE THE PLANS OF THE WICKED AGAINST YOUR PEOPLE.

DEAR LORD, BLESS THOSE WHO ARE BEING PERSECUTED FOR THEIR FAITH IN YOU.

MAY THOSE WHO PERSECUTE REPENT AND BE SAVED.

MAY THERE BE UNITY AMONG BELIEVERS IN CHRIST.

MAY FAMILIES BE IN UNITY.

MAY FAITH COME TO THOSE WHO DOUBT.

LORD, SHOW NEW BELIEVERS HOW TO GROW IN THEIR FAITH.

THANK YOU, LORD, FOR MAKING ME MORE LIKE JESUS.

MAY OUR UNSAVED LOVED ONES COME TO CHRIST.

GUIDE OUR SUPREME COURT TO JUDGE RIGHTEOUSLY.

L PRAY FOR THE VICTIMS OF NATURAL DISASTERS.

LORD, HELP ME TO HAVE A SERVANT'S HEART.

MAY OUR CHURCHES BE FILLED WITH YOUR POWER.

LORD, HELP ME TO SHOW YOUR LOVE TO OTHERS TODAY.

LORD, DO NOT LET ME ENTER TEMPTATIONS.

THANK YOU, LORD, FOR VICTORY OVER DEPRESSION.

LORD, HELP ME TO KNOW YOU BETTER.

MAY YOUR PRESENCE BE A COMFORT TO THE FAMILIES OF THOSE WHO HAVE DIED

LORD, HELP ME TO BE A GOOD WITNESS TO MY NEIGHBORS.

LORD, TOUCH THE SICK IN THE HOSPITALS TODAY WITH YOUR HOPE.

LORD, THANK YOU FOR THE INTIMATE RELATIONSHIP L HAVE WITH YOU

LORD, LET THOSE WHO FEEL UNLOVED KNOW YOUR LOVE FOR THEM.

MAY YOUR LOVE MEND BROKEN MARRIAGES.

LORD, TAKE CARE OF THE FAMILIES OF THOSE IN PRISONS.

LORD, WITH YOU AS MY SHEPHERD, L WILL NOT LACK.

I WANT THE HOLY SPIRIT TO BE IN CONTROL OF MY LIFE.

LORD, PROTECT OUR LOCAL POLICE OFFICERS.

MAY SINGLE MOTHERS HAVE ALL THEIR NEEDS MET.

MEND THE HEARTS OF THOSE DESERTED BY THEIR SPOUSES.

LORD, SHOW YOUR MIRACULOUS POWERS TODAY.

DEAR GOD, THANK YOU FOR CLEANSING ME OF CONFESSED SIN.

GOD, HELP ME TO LOOK AT PEOPLE AS YOU SEE THEM.

LORD JESUS, I THANK YOU THAT YOU ARE COMING TO EARTH TO REIGN.

MAY OUR MAYOR BE FILLED WITH THE WISDOM OF GOD.

MAY YOUR LEADERS BE SERVING FAITHFULIY.

DEEPEN MY BELIEF IN YOUR NAME (YAHWEH).

LORD, BE THE HEAD OF OUR HOME.

I PRAY FOR THE WHOLE WORLD TO RECEIVE THE GOSPEL OF CHRIST.

L WANT TO HAVE THE FULLNESS OF THE HOLY SPIRIT.

I PRAY FOR PEACE IN THE MIDDLE EAST.

LORD JESUS, I THANK YOU THAT YOU ARE COMING TO EARTH TO REIGN.

THANK YOU LORD, FOR MY HAPPY TIMES. . .

LORD, HELP ME TO USE UNHAPPY TIMES AS TIMES FOR GROWTH. . .

LORD, REVEAL YOUR PURPOSE IN MY TRIALS. . .

THANK YOU FOR THE BIBLE THAT GUIDES ME BY YOUR WORDS. . .

GUIDE ME IN MY CHOICES THAT I MAY KNOW WHICH IS THE RIGHT THING TO DO. . .

LORD, KEEP ME FROM GIVING UP BECAUSE OF WHAT SEEMS TOO HARD TO OVERCOME. . .

LORD, HELP ME TO REMEMBER THAT EVERY ACT OF KINDNESS TO OTHERS IS AN ACT OF KINDNESS TO YOU.

LORD, HELP ME TO DO TO OTHERS WHAT I WOULD WANT THEM TO DO TO ME. . .

LORD, HELP ME TO SHARE MY SPIRITUAL RICHES WITH OTHERS. . .

HELP ME TO TRUST AND NOT BE AFRAID. . .

LORD, HELP ME TO GO THROUGH DAYS WITHOUT SINNING. . .

HELP ME TO THINK THOUGHTS OF GOOD WILL, LOVE, UNDERSTANDING, AND SYMPATHY TOWARD OTHERS. . .

LORD, HELP ME TO SAY AS PAUL SAID, "TO ME TO LIVE IS CHRIST."

LORD, MAKE ME BOLD TO SPEAK AS I OUGHT TO SPEAK AT ALL TIMES AND IN ALL PLACES

LORD, FILL MY HEART WITH JOY TO MAKE KNOWN TO OTHERS THE HAPPINESS OF FOLLOWING YOUR WAY OF LIFE

THANK YOU FOR THE FELLOWSHIP MY CHURCH GIVES ME. . .

HELP ME TO LIVE IN SUCH A WAY AS TO BRING GLORY TO YOUR NAME. . .

LORD, GUIDE ME TO CHOOSE WISELY. . .

THANK YOU FOR THE FELLOWSHIP I HAVE IN OUR CHURCH. . .

LORD, HELP ME TO SHOW OTHERS THAT THE LIFE CENTERED IN YOU IS THE RICHEST AND MOST REWARDING WAY TO LIFE. . .

THANK YOU, LORD, FOR ALL MY BLESSINGS. . .

THANK YOU, LORD, FOR GIVING ME A GIVING HEART.

LORD, HELP ME TO SEE THE WAYS I NEED TO CHANGE. . .

HELP ME TO BE SENSITIVE TO THE FEELINS OF OTHERS. . .

THANK YOU FOR ALL MY FRIENDS. . .

DEAR GOD, RAISE UP YOUNG PEOPLE WHO LEAD OUR COUNTRY IN RIGHT WAYS. . .

DEAR LORD, GUIDE ME TO MAKE WISE CHOICES. . .

HOLY SPIRIT, HELPME IN MY WORSHIP. . .

DEAR LORD, HELP ME TO OVERCOME OBSTACLES THAT TEND TO GET ME DOWN. . .

THANK YOU, THANK YOU, THANK YOU, THANK YOU, THANK YOU LORD!

THANK YOU, LORD, FOR MAKING ME A HAPPY CHRISTIAN.

DEAR LORD, HELP ME TO BE JOYFUL ALL DAY TODAY. . .

LORD, I WANT TO HELP YOU BUILD YOUR CHURCH. . .

LORD, TAKE CARE OF ANY OF MY ENEMIES. . .

THANK YOU, LORD, THAT YOUR WILL IS BEING DONE ON EARTH AS IT IS IN HEAVEN IN PERSONS AND PLACES. . .

THANKS FOR SAVING ME FROM MY TROUBLES. . .

LORD, HELP ME TO LIVE LIKE YOUR DISCIPLE. . .

LORD, HELP ME TO FIND IN CRITICISM A WAY BY WHICH I GROW STRONGER. . .

DEAR GOD, I DON'T WANT TO HURT YOUR FEELINGS. . .

DEAR GOD, HELP ME TO LISTEN TO WHAT YOU HAVE TO SAY TO ME. . .

THANKS FOR THE BEAUTY OF YOUR CREATION. . .

THANK YOU JESUS FOR COMING INTO THIS WORLD TO SAVE US. . .

THANK YOU FOR YOUR GOODNESS AND BLESSINGS IN MY LIFE. . .

FATHER GOD, HELP ME TO HEAR YOUR VOICE. . .

THANK YOU, LORD, FOR YOUR WORD THAT SAYS YOU WILL NEVER LEAVE US OR FORSAKE US. . .

LORD, HELP ME TO FIND SOMEONE WITH WISDOM TO ADVISE ME. . .

MY GOD, THANK YOU FOR YOUR EXTRAVAGANT LOVE. . .

DEAR LORD, YOU GIVE AND FORGIVE. . .

DEAR GOD, YOU SHOW YOUR LOVE BY GIVING. . .

DEAR GOD, YOU GAVE YOUR BEST FOR ME, SO I WANT TO GIVE MY BEST TO YOU.

THANK YOU FOR MAKING ME A NEW PERSON.

THANKS, GOD, FOR THE GIFT OF FAMILY. . .

JESUS CHRIST, I CONFESS YOU AS MY LORD AND SAVIOR. . .

GOD, I PRAY FOR ALL THE NATIONS OF THE WORLD TO BE FOLLOWERS OF JESUS CHRIST. . .

HELP ME TO BE AN ENCOURAGER. . .

THANKS, LORD, FOR THE GIFT OF LAUGHTER. . .

THANK YOU, JESUS, FOR COMING INTO THIS WORLD TO SAVE US. . .

THANK YOU, LORD, YOU ARE NOT MAD AT ME, BUT MAD ABOUT ME.

LORD, HELP ME TO BE LIKE A CHILD IN MY FAITH.

LORD, TAKE OUT THE SELFISHNESS THAT IS IN MY HEART.

GOD, THANK YOU FOR ALL THOSE WHO TAUGHT ME YOUR WORD.

FATHER GOD, THANKS THAT YOU REMEMBER ALL MY PAST PRAYER REQUESTS THAT ARE NOT ANSWERED YET.

LORD, WHEN I RUN INTO TROUBLE, HELP ME TO FIND THE WAY OUT. . .

DEAR GOD, GUIDE ME EVERYDAY OF MY LIFE. . .

DEAR GOD, HELP MY CHILDREN TO BE ALL YOU WANT THEM TO BE. . .

THANK YOU, LORD, THAT ANYONE IN CHRIST IS A NEW CREATION. . .

LORD, I GIVE YOU EVERY HURT, SORROW AND PAIN, KNOWING THAT YOU CARE AND WILL MAKE ALL THINGS NEW AGAIN. . .

LORD, HAVE YOUR WAY IN EVERY AREA OF MY LIFE. . .

OH HAPPY DAY WHEN JESUS WASHED MY SINS AWAY

CHAPTER FIVE

"BIBLEDIGS"

Bible verses on www.youtube.com
that I put on each day.
Type "bibledig" and click on the picture of the man with a shovel and scroll down to the verse.

OLD TESTAMENT

GENESIS

Genesis 1:16 GOD MADE TRILLIONS OF STARS

Genesis 2:8 THE FIRST GARDENER WAS GOD

Genesis 2:18 GOD MAKES A "HELP MEET" FOR ADAM

Genesis 3: 16 GOD SAID MAN SHALL RULE OVER THE WOMAN.

Genesis 4:7 IF ONE DOES NOT DO WELL, IT IS BECAUSE SIN IS AT THE DOOR.

Genesis 5:2 EVE WAS CALLED ADAM, TOO

Genesis 5:24 ENOCH WAS IN HABITUAL FELLOWSHIP WITH GOD (WALKED WITH GOD) AND NEVER DIED.

Genesis 6:2-4 THE MARRIAGE OF THE SONS OF GOD AND THE DAUGHTERS OF MEN PRODUCED GIANTS.

Genesis 6:5-7, 11, 12 WICKEDNESS OF MAN WAS SO GREAT THAT GOD HAD TO DESTROY THEM OFF THE FACE OF THE EARTH.

Genesis 6:8 NOAH FOUND GRACE IN THE EYES OF THE LORD.

Genesis 9:6 CAPITOL PUNISHMENT COMMANDED BY GOD

Genesis 12:2 GOD WILL BLESS AND WE SHALL BE A BLESSING.
Genesis 14:20 FIRST EXAMPLE OF GIVING TITHES
Genesis 15:6 BELIEVING GOD IS RIGHTEOUSNESS

Genesis 17:1 LIVE BEFORE GOD AND BE PERFECT (BLAMELESS). GOD'S EXPECTATION OF US

Genesis 18: 14 "IS ANYTHING TOO HARD FOR THE LORD?" (SPOKEN BY GOD IN A BODY)

Genesis 21:6 GOD MADE SARAH LAUGH
Genesis 24:67 THERE WAS NO CEREMONY OF MARRIAGE, THE REMOVAL OF THE BRIDE FROM HER HOME TO THAT OF THE BRIDEGROOM COMPLETED THE MARRIAGE.
Genesis 45:8 GOD PERMITTED JOSEPH TO BE SOLD INTO SLAVERY SO HE COULD WORK IT OUT FOR GOOD.

Genesis 49:4 BEING UNSTABLE PREVENTS ONE FROM EXCELLING.
Genesis 49:22 A PICTURE OF A FRUITFUL BELIEVER

Genesis 50:26 GENESIS BEGINS WITH A GARDEN AND ENDS WITH A COFFIN.

EXODUS

Exodus 2:6 A BABY'S CRY TO DELIVER A NATION
Exodus 3:14 GOD'S NAME IS "I AM"
Exodus 4:24 MOSES ALMOST DIED IN SERVING THE LORD AND NEGLECTING HIS FAMILY.
Exodus 12:13 "WHEN I SEE THE BLOOD I WILL PASS OVER YOU."

Exodus 14: 13 FEAR NOT, STAND STILL AND SEE THE SALVATION OF THE LORD.
Exodus 14: 15 STOP PRAYING ABOUT IT AND GO FORWARD

Exodus 15: 1-11 SONG OF MOSES
Exodus 19:5 TWO CONDITIONS OF BLESSINGS, "OBEY MY VOICE. . .KEEP MY COVENANT."

Exodus 20:5 NEVER DOES GOD SAY VISITING THE INIQUITIES OF THE MOTHERS.
Exodus 20:26 GOD DEMANDS MODESTY OF HIS PEOPLE

Exodus 25:2 THE LORD WANTS AN OFFERING OF EVERYONE WHO GIVES IT WILLINGLY FROM THE HEART.

Exodus 28:3 GOD FILLS WITH THE SPIRIT OF WISDOM

Exodus 28:42 LINEN SHORTS (NOT WOOL) — NO SWEAT IN SERVING THE LORD.

Exodus 33:3 GOD DOES NOT WANT TO BE AMONG STIFF-NECKED PEOPLE.
Exodus 33; 14 "MY PRESENCE SHALL GO WITH THEE (YOU)."

Exodus 33:23 MOSES COULD SEE GOD'S BACK

LEVITICUS

Leviticus 3:16 "ALL THE FAT IS THE LORD'S" (SO GIVE IT TO HIM)
Leviticus 9:22 THE LIFTING UP OF THE PRIESTS HANDS TOWARDS THE PEOPLE WAS FOR A BLESSING.

Leviticus 17:11 IT IS THE BLOOD THAT MAKES ATONEMENT FOR THE SOUL.

Leviticus 19: 16 THOU SHALT NOT PEDDLE GOSSIP
Leviticus 19: 17,18 THE LAW OF LOVE

Leviticus 25:10 YEAR OF JUBILEE - 50 "YEAR. "PROCLAIM LIBERTY.. (THIS QUOTATIONIS ON THE LIBERTY BELL OF THE U.S.A. IN PHILADELPHIA, PA)

Leviticus 26:4-12 TWENTY-FOUR BLESSINGS CONDITIONED ON VERSE 3. OBEYING GOD'S COMMANDS

Leviticus 27:30 ALL THE TITHE WAS THE LORD'S

NUMBERS

Numbers 6:24-26 THE BLESSING BENEDICTION. JEHOVAH MENTIONED 3 TIMES FOR THE TRINITY.

Numbers 10:29 "COME (THERE) WITH US, AND WE WILL DO THEE GOOD."
Numbers 10:35 "RISE UP, LORD, AND LET YOUR (THINE) ENEMIES BE SCATTERED" (PSALMS 68: 1)
Numbers 11:1 WHEN THE PEOPLE COMPLAINED, IT DISPLEASED THE LORD; AND HIS ANGER WAS KINDLED; AND THE FIRE OF THE LORD BURNT AMONG THEM, AND CONSUMED THEM

Numbers 14:21 "ALL THE EARTH SHALL BE FILLED WITH THE GLORY OF THE LORD." (SONG)
Numbers 22:28 GOD CAN MAKE EVEN A DONKEY SPEAK
Numbers 24:13 "WHAT THE LORD SAITH, THAT WILL I SPEAK." (BALAAM)
Numbers 27:1 NOAH WAS A WOMAN (36:11)
Numbers 32:23 "BE SURE YOUR SIN WILL FIND YOU OUT"

DEUTERONOMY

Deuteronomy 3:22 "YE SHALL NOT FEAR THEM, FOR THE LORD YOUR GOD SHALL FIGHT FOR YOU"
Deuteronomy 4:2 NOT TO ADD OR TAKE AWAY FROM THE WORD OF THE LORD, BUT TO OBEY.
Deuteronomy 4:29 ANYONE WHO SEEKS THE LORD WITH ALL THEIR HEART AND SOUL WILL FIND HIM.

Deuteronomy 6:5 THE FIRST AND GREAT COMMANDMENT: TO LOVE GOD WITH ALL YOUR SPIRIT, SOUL, AND BODY.

Deuteronomy 6:7 TIMES OF GODLY EDUCATION OF CHILDREN BY PARENTS.

Deuteronomy 7: 15 KEEPING GOD'S COMMANDMENTS IS A CONDITION FOR HEALING.

Deuteronomy 8:18 GOD GIVES POWER TO GET WEALTH

Deuteronomy 18: 10,11 OCCULT PRACTICES ARE AN ABOMINATION TO THE LORD

Deuteronomy 24:5 LAW FOR NEWLYWEDS

Deuteronomy 28:47 SERVE THE LORD WITH JOYFULNESS

Deuteronomy 31:6,8 INSTRUCTIONS FOR VICTORY

Deuteronomy 32:9 THE LORD'S PORTION IS HIS PEOPLE

Deuteronomy 33:25 STRENGTH ALL THE DAYS OF LIFE

Deuteronomy 34:7 MOSES DIED AT 120 YRS. OF AGE AND HIS EYE WAS NOT DIM.
Deuteronomy 34:7 MOSES DIED ON HIS BIRTHDAY FEBRUARY 1 (31:2)

Deuteronomy 34:9 JOSHUA WAS FULL OF THE SPIRIT OF WISDOM FOR MOSES HAD LAID HIS HANDS UPON HIM.

JOSHUA

Joshua 1:6,7,9 THREE TIMES GOD COMMANDS JOSHUA TO BE STRONG AND COURAGEOUS. THE 4TH TIME IT WAS SAID BY THE PEOPLE V.18b
Joshua 1:8 HOW TO BE PROSPEROUS

Joshua 7:10 NO USE TO PRAY WHEN SIN HASN'T BEEN REPENTED OF.

Joshua 7:19 CONFESSION OF SIN GIVES GLORY TO THE LORD.
Joshua 14:11 CALEB TESTIFIES THAT HE WAS AS STRONG AT 85 YEARS OF AGE AS HE WAS AT 40.

JUDGES

Judges 6:24 “JEHOVAH-SHALOM” (“THE LORD IS PEACE”)

Judges 13:9 IT IS SCRIPTURAL TO PRAY FOR A VISIT FROM AN ANGEL (NOT TO BE AN ANGEL)

RUTH

Ruth 3:5 RUTH HAS AN OBEDIENT, SUBMISSIVE SPIRIT.

I SAMUEL

I Samuel 1:27 SPECIFIC PRAYER REQUEST ANSWERED BY HANNAH.

I Samuel 3: 19 IF THEY ARE NOT THE WORDS OF THE LORD THEY SHOULD FALL TO THE GROUND.
I Samuel 10:6 TURNED INTO ANOTHER PERSON BY THE HOLY SPIRIT.

I Samuel 10:26 “THERE WENT WITH HIM A BAND OF MEN WHOSE HEARTS GOD HAD TOUCHED.”

I Samuel 12:23,24 MY MINISTRY AND LIFE SCRIPTURE (ALONG WITH PHILIPPIANS 2:13)

I Samuel 15:22 “TO OBEY IS BETTER THAN SACRIFICE”
I Samuel 15:23 REBELLION = WITCHCRAFT. STUBBORNESS = WICKEDNESS + IDOLATRY
I Samuel 15:24 DISOBEYING GOD’S WORD BECAUSE OF FEARING THE PEOPLE AND OBEYING THEIR VOICE.

I Samuel 16:7 A WARNING ABOUT LOOKING ON OUTWARD APPEARANCE ONLY.

I Samuel 16:23 GOOD MUSIC CAN MAKE EVIL SPIRITS LEAVE A PERSON.

I Samuel 17:45 DAVID CAME AGAINST GOLIATH IN THE "NAME OF THE LORD OF HOSTS."

I Samuel 30:6 IN THE MIDST OF CALAMITY, "DAVID ENCOURAGED HIMSELF IN THE LORD"

II SAMUEL

II Samuel 6:14 DAVID DANCED BEFORE THE LORD WITH ALL HIS MIGHT (v. 16 Leaping also)

II Samuel 7: 14 GOD USES PEOPLE TO CHASTISE US WHEN WE SIN.

I KINGS

IKings2:3HOWTOPROSPER(KEEPHISCHARGE,COMMANDMENTS, AND WALK IN HIS WAYS).
I Kings 3:10 THE REQUEST THAT PLEASED GOD V. 9- DESIRING AN UNDERSTANDING HEART (v.11)

I Kings 3:14 HOW TO LIVE LONGER (WALK IN GOD'S WAYS AND KEEP HIS COMMANDMENTS)

I Kings 8:56 "THERE HAS NOT FAILED ONE WORD OF ALL HIS GOOD PROMISE."
I Kings 19:6,8 ANGEL FOOD CAKE HAD A LOT OF NUTRITION.

II KINGS

II Kings 2:11 ELIJAH WENT TO HEAVEN WITHOUT DYING. ENOCH WAS THE ONLY OTHER.

II Kings 5: 14 NAAMAN HEALED BY OBEYING THE INSTRUCTIONS OF ELISHA.

II Kings 6:16 "FEAR NOT: FOR THEY THAT BE WITH US ARE MORE THAN THEY THAT BE WITH THEM."

II Kings 6:17 PRAYER FOR OPENING THE EYES OF ONE TO SEE SPIRITUALLY.

II Kings 7:9 "THIS DAY IS A DAY OF GOOD TIDINGS, AND WE HOLD OUR PEACE."
II Kings 22:19 GOD LIKES A TENDER HEART

I CHRONICLES

I Chronicles 4:10 THE 5 REQUESTS OF JABEZ WHICH GOD GRANTED.

I Chronicles 10:13 SAUL DIED FOR HIS SIN OF NOT KEEPING GOD'S WORD AND CONSULTING A MEDIUM.

I Chronicles 16:29 "WORSHIP THE LORD IN THE BEAUTY OF HOLINESS."
I Chronicles 22:19 "NOW SET YOUR HEART AND SOUL TO SEEK THE LORD YOUR GOD."
I Chronicles 23:5 4,000 PRAISED THE LORD WITH INSTRUMENTS.

II CHRONICLES

II Chronicles 5: 13,14 THE GLORY OF THE LORD FILLED THE HOUSE OF GOD WHEN ALL PRAISED GOD IN UNITY.
II Chronicles 6:29 SPREAD FORTH THE HANDS IN THE HOUSE OF GOD WHEN PRAYING FOR HEALING OR PLAGUE.

II Chronicles 7: 14 CONDITIONS FOR ANSWERED PRAYER
II Chronicles 20:15 "FOR THE BATTLE IS NOT YOURS, BUT GOD'S (V. 17)

II Chronicles 20:20 "BELIEVE HIS PROPHETS, SO SHALL YOU PROSPER."

II Chronicles 20:22 WHEN THEY BEGAN TO SING AND PRAISE THE LORD, VICTORY CAME.

II Chronicles 26:5 "AS LONG AS HE (UZZIAH) SOUGHT THE LORD, GOD MADE HIM TO PROSPER."

II Chronicles 29:30 "THEY SANG PRAISES WITH GLADNESS"

II Chronicles 33:12 AFFLICTION SOMETIMES CAUSES THE PERSON TO SEEK THE LORD AND BE HUMBLE.

EZRA

Ezra 3:11 "ALL THE PEOPLE SHOUTED WITH A GREAT SHOUT WHEN THEY PRAISED THE LORD."

Ezra 7:10 PREPARE THE HEART TO SEEK THE LAW OF THE LORD AND DO IT.

Ezra 8:23 FASTING AND PRAYER BRINGING FORTH GOD'S HELP (v. 21, 31)

NEHEMIAH

Nehemiah 2:20 "THE GOD OF HEAVEN, HE WILL PROSPER US."

Nehemiah 8:10 "THE JOY OF THE LORD IS YOUR STRENGTH."

ESTHER

Esther 4:14 YOU HAVE COME FOR SUCH A TIME AS THIS.

JOB

Job 3:25 "THAT WHICH I WAS AFRAID IS COME UNTO ME."

Job 5:17 "HAPPY IS THE MAN WHOM GOD CORRECTS."

Job 13:15 "THOUGH HE SLAY ME, YET WILL I TRUST HIM."

Job 14:5 A PERSON'S DAYS ARE ALREADY DETERMINED. . .HIS TIME IS ALLOTTED

Job 23:12 WORDS OF HIS MOUTH BETTER THAN NECESSARY FOOD

Job 42: 12 "THE LORD BLESSED THE LATTER END OF JOB MORE THAN HIS BEGINNING." v.10 (Double or nothing)

PSALMS

Psalms 2:4 GQD LAUGHS

Psalms 2:12 "KISS THE SON." (lest the Father be angry)

Psalms 4:8 NOW I "LAY ME DOWN IN PEACE AND SLEEP."
Psalms 16:11 IN THE PRESENCE OF THE LORD IS FULLNESS OF JOY.

Psalms 27:14 HOW TO HAVE A STRONG HEART
Psalms 35:13 HUMBLING THE SOUL WITH FASTING

Psalms 35:27 THE LORD TAKES PLEASURE IN THE PROSPERITY OF HIS SERVANTS.

Psalms 57:7 "MY HEART IS FIXED." (108:1) (112:7)

Psalms 60:12 "THROUGH GOD WE SHALL DO VALIANTLY"

Psalms 68:6 GOD SETS THE LONELY IN FAMILIES, BUT THE REBELLIOUS LIVE IN DRYNESS.

Psalms 68:19 WE ARE "LOADED" (NIV- WHO DAILY BEARS OUR BURDENS)

Psalms 70:4 CONTINUOUSLY SAY, LET GOD BE MAGNIFIED.

Psalms 71:18 GOOD OLD AGE DESIRES
Psalms 77:3 COMPLAINING DOESN'T HELP

Psalms 84:7 "GO FROM STRENGTH TO STRENGTH"
Psalms 84: 11 "THE LORD WILL GIVE GRACE AND GLORY NO GOOD THING WILL HE WITHHOLD F ROM THEM THAT WALK UPRIGHTLY."

Psalms 85:6 "REVIVE US AGAIN"

Psalms 85:10 MONEY AND TRUTH MEET; RIGHTEOUSNESS AND PEACE KISS EACH OTHER.

Psalms 90:17 "LET THE BEAUTY OF THE LORD OUR GOD BE UPON US."

Psalms 92:13.14 THOSE THAT ARE PLANTED IN THE HOUSE OF THE LORD SHALL BE FRUITFUL EVEN IN OLD AGE.

Psalms 97: 10 IF WE LOVE GOD 'WE SHOULD HATE EVIL.
Psalms 100:2 "SERVE THE LORD WITH GLADNESS"
Psalms 103:12 "FAR OUT" FORGIVENESS OF OUR SINS
Psalms 103:21 "MINISTERS OF HIS: THAT DO HIS PLEASURE"
Psalms 104:35 THE FIRST "HALLELUJAH" IN THE BIBLE
Psalms 105:15 "DO MY PROPHET NO HARM"
Psalms 106: 15 "HE GAVE THEM THEIR REQUEST; BUT SENT LEANNESS INTO THEIR SOUL."
Psalms 107:8 "OH THAT MEN WOULD PRAISE THE LORD FOR HIS GOODNESS, AND FOR HIS WONDERFUL WORKS. . ." (repeated in vs. 15, 21,31)
Psalms 107:9 "FOR HE SATISFIES. . ."
Psalms 107:20 "HE SENT HIS WORD AND HEALED THEM."
Psalms 109:24 THE PHYSICAL RESULTS OF FASTING

Psalms 111:10 'WE WILL UNDERSTAND AS WE DO GOD'S COMMANDS

Psalms 112:7 A FIXED HEART TS ONE THAT TS TRUSTING IN THE LORD.
Psalms 113:3 PRAISE THE LORD FROM SUN UP TO SUN DOWN.

Psalms 116:15 PRECIOUS DEATH

Psalms 117 SHORTEST CHAPTER IN THE BIBLE
Psalms 118:6 IF THE LORD IS ON MY SIDE I FEAR NOT.
Psalms 119:11 MEMORIZE AND MEDITATE ON GOD'S WORD
Psalms 119:12 SEEK TO MAKE GOD HAPPY (124:6) (BY PRAISING HIM)

Psalms 119:18 ASK GOD TO REMOVE HINDRANCES TO SPIRITUAL SIGHT.
Psalms 119:36 LORD, INCLINE MY HEART TO YOUR WORDS.

Psalms 119:67 GOING ASTRAY FROM GOD'S WORD BRINGS AFFLICTION.
Psalms 119:71 TROUBLES WORK FOR GOOD

Psalms 119:89 FOREVER, THE WORD OF GOD IS SETTLED IN HEAVEN.
Psalms 119:105 GOD'S WORD IS LIGHT

Psalms 119:164 DAVID SAID HE PRAISED THE LORD SEVEN TIMES A DAY.
Psalms 119:165 HOW TO HAVE GREAT PEACE. HOW TO HAVE NOTHING OFFEND YOU.
Psalms 122:1 GLAD WHEN INVITED TO GOD'S HOUSE
Psalms 122:6 PRAY FOR THE PEACE OF JERUSALEM. PROSPERITY IS PROMISED TO THOSE WHO DO.
Psalms 126:3 "THE LORD HAS DONE GREAT THINGS FOR US; WHEREOF WE ARE GLAD."
Psalms 126: 5,6 SOWING AND REAPING
Psalms 133:1 HOW TO HAVE A GOOD AND PLEASANT TIME
Psalms 134: 1-3 SECOND SHORTEST CHAPTER IN THE BIBLE(44 words) (Ps. 117, 33 Words)(vs 1,2song)
Psalms 134:2 "LIFT UP YOUR HANDS IN THE SANCTUARY, AND BLESS THE LORD"
Psalms 138:1 "I WILL PRAISE YOU WITH MY WHOLE HEART."

Psalms 142:7 "BRING MY SOUL OUT OF PRISON, THAT I MAY PRAISE YOUR NAME."

Psalms 143:10 "TEACH ME TO DO YOUR WILL"
Psalms 144: 15 "HAPPY IS THAT PEOPLE WHOSE GOD IS THE LORD."

Psalms 147:3 GOD HEALS THE BROKENHEARTED AND BANDAGES THEIR WOUNDS

Psalms 148 36 ADMONITIONS AND 33 THINGS TO PRAISE THE LORD

Psalms 149:3 “PRAISE HIS NAME IN THE DANCE”

PROVERBS

Proverbs 1:7 “THE FEAR OF THE LORD IS THE BEGINNING OF KNOWLEDGE.” (AND WISDOM 9:10)

Proverbs 3:5,6 CONDITIONS FOR GUIDANCE

Proverbs 3:21,24 SOUND WISDOM AND DISCRETION WILL GIVE SWEET SLEEP
Proverbs 3:27 WHEN YOU CAN DO GOOD TO THE DESERVING, DO IT.

Proverbs 4:22 GOD’S WORD IS HEALTH

Proverbs 6: 16-19 7 THINGS GOD HATES

Proverbs 8: 13 THE FEAR OF THE LORD IS TO HATE EVIL

Proverbs 9:8 “REBUKE A WISE MAN AND HE WILL LOVE YOU.”
Proverbs 11:14 SAFETY IN MANY COUNSELORS

Proverbs 14:34 “RIGHTEOUSNESS EXALTS A NATION”

Proverbs 15:33 “BEFORE HONOR HUMILITY”

Proverbs 16:3 COMMIT OUR WORKS UNTO THE LORD AND OUR THOUGHTS WILL BE SUCCESSFUL.

Proverbs 16:18 THE BAD EFFECTS OF PRIDE AND HAUGHTINESS.

Proverbs 16:24 “PLEASANT WORDS ARE. . .HEALTH TO THE BONES”

Proverbs 16:32 HE WHO RULES HIS SPIRIT IS BETTER THAN ONE WHO CAPTURES A CITY.

Proverbs 16:33 THAT WHICH MAY SEEM CHANCE IS ALSO ORDERED BY THE LORD.

Proverbs 17:4 "A NAUGHTY TONGUE"
Proverbs 17:6 GRANDCHILDREN ARE A CROWN FOR THE OLD. FATHERS ARE THE CHILDREN'S GLORY.
Proverbs 17: 17 "A FRIEND LOVES AT ALL TIMES"
Proverbs 18:10 THE NAME OF THE LORD IS A PLACE OF SAFETY.

Proverbs 18:16 A VALUABLE GIFT WILL BRING ONE INTO THE PRESENCE OF GREAT MEN.

Proverbs 18:21 "DEATH AND LIFE ARE IN THE POWER OF THE TONGUE."

Proverbs 19:17 HE WHO GIVES TO THE POOR LENDS TO THE LORD.

Proverbs 22:6 THE LAW OF CHILD REARING

Proverbs 23:7 "AS HE THINKS IN HIS HEART, SO IS HE"
Proverbs 26:18,19 "I WAS ONLY JOKING" IS SOMETIMES NO JOKE.

Proverbs 26:28 "A FLATTERING MOUTH WORKS RUIN."
Proverbs 27: 19 THE FACE IS THE MIRROR OF THE HEART
Proverbs 28:1 THE RIGHTEOUS ARE BOLD AS A LION

Proverbs 28:9 HE WHO DOESN'T LISTEN TO TRUTH WILL NOT HAVE HIS PRAYERS ANSWERED.

Proverbs 28: 13 CONFESSING AND FORSAKING ONE'S SIN BRINGS PROSPERITY AND MERCY.

Proverbs 29:18 "WHERE THERE IS NO VISION THE PEOPLE PERISH."

Proverbs 3 1:30 MANNERS AND BEAUTY ARE DECEITFUL, BUT A WOMAN WHO FEARS THE LORD SHALL BE PRAISED.

ECCLESIASTES

Ecclesiastes 3:1 THERE IS A TIME FOR EVERYTHING

Ecclesiastes 4: 12 A THREEFOLD CORD IS NOT EASILY BROKEN.

Ecclesiastes 7:1 THE DAY OF DEATH IS BETTER THAN THE DAY OF ONE'S BIRTH.

Ecclesiastes 12:3-7 DESCRIPTION OF THE AGING OF THE BODY BEFORE DEATH.

SONG OF SOLOMON

Song of Solomon 2:16 "MY BELOVED IS MINE, AND I AM HIS"
Song of Solomon 5:16 "HE IS ALTOGETHER LOVELY'
Song of Solomon 8:7 "MANY WATERS CANNOT QUENCH LOVE"

ISAIAH

Isaiah 2:4 UNIVERSAL PEACE IS COMING

Isaiah 10 ALL ABOUT THE ASSYRIANS

Isaiah 10:5 GOD USED THE ASSYRIAN KING LIKE A ROD TO CHASTISE ISRAEL.

Isaiah 11:2 THE SEVENFOLD ANNOINTING OF THE MESSIAH

Isaiah 14:12 SATAN'S FALL

Isaiah 14:24 WHAT GOD EVEN THINKS WILL COME TO PASS

Isaiah 19:25 "BLESSED BE. . .ASSYRIA THE WORK OF MY HANDS."

Isaiah 28:11 THE PREDICTION OF SPEAKING IN TONGUES

Isaiah 28:16 THE ONE WHO BELIEVES IN CHRIST SHALL NOT PANIC.

Isaiah 30:19 GOD IS VERY GRACIOUS AND WILL ANSWER OUR CRY (38:5)

Isaiah 30:21 OUR EARS SHALL HEAR WORDS OF GUIDANCE.

Isaiah 32:17 THE EFFECT OF RIGHTEOUSNESS IS PEACE

Isaiah 37:36 ONE ANGEL KILLING 185,000 TROOPS OF THE ASSYRIANS.

Isaiah 38:5 PRAYER AND TEARS CAN CHANGE THE DECISION OF GOD (v.1). THIS IS THE ONLY TIME THAT GOD EVEN TOLD A PERSON HOW LONG HE WOULD LIVE.
Isaiah 40:29 GOD GIVES POWER AND STRENGTH TO THE FAINT AND WEAK.
Isaiah 40:31 HOW TO RENEW OUR STRENGTH

Isaiah 48:22 THERE IS NO PEACE FOR THE WICKED (57:21)

Isaiah 49:25b "I WILL SAVE YOUR CHILDREN"

Isaiah 50:7 "GOD WILL HELP ME

Isaiah 52:7 BEAUTIFUL FEET OF THE EVANGELISTS

Isaiah 52:10 THE LORD HAS ROLLED UP HIS SLEEVE TO DO A MIGHTY WORK.

Isaiah 64:8 GOD MOLDS US

Isaiah 65:24 SOMETIMES GOD ANSWERS PRAYER BEFORE WE PRAY IT

JEREMIAH

Jeremiah 3:12,13 GOD'S MERCY IS CONDITIONED BY REPENTANCE.

Jeremiah 17:9 THE NATURAL HEART IS DECEITFUL

Jeremiah 20:9 HOLY HEART BURN

Jeremiah 24:7 GOD GIVES AN UNDERSTANDING HEART

Jeremiah 30:17 GOD RESTORES HEALTH AND HEALS WOUNDS.

Jeremiah 33:3 GOD'S PHONE NUMBER

Jeremiah 46:11 THERE ARE TIMES WHEN MEDICINES WILL NOT CURE.

Jeremiah 48:10 CURSED IS ANYONE WHO DOES GOD'S WORK NEGLIGENTLY (DECEITFULLY)

LAMENTATIONS

Lamentations 3:23 "GREAT IS YOUR FAITHFULNESS'

Lamentations 3:41 LIFT UP HEART AND HANDS UNTO GOD

EZEKIEL

Ezekiel 11:19 GOD WILL PUT A NEW SPIRIT WITHIN

Ezekiel 16:6 A COMMAND TO THE BLEEDING — "LIVE"

Ezekiel 20:38 GOD WILL PURGE OUT THE REBELS FROM AMONG HIS PEOPLE.

Ezekiel 22:30 NO INTERCESSOR FOUND TO SAVE ISRAEL

Ezekiel 23:12 THE ASSYRIANS WERE FAMOUS FOR THEIR ELEGANT CLOTHES.

Ezekiel 34:26 "THERE SHALL BE SHOWERS OF BLESSING."
Ezekiel 36:26 GOD CAN GIVE US A NEW HEART AND A NEW SPIRIT.

DANIEL

Daniel 3:17 "OUR GOD WHOM WE SERVE IS ABLE TO DELIVER US.. . . "

Daniel 7:13,14 THE SECOND COMING OF CHRIST

Daniel 7:15 MAN 'S TRIUNE BEING SEEN HERE: SPIRIT, BODY, MIND

Daniel 11:32 "THE PEOPLE THAT DO KNOW THEIR GOD SHALL BE STRONG AND DO EXPLOITS."

DANIEL 12:3 REWARDS FOR CONVERTING OTHERS TO RIGHTEOUSNESS

HOSEA

Hosea 4:6 "MY PEOPLE ARE DESTROYED FOR LACK OF KNOWLEDGE."
Hosea 6:6 TWO THINGS GOD DESIRES MORE THAN SACRIFICE OFFERINGS: MERCY AND THE KNOWLEDGE OF GOD

Hosea 10:12 "IT IS TIME TO SEEK THE LORD, 'TILL HE COMES AND RAINS RIGHTEOUSNESS UPON YOU." "SOW. . . REAP."

JOEL

JOEL 2:25 GOD WILL RESTORE TO YOU THE YEARS THAT THE LOCUST HAS EATEN.
Joel 2:28,29 THE OUTPOURING OF THE HOLY SPIRIT

Joel 3:10 “LET THE WEAK SAY, I AM STRONG”

AMOS

Amos 3:3 TWO CAN’T WALK TOGETHER UNLESS THEY ARE AGREED.

Amos 3:7 GOD REVEALS HIS SECRETS TO THE PROPHETS.

JONAH

Jonah 3:4 JONAH PREDICTED THAT NINEVEH WOULD BE DESTROYED IN FORTY DAYS, BUT NINEVEH REPENTED AND SO DID GOD (V10). JONAH WAS ANGRY ABOUT IT (4:1)

MICAH

Micah 6:8 WHAT THE LORD REQUIRES

NAHUM

Nahum 1:7 THE LORD IS A STRONG HOLD IN THE DAY OF TROUBLE.

HABAKKUK

Habakkuk 2:4 “THE JUST SHALL LIVE BY HIS FAITH”

Habakkuk 2:14 GOD’S ULTIMATE PURPOSE ON EARTH

ZEPHANIAH

Zephaniah 3: 17 SONG

HAGGAI

Haggai 1:5,7 "CONSIDER YOUR WAYS"

Haggai 2:9 "THE GLORY OF THE LATTER HOUSE SHALL BE GREATER THAN OF THE FORMER."

Haggai 2:19 "FROM THIS DAY WILL I BLESS YOU"

ZECHARIAH

Zechariah 4:6 THE TRUE SOURCE OF OUR POWER IS THE HOLY SPIRIT.

MALACHI

Malachi 3:11 GOD WILL REBUKE THE DEVOURER FOR OUR SAKES WHEN WE ARE TITHERS (3:10)

Malachi 3:17 WE ARE JEWELS TO THE LORD

Malachi 4:6 GOD WILL TURN THE HEARTS OF THE FATHERS TO THE CHILDREN AND THE CHILDREN TO THEIR FATHERS.

NEW TESTAMENT

MATTHEW

Matthew 1:20 GETTING A MESSAGE FROM THE LORD IN A DREAM.

Matthew 4: 1-11 JESUS OVERCAME THE DEVIL BY THE SCRIPTURE, AND THE DEVIL LEFT AND THE ANGELS CAME.

Matthew 4: 19 FOLLOW JESUS AND HE WILL MAKE US FISHERS OF MEN.
Matthew 5:13 DON'T BE A "GOOD FOR NOTHING"

Matthew 5:19 GREATNESS WITH JESUS IS TO KEEP AND TEACH GOD'S COMMANDMENTS.

Matthew 5:48 GO FOR PERFECTION

Matthew 6: 14,15 JESUS STRESSED FORGIVENESS AS A CONDITION TO ANSWERED PRAYER

Matthew 6:21 WHERE IS MY HEART? WHERE IS MY TREASURE?

Matthew 6:33 FIRST THINGS FIRST!

Matthew 7:11 GOD WILL ALWAYS GIVE GOOD THINGS TO THOSE WHO ASK.

Matthew 7: 12 THE SUMMARY OF ALL THE LAW AND PREACHERS

Matthew 8:10 GREAT FAITH IS MARVELOUS TO JESUS (AMAZING)

Matthew 9: 13 THE LORD PREFERS MERCY TO OFFERINGS.

Matthew 9:38 PRAY FOR CHRISTIAN LABORERS

Matthew 11:16-19 YOU CAN'T PLEASE EVERYBODY

Matthew 11:25 DON'T THINK YOU ARE SO SMART

Matthew 13:57,58 WHEN YOU ARE OFFENDED AT GOD'S SERVANT, HE CAN 'T DO MUCH FOR YOU

Matthew 14:26 SOMETIMES IT IS EASIER TO BELIEVE IN GHOSTS THAN MIRACLES.

Matthew 14:31,32 EVEN WHEN WE FAIL, JESUS WILL BE THERE TO HELP.

Matthew 22:29 WHY WE ERR

Matthew 24:24 IT WILL NOT BE POSSIBLE TO DECEIVE GOD'S CHOSEN ONES.

MARK

Mark 3:5 JESUS HAD THE LOOK OF ANGER AT HARDNESS OF HEARTS.

Mark 3:21 CHRIST'S RELATIVES AND FRIENDS WERE TRYING TO RESTRAIN HIM. THEY THOUGHT HE WAS OUT OF HIS MIND.

Mark 3:22 THE SCRIBES SAID THAT JESUS WAS POSSESSED BY THE DEVIL.
Mark 3:30 SAYING "CHRIST HAS A DEMON" IS A SIN THAT IS ETERNAL. (v.29)

Mark 4:40 FEAR CAN OVERCOME FAITH AND FAITH CAN OVERCOME FEAR.

Mark 5:36 "BE NOT AFRAID, ONLY BELIEVE"

Mark 6:6 JESUS MARVELED (WAS ASTONISHED) AT THEIR UNBELIEF.

Mark 6:50 CHEER UP — "HERE COMES JESUS" — BE NOT AFRAID.

Mark 6:56 AS MANY AS TOUCHED JESUS WERE HEALED.

Mark 8:38 "SHAME, SHAME, DOUBLE SHAME

Mark 9:35 HOW TO BE FIRST AND GREAT. MAKE YOURSELF A SERVANT.

Mark 9:40 JESUS SAID THAT ONE WHO IS NOT AGAINST HIM IS ON HIS SIDE.

Mark 11:22,23 BY FAITH "SAY" AND DON'T DOUBT

Mark 12:30 #1 LOVE GOD WITH ALL OUR STRENGTH v.31 #2 LOVE YOUR NEIGHBOR AS YOURSELF

Mark 13:24,26 CHRIST COMES AGAIN AFTER THE TIME OFTRIBULATION.

Mark 14:3 JESUS SMELLED SWEET

Mark 14:26 JESUS SANG A PSALM WITH THE DISCIPLES.

Mark 14:30 BEWARE OF COCKINESS

Mark 14:33,34 JESUS ALMOST HAD A HEART ATTACK IN THE GARDEN.

Mark 14:36 "NOT WHAT I WANT, BUT WHAT YOU WANT."

Mark 14:38 HOW TO AVOID TEMPTATION: "WATCH AND PRAY."

Mark 16:20 THE PREACHING OF GOD'S WORD IS CONFIRMED BY MIRACLES. AMEN

LUKE

Luke 1:37 "NOTHING IS IMPOSSIBLE WHEN YOU PUT YOUR TRUST IN GOD."
Luke 1:46,47 MY SOUL MAGNIFIES THE LORD AND MY SPIRIT REJOICES IN GOD MY SAVIOR.

Luke 1:49 HE HAS DONE GREAT THINGS FOR ME

Luke 2:13 THE HEAVENLY TROOPS PRAISE GOD

Luke 2:51 JESUS LEARNED OBEDIENCE IN HIS HOME

Luke 2:52 JESUS GREW IN WISDOM

Luke 3:21 WHEN JESUS WAS BAPTIZED, HE WAS ALSO PRAYING WHEN HEAVEN OPENED AND THE HOLY SPIRIT CAME UPON HIM. (V. 22) AND GOD SPOKE FROM HEAVEN.

Luke 4:1 JESUS BEING FULL OF THE HOLY SPIRIT WAS LED OF THE SPIRIT INTO THE WILDERNESS TO BE TESTED BY THE DEVIL FOR FORTY DAYS. (v.2)

Luke 4:16 JESUS FOLLOWED CUSTOM. HE ATTENDED THE SYNAGOGUE EVERY SABBATH. HE EVEN TOOK PART BY READING THE SCRIPTURE (v.17)

Luke 6:23 “LEAP FOR JOY” (v.22) WHEN HATED AND EXCLUDED BECAUSE OF LOYALTY TO JESUS

Luke 7:34 THEY SAID JESUS WAS A GLUTTON, DRUNKARD AND IN BAD COMPANY

Luke 7:50 JESUS SAID OUR FAITH SAVES US —GO IN PEACE.

Luke 8:2 WOMEN WHO WERE HEALED SUPPORTED JESUS FINANCIALLY. (v.3)

Luke 8:21 HOW TO BE A RELATIVE OF JESUS

Luke 8:50 “FEAR NOT, BELIEVE ONLY

Luke 10:7 JESUS SAID THE PREACHER DESERVES HIS WAGES AND EARNS HIS PAY.

Luke 10:20 SOMETHING ALWAYS TO REJOICE OVER - (NAMES WRITTEN IN HEAVEN)

Luke 11:28 MORE BLESSED THAN THE MOTHER OF JESUS ARE THOSE WHO HEAR GOD'S WORD AND OBEY IT.

Luke 12:29 DON'T HAVE A "DOUBTFUL MIND"

Luke 12:53 IN-LAW TROUBLE OVER JESUS

Luke 14:23 THE LORD WANTS HIS HOUSE FULL

Luke 17:3 JESUS SAID WE SHOULD FORGIVE IF THE OFFENDER REPENTS.

Luke 17:5,6 IT'S NOT HAVING MORE FAITH, BUT USING WHAT LITTLE YOU HAVE.

Luke 17:10 ARE WE EVEN DOING OUR DUTIES? OVER AND ABOVE THE CALL OF DUTY IS REQUIRED OF JESUS.

Luke 17: 14 AS THEY WENT IN OBEDIENCE THEY WERE HEALED

Luke: 17:21 THE KINGDOM OF GOD IS IN US WHEN THE KING REIGNS IN THE LIFE.

Luke 18:27 THE THINGS WHICH ARE IMPOSSIBLE WITH MAN ARE POSSIBLE WITH GOD.

Luke 19:5 JESUS INVITES HIMSELF IN. WE MUST RECEIVE HIM.

Luke 19:41 JESUS WEPT AGAIN

Luke 21:26 HEART FAILURE THROUGH FEAR

Luke 24:27 HOW WOULD YOU LIKE JESUS EXPLAINING THE SCRIPTURES?

Luke 24:15 JESUS ENLIGHTENED THEIR MINDS TO UNDERSTAND THE SCRIPTURES.

Luke 24:47 REPENTANCE LEADING TO FORGIVENESS OF SINS SHOULD BE PREACHED IN JESUS NAME.

Luke 24:49 WE MUST BE INVESTED WITH HOLY SPIRIT POWER

JOHN

John 1:16 OF HIS ABUNDANCE WE RECEIVE BLESSING AFTER BLESSING.

John 2:17 JESUS HAD RESPECT AND ZEAL FOR THE HOUSE OF GOD.

John 4:36 GOD'S WORK IS GATHERING A HARVEST FOR ETERNAL LIFE.

John 6: 12 JESUS DOESN'T WASTE ANYTHING

John 6:21 IT WAS A POWER BOAT WHEN JESUS CAME INTO IT.

John 6:29 BELIEVING IS WORKING FOR GOD
John 6:64 JESUS KNOWS.

John 10:20 MANY SAID JESUS HAD A DEMON AND WAS INSANE AND SHOULD NOT LISTEN TO HIM.

John 11:4 SOME SICKNESSES DO NOT END IN DEATH BUT TO BRING GLORY TO GOD IN ITS HEALING.

John 11:33 JESUS WAS EMOTIONAL AND WAS TROUBLED. (v.38)

John 12:26 THE FATHER WILL HONOR THOSE WHO SERVE JESUS.

John 12:37 SOME JUST WILL NOT BELIEVE EVEN IF THEY SEE MANY MIRACLES.

John 13:35 THE MARK OF A DISCIPLE - LOVE!

John 14:9 TO KNOW AND SEE THE FATHER IS TO KNOW AND SEE CHRIST.

John 14:12 WITH FAITH IN CHRIST, YOU WILL DO GREATER WORKS THAN HE.

John 16:22 NO MAN CAN TAKE OUR JOY AWAY FROM US.

John 16:24 ASKING AND RECEIVING IN JESUS NAME BRINGS FULL JOY.

John 17:23 THE FATHER LOVES US AS MUCH AS HE LOVES JESUS.

ACTS

Acts 1:14 THEY WERE PRAYING IN UNITY

Acts 2:4 IN THEIR BAPTISM IN THE HOLY SPIRIT, THEY WERE FILLED WITH HIM.

Acts 2:11 THEY WERE SPEAKING IN TONGUES OF THE WONDERFUL WORKS OF GOD.

Acts 4:24 RAISING THEIR VOICES TO GOD IN UNITY

Acts 4:29 PRAY FOR BOLDNESS IN SPEAKING GOD'S WORD.

Acts 5:29 "WE OUGHT TO OBEY GOD RATHER THAN MEN."

Acts 5:32 THE HOLY SPIRIT IS GIVEN BY GOD TO THOSE WHO OBEY HIM.

Acts 5:41 REJOICING TO SUFFER FOR THE NAME OF JESUS.

Acts 7:56 JESUS IS AT THE RIGHT HAND OF THE FATHER.

Acts 8:39 THE HOLY SPIRIT CARRIED PHILLIP AWAY AND TRANSPORTED HIM SOMEWHERE ELSE.

Acts 10:35 ANYONE WHO REVERENCES GOD AND DOES WHAT IS RIGHT IS ACCEPTABLE WITH HIM.

Acts 10:44 AS PETER PREACHED THE LISTENERS WERE BAPTIZED IN THE HOLY SPIRIT AND SPOKE IN TONGUES (V. 46)

Acts 11:15,16 THE HOLY SPIRIT FALLING ON THEM AND THEY SPEAKING IN TONGUES, IS THE BAPTISM OF THE HOLY SPIRIT.

Acts 12: 15 UNBELIEVING BELIEVERS

Acts 13:48 "AS MANY AS WERE ORDAINED (CHOSEN) TO ETERNAL LIFE, BELIEVED."

Acts 13:52 THE DISCIPLES WERE FILLED WITH JOY AND THE HOLY SPIRIT.

Acts 16:15 THE FIRST WOMAN REPORTED BAPTIZED AND THE FIRST CONVERT IN EUROPE.

Acts 17:6 TESTIMONY OF THE UNSAVED ABOUT THE BELIEVERS — "THEY HAVE TURNED THE WORLD UPSIDE DOWN."

Acts 17:11 EAGER HEARERS AND READERS AND BELIEVERS (v.12)

Acts 19:11 THERE ARE SPECIAL MIRACLES GOD WORKS THROUGH MEN.

Acts 20:7 THE DISCIPLES HAD COMMUNION ON THE FIRST DAY OF THE WEEK. (THE NEW DAY BEGAN AT SUNSET. THIS WOULD BE AT MIDNIGHT, 7b)

Acts 20:28b "FEED THE CHURCH OF GOD"

Acts 20:32 THE WORD OF GOD IS ABLE TO MAKE ONE STRONG.

Acts 22:15 A WITNESS TELLS WHAT HE HAS SEEN AND HEARD.

ROMANS

Romans 1:17 "LIVE BY FAITH"

Romans 4:17 GOD CALLS THOSE THINGS WHICH ARE NOT AS THOUGH THEY WERE. (HE CALLS INTO EXISTENCE THE THINGS WHICH DO NOT EXIST) (MARK 11:24)

Romans 8:1 NO CONDEMNATION IF WE WALK IN THE SPIRIT.

Romans 8:27 THE HOLY SPIRIT MAKES A PERFECT PRAYER FOR US.

Romans 8:32 WE ARE MORE THAN CONQUERORS THROUGH CHRIST.

Romans 10:17 FAITH COMES FROM HEARING THE WORD OF GOD.

Romans 11:33 GOD'S WAYS OF DOING THINGS ARE OVER OUR HEADS.

Romans 12:1 PRESENTING OUR BODIES TO GOD IN SPIRITUAL WORSHIP.

Romans 12:2 TRANSFORMING THE LIFE BY RENEWING THE MIND.

Romans 12:9 LET LOVE BE WITHOUT HYPOCRISY

Romans 13:1 EVERYONE IS TO BE SUBMITTED TO GOVERNING AUTHORITIES.

Romans 13:8 LEAVE NO DEBT UNPAID INCLUDING DEBT OF LOVE.

Romans 13:14 OUR ARMOR OF LIGHT IS THE ARMOR OF GOD (EPH. 6)

Romans 14:17 THE KINGDOM OF GOD IS RIGHTEOUSNESS, PEACE, AND JOY IN THE HOLY SPIRIT.

Romans 14:19 FOLLOW AFTER THINGS THAT CONTRIBUTE TO PEACE.

Romans 14:23 WHATEVER IS NOT OF FAITH IS SIN

Romans 15:13 WE ABOUND IN HOPE THROUGH THE POWER OF THE HOLY SPIRIT.

Romans 16:4 RISKING OUR NECKS FOR ONE ANOTHER

Romans 16:20 GOD BRUISES SATAN UNDER OUR FEET

I CORINTHIANS

I Corinthians 1:4 BEING THANKFUL FOR THE CHURCH AS THE RECIPIENT OF GOD'S GRACE.

I Corinthians 1:17 PREACHING THE GOSPEL IS MORE IMPORTANT THAN BAPTIZING.

I Corinthians 1:21 THE WORLD BY ITS OWN WISDOM CANNOT KNOW GOD.

I Corinthians 1:23 PREACH CHRIST CRUCIFIED

I Corinthians 1:31 GLORY IN THE LORD

I Corinthians 2:10 GOD REVEALS HIS HIDDEN WONDERS BY HIS SPIRIT.

I Corinthians 2:16 WE HAVE THE MIND OF CHRIST (THE SPIRITUALLY MINDED HAVE THE VERY THOUGHTS OF CHRIST).

I Corinthians 3:14 WE SHALL BE REWARDED FOR OUR SPIRITUAL WORKS AFTER SALVATION

I Corinthians 3:21 LET NO ONE GLORY IN MEN

I Corinthians 4:1 WE ARE TRUSTEES TO DISTRIBUTE THE HIDDEN TRUTHS OF GOD.

I Corinthians 4:2 THE REQUIREMENT OF A TRUSTEE IS TO BE TRUSTWORTHY.

I Corinthians 4:20 THE KINGDOM OF GOD DOES NOT SHOW ITSELF IN TALK BUT IN POWER.

I Corinthians 5:11 DON'T HAVE FELLOWSHIP WITH ONE WHO CALLS HIMSELF A CHRISTIAN BUT LIVES AS A FORNICATOR, COVETOUS, IDOLATER, SLANDERER, DRUNKARD, OR SWINDLER.

I Corinthians 5:12 WE DON'T JUDGE OUTSIDERS, BUT THOSE IN THE CHURCH.

I Corinthians 6:12 SOMETHING MAY BE LAWFUL FOR YOU BUT NOT GOOD FOR YOU.

I Corinthians 7:5 SATAN TEMPTS US THROUGH OUR LACK OF SELF-CONTROL.

I Corinthians 7:39 BE MARRIED ONLY IN THE LORD

I Corinthians 8:12 SINNING AGAINST THE BRETHREN IS SINNING AGAINST CHRIST.

I Corinthians 12:1 DON'T BE IGNORANT CONCERNING SPIRITUAL GIFTS.

1 Corinthians 12:31 SEEK THE BEST GIFTS AND USE THEM IN LOVE (1 Cor.13)

I Corinthians 13:2 THE GIFTS WITHOUT LOVE ARE WORTH NOTHING.

I Corinthians 14:1 FOLLOW AFTER LOVE AND SPIRITUAL GIFTS.

I Corinthians 14:2 SPEAKING IN TONGUES IS SPEAKING HIDDEN TRUTHS.

I Corinthians 14:14 OUR SPIRIT PRAYS IN THE UNKNOWN TONGUE.

I Corinthians 14:16 WE BLESS IN THE SPIRIT OF TONGUES

I Corinthians 15:33 BAD COMPANY RUINS GOOD HABITS

I Corinthians 15:57 WE HAVE BEEN GIVEN THE VICTORY BY GOD THROUGH JESUS.

I Corinthians 16:14 LET ALL OF OUR AFFAIRS BE DONE IN LOVE.

II CORINTHIANS

II Corinthians 2:11 SATAN CAN GET AN ADVANTAGE OVER US IF WE DO NOT FORGIVE LIKE WE SHOULD (v. 10)

II Corinthians 2:14 IN CHRIST WE ARE CONTINUALLY TRIUMPHANT.

II Corinthians 2:16 WE CAN BE THE ODOR OF DEATH OR LIFE TO OTHERS.

II Corinthians 4:4 THE MIND GETS BLINDED BY SATAN WHEN THE PERSON WILL NOT BELIEVE

II Corinthians 4:8-10 DOWN BUT NOT OUT!

II Corinthians 4:17 OUR AFFLICTIONS WORK FOR US

II Corinthians 5:7 "WE WALK BY FAITH, NOT BY SIGHT"

II Corinthians 5:14 THE LOVE OF CHRIST COMPELS US

II Corinthians 9:6 SCANTY SOWING; SCANTY HARVEST

II Corinthians 10:4 OUR WEAPONS ARE NOT HUMAN POWER BUT GOD POWER.

II Corinthians 10:17 IF YOU WANT TO BRAG, GO AHEAD AND BRAG ON THE LORD.

II Corinthians 11:23-29 SO YOU THINK YOU'VE GOT TROUBLES?

GALATIANS

Galatians 1:19 THE LORD'S BROTHER, JAMES, BECAME AN APOSTLE.

Galatians 2:2 PAUL SUBMITTED HIS TEACHINGS TO THE CHURCH LEADERS IN JERUSALEM.
Galatians 2:20 "I LIVE BY THE FAITH OF THE SON OF GOD."

Galatians 4:19 "SHAPE UP."

Galatians 5:6 WHAT COUNTS IS FAITH ACTING THROUGH LOVE.

Galatians 5:14 ALL THE LAW IS FULFILLED IS ONE WORD - “LOVE”.

Galatians 6:2 THE LAW OF CHRIST IS TO BEAR ONE ANOTHER’S BURDEN.

Galatians 6:7,8 THE LAW OF SOWING AND REAPING

Galatians 6:9 DON’T GET TIRED OF DOING RIGHT, WE WILL REAP A HARVEST OF BLESSING IF WE DON’T GIVE UP.

Galatians 6:10 PREFERENTIAL TREATMENT TO BRETHREN IN CHRIST

EPHESIANS

Ephesians 1:4 CHOSEN IN CHRIST BEFORE THE CREATION OF THE WORLD

Ephesians 1:5 CHOSEN THEN PREDESTINATED (DESTINED) TO BE HIS SONS

Ephesians 1:12 WE SHOULD BE TO THE PRAISE OF HIS GLORY (PTL)

Ephesians 2:14 CHRIST IS OUR PEACE (HE PRODUCES PEACE V. 15)

Ephesians 3:20 GOD IS ABLE TO DO MORE THAN WE ASK BY THE POWER WHICH IS AT WORK WITHIN US.

Ephesians 6:11 PUT ON THE WHOLE ARMOR OF GOD TO STAND AGAINST THE SCHEMES OF THE DEVIL.

PHILIPPIANS

Philippians 1:1 THREE CLASSES OF BELIEVERS IN THE CHURCH: SAINTS, BISHOPS (ELDERS, OVERSEERS) AND DEACONS (ASSISTANTS)

Philippians 1:4 MAKING REQUEST WITH JOY IN PRAYER

Philippians 1:6 GOD WHO BEGINS SOMETHING CAN COMPLETE IT IN US.

Philippians 1:20 MAGNIFY CHRIST

Philippians 1:23 A GODLY DILEMMA

Philippians 2:5 HAVE THE SAME ATTITUDE AS CHRIST (6 - 8)

Philippians 2:11 EVERY TONGUE SHOULD CONFESS THAT JESUS CHRIST IS LORD

Philippians 2:13 GOD NOT ONLY WORKS TO MAKE US WILLING TO DO HIS WILL, BUT ALSO GIVES US THE ENERGY.

Philippians 2:14 DO ALL THINGS WITHOUT GRUMBLING AND FAULT-FINDING.

Philippians 2:16 HOLDING FORTH THE WORD OF LIFE TO A CROOKED WORLD

Philippians 3:20 WE ARE CITIZENS OF THE STATE OF HEAVEN.

Philippians 4:4 ALWAYS BE GLAD IN THE LORD

Philippians 4:8 WHAT TO THINK ABOUT

Philippians 4:11 CONTENTMENT IN ANY STATE (13, 14)

COLOSSIANS

Colossians 1:16 ALL THINGS WERE CREATED BY CHRIST AND FOR HIM.

Colossians 3:5 COVETOUSNESS IS IDOLATRY

Colossians 3:15 "LET THE PEACE OF CHRIST RULE IN OUR HEARTS."

Colossians 4:2 DEVOTE OURSELVES TO PRAYER WITH THANKSGIVING

I THESSALONIANS

I Thessalonians 1:5 THE PREACHING OF THE GOSPEL MUST BE ACCOMPANIED WITH HE POWER OF THE HOLY SPIRIT AND FULL CONVICTION.

I Thessalonians 5:18 THIS IS THE WILL OF GOD FOR US (vs.16-22)

II THESSALONIANS

II Thessalonians 2: 10 LOVE THE TRUTH OR PERISH (vs. 11,12)

II Thessalonians 3:10 ANOTHER COMMAND: "IF ANY WOULD NOT WORK, NEITHER SHOULD HE EAT."

I TIMOTHY

I Timothy 1:5 THE END OF THE COMMANDMENT IS LOVE FROM A PURE HEART AND OF A GOOD CONSCIENCE, AND OF FAITH WITHOUT HYPOCRISY.

I Timothy 2:8 IT IS DESIRABLE TO PRAY WITH HANDS LIFTED UP AS A SIGN OF PEACE AND FAITH.

I Timothy 4:4 EVERYTHING THAT GOD HAS CREATED IS GOOD AND NOT TO BE REFUSED IF IT IS RECEIVED WITH THANKS.

I Timothy 6:6 BIG PROFIT!

II TIMOTHY

II Timothy 3: 16 "ALL SCRIPTURE IS GOD-INSPIRED AND PROFITABLE."

TITUS

Titus 1:16 DISOWNING GOD WITH OUR ACTIONS

PHILEMON

Philemon 22 "THROUGH YOUR PRAYERS I SHALL BE GIVEN TO YOU."

HEBREWS

Hebrews 1:2 GOD IS SPEAKING LOUD AND CLEAR BY HIS SON.

Hebrews 1:3 JESUS IS THE IMAGE OF GOD

Hebrews 1:14 ANGELS ARE MINISTERING SPIRITS TO US

Hebrews 2:12 JESUS SINGS PRAISES IN THE CONGREGATION.

Hebrews 3:13 ENCOURAGE ONE ANOTHER DAILY

Hebrews 3: 17 GRIEVE NOT THE SPIRIT OF GOD OR ELSE

Hebrews 4:12 THE WORD OF GOD IS A DISCERNER OF THE THOUGHTS AND INTENTS OF THE HEART.

Hebrews 5:8 JESUS LEARNED OBEDIENCE THROUGH SUFFERING.

Hebrews 6:4-6 AN UNPARDONABLE SIN

Hebrews 6:12 "THROUGH FAITH AND PATIENCE YOU INHERIT THE PROMISES."

Hebrews 6: 19 HOPE IS AN ANCHOR OF THE SOUL

Hebrews 9:27 TWO APPOINTMENTS FOR ALL UNSAVED

Hebrews 10:25 ENCOURAGE ONE ANOTHER

Hebrews 10:36 AFTER WE HAVE DONE THE WILL OF GOD WE WILL RECEIVE THE PROMISE.

Hebrews 11:1a FAITH IS THE SOLID GROUND FOR WHAT IS HOPED FOR. IT IS THE REALIZATION OF THINGS HOPED FOR.

Hebrews 11:1b IT IS PROOF OF THE REALITY OF THE THINGS NOT SEEN. IT MAKES US CERTAIN OF REALITIES WE DO NOT SEE.

Hebrews 11:6 WE PLEASE GOD BY FAITH

JAMES

James 1:2 CONSIDER OURSELVES HAPPY WHEN IN TRIALS

James 1:3 TRIALS TEST OUR FAITH AND PRODUCES PATIENCE.

James 1:5,6 IF WE LACK, ASK OF GOD IN FAITH WITHOUT DOUBT.

James 1:17 EVERY GOOD GIFT IS FROM GOD

James 2:18 FAITH IS SEEN BY WORKS (V. 20)

James 4:6 GOD GIVES MORE GRACE TO THE HUMBLE, BUT RESISTS THE PROUD

James 4:7,8 HOW TO SEE THE DEVIL RUN AWAY FROM YOU

James 4:10 HUMBLE OURSELVES IN THE SIGHT OF THE LORD AND HE SHALL EXALT US.
James 4:17 THE SINS OF OMISSION

James 5:15 THE PRAYER OF FAITH SHALL SAVE THE SICK AND THE SINS WILL BE FORGIVEN

James 5:16 CONFESS OUR SINS ONE TO ANOTHER AND PRAY FOR EACH OTHER THAT HEALING MAY COME.

I PETER

I Peter 1:4 WE HAVE AN INHERITANCE RESERVED IN HEAVEN.

I Peter 2:2 HOW TO GROW IN CHRIST? DESIRE THE WORD.

I Peter 2:21 "YOU SHOULD FOLLOW HIS STEPS"

I Peter 2:24 "BY WHOSE STRIPES YOU WERE HEALED"

I Peter 1-7 GOOD HUSBAND AND WIFE RELATIONS HELP IN PRAYER.

I Peter 3:12 DOING EVIL CLOSES GOD'S EARS TO OUR PRAYERS.

I Peter 3:16 KEEP A CLEAR CONSCIENCE

I Peter 5:9 SATAN IS TO BE RESISTED BY STRONG FAITH.

II PETER

II Peter 1:10 HOW TO KEEP FROM FALLING (w. 5-7)

II Peter 3:9 GOD'S WILL: THAT NONE SHOULD PERISH AND ALL SHOULD COME TO REPENTANCE

I JOHN

I John 2:3 THIS IS HOW WE MAY BE SURE THAT WE KNOW CHRIST, BY OBEYING HIS COMMANDMENTS (v.4)

I John 3:2,3 WHEN CHRIST COMES WE SHALL BE LIKE HIM.

I John 4:4 "GREATER IS HE THAT IS IN YOU THAN HE THAT IS IN THE WORLD."

I John 4:18 "PERFECT LOVE CASTS OUT FEAR"
I John 5:1 ONE IS BORN OF GOD WHO BELIEVES THAT JESUS IS CHRIST.

I John 5:3 "THIS IS LOVING GOD WHEN WE OBEY HIS COMMANDS. HIS COMMANDMENTS ARE NOT BURDENSOME."

I John 5:13 "YOU MAY KNOW THAT YOU HAVE ETERNAL LIFE."

I John 5:14,15 PRAYER CONFIDENCE

I John 5:20 JESUS CHRIST IS THE TRUE GOD AND ETERNAL LIFE.

II JOHN

II John 6 "THIS IS LOVE" — OBEYING CHRIST'S COMMANDS

III JOHN

III John 2 GOD'S WISH OF PROSPERITY FOR HIS CHILDREN: IN SPIRITUAL AND PHYSICAL REALM

JUDE

Jude 2 MERCY, PEACE, AND LOVE BE MULTIPLIED

Jude 20 BUILDING OURSELVES UP IN OUR FAITH BY PRAYER IN THE SPIRIT.

Jude 24 OUR LORD IS ABLE TO KEEP US FROM FALLING AND TO PRESENT US WITHOUT BLEMISH IN THE PRESENCE OF HIS GLORY WITH GREAT JOY.

REVELATION

Revelation 1:3 HAPPY IS THE ONE WHO READS ALOUD AND THOSE WHO HEAR THE WORDS, AND THOSE WHO HEED THE WORDS.

Revelation 1:7 WHEN CHRIST COMES WITH CLOUDS EVERY EYE WILL SEE HIM.

Revelation 1:18 CHRIST HAS THE KEYS OF DEATH AND HADES.

Revelation 5:11,12 OVER 100 MILLION ANGELS SHOUTED PRAISE OF GOD (v. 12)

Revelation 12:11 HOW TO OVERCOME SATAN: BLOOD OF CHRIST, WORD OF TESTIMONY, WILLINGNESS TO BE MARTYRED.

Revelation 14:13 HAPPY ARE THE ONES WHO DIE AS CHRISTIANS. WHAT WE HAVE DONE FOLLOWS US IN DEATH.

Revelation 17:17 GOD PUTS INTO HEARTS THAT WHICH FULFILLS HIS WILL.

Revelation 19:1 A GREAT CROWD OF PEOPLE IN HEAVEN WERE SHOUTING "PRAISE THE LORD."

Revelation 19:7 "LET US BE GLAD AND REJOICE"
Revelation 22:12 EVERYONE WILL BE REWARDED ACCORDING TO HIS WORKS.

Revelation 22: 17 "COME. . .COME. . .COME"

Revelation 22:20 THE LAST WORDS OF JESUS IN THE BIBLE

Revelation 22:20b THE LAST PRAYER IN THE BIBLE

Revelation 22:21 THE BIBLE ENDS WITH "THE GRACE OF THE LORD JESUS BE WITH GOD'S PEOPLE."

CHAPTER SIX

My Assyrian Ministry

SINCE RETIRING FROM PASTORING FOUR CHURCHES SINCE 1992, MY ASSYRIAN MINISTRY HAS TAKEN ME ON SPEAKING ENGAGEMENTS TO:

15 Foreign Countries, 15 States in the USA, 94 Cities in the USA and the World, 18 Denominations, 80 different Churches, 44 Conferences and Organizations, 15 Television and Radio stations.

Rev. John Booko, an Assyrian American, has studied the Scriptures related to the Assyrian people in great depth with its prophetic promise in Isaiah 1 9:23-25 which states:

"In that day there will be a highway from Egypt to Assyria. . .In that day Israel will be third along with Egypt and Assyria, a blessing on the earth. The Lord Almighty will bless them, saying. . .Assyria my handiwork. . ."(NIV)

God used Assyria in the past when it was a powerful nation and He used Assyrians to spread the Gospel to far away lands. So, He plans to use the restored Assyria in His future.

Over 150 times, the Bible refers to Assyria and the Assyrians. Jesus grew up among the Assyrians in Galilee and spoke the Assyrian language which is Aramaic. Jesus and the apostles preached in the Assyrian language and the New Testament was first written in the Assyrian language.

While persecution drove many Assyrian Christians from the areas of present day Iraq, Turkey, and Iran, they are being stirred by the Holy Spirit to again seek their destiny according to the Scripture.

HERE IS A BRIEF HISTORY OF MY PEOPLE

I am an Assyrian American. I am not to be confused with Syrians from Syria. My ancestors were of the rich and powerful land of Mesopotamia which lies between the Tigris and the Euphrates Rivers, just north of the Garden of Eden. Today this entire area is now Iran and Iraq. We are not Arabs or Moslems, we are Christians. We still speak our ancient mother tongue, Aramaic, which is also the language which Christ spoke, and were among the first converts to Christianity. The Assyrians played an important part in the history of the Near East, of the Bible, and of religion in general. Our ancient city of Nineveh was converted to the Lord by Jonah. The Assyrian Church, or as it is known the Ancient Apostolic Church of the East, was one of the strongest Christian Churches in the world and was noted for its missions in the Middle East, India, China, Mongolia, Indonesia, Japan and other parts of the world. The Assyrians were also the originators of the Alphabet.

The destruction of Nineveh in 612 B.C. scattered the Assyrians all over the world. Many of the Assyrians still live in Middle Eastern countries. Presently there are about 80,000 Assyrians living in Chicago.

We have upheld all our traditions and customs and still speak our ancient mother tongue. Even though we do not have a country anymore, we have survived through the centuries and we're still going strong. Further history of the Assyrians can be found throughout the Old Testament of the Bible.

Isaiah 19:23-25, is a good example of the Lord's promise to the Assyrians. People think we do not exist anymore because we do not have a country, but we are alive, well, and united. The Jews only recently got their country in 1948, does this mean that they did not exist up until then?

Having stated that I am an Assyrian, you should know that I am an Assyrian born in the right place. I must admit that sometimes I pray and ask God, "Lord, how come I was so blessed to be born in Chicago, Illinois, in 1922, when I could have been born in the mountains of Northern Iraq where my father was a shepherd?"

As you can imagine, life in Iraq as a shepherd was extremely difficult for my father, Avrahim (Abraham).

My dad left his hometown of Asheta about 1910, before World War I, and traveled through Persia, Russia (now called the Commonwealth of Independent States), Germany and Poland, arriving in the United States about 1912. His father was a priest in the Church of the East. His family is known as the family of priests. It looks like the sons are maintaining that tradition through the sovereignty of God. He settled in Chicago, where he soon discovered there was not much of a job opportunity for shepherds (but, praise God, thanks to His heavenly hand, today, I am a shepherd of a spiritual flock)!

My mother (her father was a deacon in the Nestorian Church) journeyed to America because of a persecution that broke out. Her village was Zarni which was north of the former capital of Assyria, Nineveh, which is presently named "Mosul" in Iraq.

Let me share with you a bit of that history. When Assyria lost its land, the Assyrians settled mostly in what is now known as Northern Iraq. During World War I, the nations which were united against Germany and Turkey were the United States, Great Britain, and others. Here are some verses from one of their war songs at that time by Shamasha Ephraim of Van.

"Forth we go to battle, ranging o'er the mountains;
Hearts all yearning forward to Mosul's fertile plains.
Nineveh 's fair city summons back her children.
Forth we go to battle in thy name, O Mar Shimun (their spiritual leader).
On the Tigris' banks lies Nineveh the holy;
Her old walls shall be to us a diadem and crown.
There alone, Assyrians, can our race be established.
Forth we go to battle in thy name, O Mar Shimun.
Hark, our Nation calls - our great Assyrian Mother;
Hark, young men, she calls you - calls each one of you by name.

Blest that youth for ever who will hear her calling.
Forth we go to battle in thy name, O Mar Shimun."

Now, the Assyrians were right up there in Northern Iraq; there were many of them inside the Turkish border. The British asked the Assyrians if they would not consider holding that region for the Allies.

The Assyrians agreed.

The British armed them, and the Assyrians fought and held the Middle East for the Allies; they were promised by the British Government that they would have their own land after the fighting was over (of course, that is what the Assyrians had been desiring).

When the war ended, instead of the British keeping their promise, they gave the land promised to the Assyrians to the Moslem Arabs!

Turkey, when attacked by the Christian states of Europe, took the war to be a kind of "jihad" (holy war) against the Christian "infidels."

Soon, friction erupted between the Turkish authorities and their Assyrian subjects, to the point of an Assyrian uprising, A number of scholars hold that the Russians (and probably the British, as well), encouraged this revolt by promising the Assyrians autonomy or full independence after the defeat of the Turks.

It is beyond question, however, that the insurrection cost the Assyrians dearly. Initially, they succeeded in repulsing a number of attacks by government forces assisted by units of Kurds (who had been the Assyrians' sworn enemies since time immemorial).

But soon afterward, they found themselves under siege and had to fight their way out to move their entire community - from infants to the elderly, a total of some seventy-thousand souls - through sub-zero weather over snow-covered mountains to Iran.

For a while thereafter, they enjoyed the patronage of the Russians, who provided them with weapons for self-defense.

With Russia's withdrawal from the war (following the Bolshevik Revolution) and the subsequent stabilization of British rule in Iraq, His Majesty's Government extended its protection to the Assyrians and brought to Iraq those who had survived the sword, disease, the hardships of exile, and their journey - altogether their numbers were reduced to some thirty-five to forty thousand people.

Then, the British recruited fighting units among the Assyrians, using them to squash sporadic rebellions within the country and in border clashes with the Turks. Taking full advantage of the Assyrians' loyalty and eagerness to please, they also cultivated the illusion of a "common fate," and went so far as to dub the Assyrians "our smallest ally" – an expression that bespoke both affection and contempt.

Further, the British continually nurtured their ally's hopes of settling in the mountainous region of northern Iraq, where they felt at home.

Such illusions were shattered one after another as the British mandate drew to a close.

For although the Anglo-Iraqi Pact of 1930 referred to the status of the various minorities in Iraq, including the Assyrians, when the mandate came to an end, the Assyrians found that all they had to show for their loyalty were vague and empty promises - and no tangible territory.

Worse yet, when they realized they were unwelcome in independent Iraq, some tried to return to Turkey; the Turks greeted them with machine-gun fire.

When they tried to enter Syria - in the hope that the French mandatory authorities would allow them to settle in the country's broad plain in the north - they were turned back at the border.

That is why a wave of Assyrians came to America after World War I, most making it to Chicago, where the nation's largest Assyrian population now thrives.

The Assyrians, it should be noted, are all professing Christians.

There is not a Moslem among them!

You could put a gun to an Assyrian's head and say, "Now, you must change from Christianity to the Moslem faith, or we will kill you," and each Assyrian would answer, "Kill me, I'll never do it."

That is how strong the Assyrians are for Christianity.

Today, there are about 3,000,000 Christian Assyrians living in the Middle East!

Most of the Assyrians were left in Northern Iraq, exposed to the wrath of the Turks under whom they were ruled. For over four-hundred years, in the Ottoman Empire, all that region was under the Turks, including the Assyrians.

Can you imagine how the Turks felt since they are Moslems and the Assyrians are Christians?

The Assyrians had fought on the side of the Allies, and now, here are the Assyrians left holding an empty bag of false promises, and the Turks and the Kurds, who are also Moslem, turned on the Assyrians and massacred thousands of them.

The Assyrians had to flee.

My mother was one of those who had to flee into Iran (known as Persia in those days).

My mother fled to Persia, and while there she went to a Presbyterian school for girls, where she became a teacher and became "born again."

Then, in 1920, she came over to the United States, and that is where she met my father.

They were married in Chicago in 1921, where I was born in 1922, and raised with my family, ultimately consisting of my brothers, Benjamin, George and Joseph, and my sister, Bertha.

The first language I spoke as a child was Assyrian, since my father could not speak English. My mother taught me English to prepare me for kindergarten.

I remember how Assyrians living in the near north side of Chicago would gather together in Lincoln Park on Sundays after church to share their stories, tea and Khada (a flat bread with butter and flour filling), and the delicious Dolma (grape leaves stuffed with rice, lamb and spices).

They all spoke in Assyrian, but we children stuck with English because we did not want to seem like foreigners.

Right now, there are about 70,000 Assyrians in Chicago, but many of them have been going to California and one of the largest Assyrian populations in the United States is in Los Angeles, California. Assyrians like California because the temperature and weather are similar to that in Iraq.

There is a prophecy in the Bible which has seemingly been forgotten or overlooked by many biblical scholars. Yet, its meaning and content are not forgotten by God.

The prophecy is like the missing piece of the gigantic puzzle we call the end time hour.

Many Christians have a fairly good understanding about the God-given role of Israel in prophecy, but when they first hear that God has a special role for another favored nation called Assyria, they are astounded.

Assyria! What's that? Where is it? Is it Syria? No, not Syria; put an "As" in front of it and it spells Assyria. Syria is a country that exists today, which is Arab and mostly Moslem, but currently there is no country called Assyria. But in its place there is the country named Iraq.

The country, Assyria, has vanished from current maps of geography, but not the people, Assyrians. I am an Assyrian/ American and there are almost 4 million Assyrians living all across our globe.

Assyria was a once-powerful nation that conquered most of the Middle East between the years 824 - 612 BC. Assyria is mentioned over 150 times in the Bible. More is said in the Bible about Assyria and Assyrians than any other nation beside Israel and Egypt.

Just as Israel did not have a homeland for 2,500 years until 1948, so Assyrians will one day have their own homeland as predicted by God in Isaiah 19:23-25.

God's other favored nation in the Bible is Assyria and the Assyrians will once again be given their own country by God to be used by him! God said it and it is recorded in the book of Isaiah chapter 19 verses 23-25: "In that day there will be a highway from Egypt to Assyria. The Assyrians will go to Egypt and the Egyptians to Assyria. The Egyptians and Assyrians will worship together. In that day Israel will be the third along with Egypt and Assyria, a blessing on the earth. The Lord Almighty will bless them, saying, 'Blessed be Egypt my people, Assyria my handiwork, and Israel my inheritance'." (NIV)

God used Assyria in the past in a punishing way, Isaiah 10:5,6.
God will use Assyria in the future in a blessing way, Isaiah 19:25.

As you read this, you will discover many biblical and historical surprises about Assyria in the Bible:

1. Assyrians living throughout the world are not Arabs or Moslems, they are Assyrians and Christian.
2. Jesus grew up with Assyrians in Galilee.
3. Jesus spoke and preached in the Assyrian language (Aramaic).
4. The Assyrians were the first nation of people to accept Christ.
5. The Gospels were first written in Assyrian language as Christ and the apostles spoke it.
6. Assyrians carried the message of Christ into the remote corners of the world such as Tibet, Mongolia, China, Japan, Indonesia, and India.

DO YOU KNOW?

God actually calls Assyria "the work of my hands" Isa. 19:25

Jesus grew up among the Assyrians in Galilee

Jesus and the apostles spoke and preached in the Assyrian language (Aramaic)

Jesus spoke well of the Assyrians in the Gospel of Matt & Luke

The founder of Assyrians was the grandson of Noah
The Prophet Jonah preached to the Assyrians in Nineveh
Assyria will be restored as a nation in the place of Iraq
The garden of Eden was in Assyria where God walked
There is a city in the State of Michigan named Assyria
There are 389 verses in the Old Testament about Assyria and Assyrians and 30 Aramaic (Assyrian) Words in the New Testament

Jesus did not say he was forsaken by God on the cross

Abraham was an Assyrian

The Assyrians were the first nation of people to accept Christ and carry his message to the Asian World

In August 1993 the 103rd Congress passed a join resolution honoring the Assyrians.

103D CONGRESS
1ST SESSION

H. J. RES. ___

IN THE HOUSE OF REPRESENTATIVES

Mr. GUTIERREZ introduced the following joint resolution; which was referred to the Committee on ______________

JOINT RESOLUTION

Expressing the sense of Congress to establish "Assyrian Pride and Remembrance Day" to recognize the tremendous legacy of the Assyrian community and to encourage all Americans to participate in the commemoration.

Whereas the Assyrian people have a proud history around the world and in the United States, dating to the earliest moments of civilization;

Whereas the Assyrian people desire, above all else, to live in peace with their neighbors;

Whereas Americans of Assyrian heritage have contributed demonstrably to the well-being of all in the United States through hard work, sympathy for others, and maintenance of unique cultural traditions;

Whereas the history of Assyrians consists of triumphant memories as well as painful ones, including the tragic massacre at Simel;

Whereas the Assyrian people have persevered in spite of such sadness, and have, indeed, thrived in a full range of endeavors undertaken as a whole and as individuals;

Whereas Assyrians have long been allies of the United States, adding vitally to victory in the First World War and to the continued struggle for peace;

Whereas the United States is a Nation that welcomes, and depends upon, people of all backgrounds, each with a story to offer others, from which America is able to craft itself into a Nation that is the envy of the world; and

Whereas all Americans, young and old, would benefit from a stronger knowledge of the Assyrian experience: Now, therefore, be it

1 *Resolved by the Senate and House of Representatives*
2 *of the United States of America in Congress assembled,*
3 That August 7, 1993, be recognized nationwide as "Assyr-
4 ian Pride and Remembrance Day," an occasion for all
5 Americans to appreciate the contributions, culture, and
6 history of the Assyrian community. The President is au-
7 thorized and requested to issue a proclamation calling
8 upon the people of the United States to observe the day
9 with appropriate ceremonies and activities.

Dear Assyrians and friends of Assyrians: Shlama!

I want to encourage all of you who are hoping, praying and working for the Assyrian cause in Iraq.

God Almighty has given His Word in Isaiah 19:23-25 that there will be the restoration of Assyria in the future, God Himself has ordained the restoration of Assyria. We are a chosen people "the work of His hands."

All the people of God must align themselves with Assyria since God has revealed in His word that He intends to restore Assyria.

It would be well for all other nations to cooperate with God's purposes for Assyria. To reject Assyria would be equivalent to rejecting God's word and thus suffer the consequences.

May the world leaders understand and be submissive to God's plan and purpose for Assyria.

May all of God's people pray and support the blessing that God has promised for and through Assyrla. "The Lord Almighty will surely bless Assyria."God said it, I believe it and that settles it!

Isaiah 66:8 and 60:22: "Can a country be born in a day or a nation be brought forth in a moment? The least of you will become a thousand, the smallest a mighty nation; I am the Lord; in its time I will do this swiftly."

"Consider Assyria. . . . I made it beautiful. . . . . ." Ezekiel 31:33. (New International Version)

ASSYRIAN MINISTRY

Rev. John Booko, Missionary To And For Assyrians in the World

STATEMENT OF MISSION

To promote and prepare the way for the fulfillment of God's prophecy through Isaiah 19:23-25 for the establishment of the country of Assyria to be the work of God's hand to bless the world THROUGH:

Intercessory prayer

Distribution of my two books and my audio and video tapes
My speaking engagements and travels
The internet and my website: www.assyria.freeservers.com
My exhibits at conferences
TV and radio interviews
Short wave radio every Sunday, 7:30-8:00 PM, EST, 9320 KHZ

COUNTRIES VISITED
Israel, Jordon, Italy, N. Ireland, England, France, Mexico, Canada, Egypt, Kenya, South Africa, Malasia, India, Japan, Sweden, Austria, Germany, Holland, Switzerland

INTERCESSORS FOR ASSYRIA
INTERCESSION FOR THE ASSYRIANS – (the Iraqi Christians)
PRAY FOR:

1. Revival of their Christianity into a vital relationship with Christ, and for the Assyrian Churches around the World to be Spirit led.
2. Restoration of their country of Assyria (now Iraq).
3. Their safety in Iraq and in other Middle East countries.
4. Iraqi constitution to give Assyrians their rights.
5. Displaced Assyrians to be able to return to their cities and villages.
6. Rebuilding of their destroyed church buildings.
7. Terrorism against Assyrians to stop in Iraq and in the Middle East.
8. Assyrians in the Middle East to lead their Moslem neighbors to Christ.
9. John Booko's Assyrian Ministry (speaking, books, shortwave radio).
10. Isaiah's prophecy in Is 19:23-25 to be fulfilled.

Psalm 50:15 "Call upon Me in the day of trouble; I will deliver you, and you will honor Me." (NIV)

THE LORD'S MODEL PRAYER
In The Language of Jesus Christ — Aramaic / Assyrian language
Babin bi shmeya, - Our Father in heaven
Pa – esh m'kootsha shimookh - hallowed be Your name.

Etya melkootookh, - Your kingdom come.
Hawi rizi-yookh — Your will be done.
Dakhi bi shmeya, oop uhrah — On earth as it is in heaven.
Hulun luckhma sun-kahnin idyo yoma - Give us this day our daily bread
Shuklun khobayn dakhit oop ukhnan shweklun daynun dahrun - And forgive us our debts as we forgive our debtors.
La moritlun ul jurahba — *Do not let us enter temptation *(Lamsa)
Illa poseelun min beesha — but deliver us from the evil one.
Sahbip deyookh eela melkewta oo khela oo tishbukhta - For Yours is the kingdom and the power and the glory
Hul ahlum, ahbadeen, ahmeen — forever. Amen.

SPEAKING ENGAGEMENTS OF REV JOHN BOOKO, THE ASSYRIAN AMERICAN, ON THE SUBJECT OF HIS BOOKS: "ASSYRIA - THE FORGOTTEN NATION IN PROPHECY" and "THE ASSYRIAN REVELATION" IN THE VARIOUS CHURCHES, CONFERENCES, CLUBS, ORGANIZATIONS AND MEDIA.

CHURCHES

ASSEMBLY OF GOD

The Carpenter's Church - Lakeland, Florida
Lighthouse Christian Center - West Palm Beach, Florida
Evangel Christian Life Center - Louisville, Kentucky
First Assembly of God — Kalamazoo, Michigan
Word of Life - Springfield, Virginia
Abundant Life Assembly - Etobicoke, Canada

BAPTIST

Montrose Baptist (American) — Chicago, Illinois
Edgewater Baptist (General Conference) — Chicago, Illinois
Bethel Baptist (NBC) - Three Rivers, Michigan

Jerusalem Baptist (Southern) - Fairfax Station, Virginia
Oakton Baptist (Southern) - Chantilly, Virginia
Calvary Baptist (GARB) - Wakefield, Michigan
Beacon Hill Missionary Baptist (Southern) — Herndon, Virginia
Judson Baptist Church (American) — Burton, Michigan
Kings Highway Baptist Church (Southern) — Fredericksburg, Virginia

BIBLE

Monte Vista Chapel - Turlock, California
Northwoods Chapel - Guerny, Wisconsin
Heritage Hills Bible Church - Assyria, Michigan
Chatham Bible Church - Hazelwood, Missouri
Grace Chapel - Tokyo, Japan
Community Bible Church — Fairfax, Virginia
McLean Bible Church — McLean, Virginia

CHURCH OF GOD

Christian Victory Center - Stuart, Florida
Church of God in Michiana (Sabbatarian) — Mishawaka, Indiana

COVENANT

Evangelical Covenant - Chicago,Illinois
Covenant Church - Tampa, Florida
Twin Cities Christian Covenant Church, Benton Harbor, Michigan
New Covenant Christian Church - Webberville, Michigan

FOUR SQUARE

First Foursquare Church - Lakeland, Florida

FULL GOSPEL

Homewood Full Gospel Church - Chicago, Illinois
Full Gospel Assembly - Knox, Indiana

INDEPENDENT

Cornerstone Community Bible Church (IF CA) — Kalkaska, Michigan

INTERDENOMINATION

Riverside Church - Three Rivers, Michigan
Holland Christian Fellowship - Holland, Michigan
Bear Lake Christian Church - Kalkaska, Michigan
Battle Creek Area Christian Fellowship - Battle Creek, Michigan
Love International Church - Springfield, Virginia
Christian Fellowship Church - Ashhurn, Virginia
River Valley Community Church — Mishawaka, Indiana
JEWISH

Congregation of Moses — Kalamazoo, Michigan

LUTHERAN

St. John's Lutheran Church (ELCA) — Three Rivers, Michigan

MENNONITE

Shiloh Fellowship - Constantine,Michigan
Pilgrim Fellowship — Nottawa, Michigan

METHODIST

Devon Methodist Telugu Fellowship – Chicago, Illinois
Wakelee United Methodist - Marcellus,Michigan

NAZARENE

Church of the Nazarene - Three Rivers, Michigan
Central Church of the Nazarene — Flint, Michigan

NON-DENOMINATION

Abundant Life Community - Willimantic, Connecticut
Bethesda Blessings Fellowship - Middlebury, Indiana
New Hope Christian Center - Waterloo,Indiana
Church of the Living God - Traverse City, Michigan
Central Michigan Christian Church - Mt.Pleasant, Michigan
Agape Christian Church - Kalamazoo, Michigan
Grace Fellowship - Kalamazoo, Michigan
The Living Word Church - Staunton,Virginia
Redeeming Love Fellowship - Shenendoah, Virginia
Family Worship Center - Harrisonburg, Virginia
Christ Fellowship Church - Herndon, Virginia
The Elijah Gate Christian Center - Leesburg, Virginia
Oakbrook Church - Reston, Virginia
King of Kings Worship Center - Purcellville, Virginia
Immanuel's Church - Silver Spring, Maryland
Southside Christian Church - Milwaukee, Wisconsin
River of Life Fellowship — Middlebury, Indiana

ORTHODOX

Orthodox Christian Center (Greek) - Tarpon Springs, Florida
Assyrian Church of the East - Phoenix,Arizona
Assyrian Church of the East - Fullerton, California
St. Mary's Assyrian Church of the East - Warren, Michigan
Assyrian Church of the East - Vienna, Austria
Mar Gewargis Assyrian Church of the East - Goteborg, Sweden

PENTECOSTAL

Assyrian Christian Church - Turlock, California
Indian Pentecostal Church - Lakeland, Florida
Assyrian Pentecostal Church - Chicago, Illinois
Assyrian Church of Nineveh - Panorama City, California

PRESBYTERIAN

St. John's Assyrian - Turlock,California
Carter-Westminister United - Skokie, Illinois
Christ Church - Arlington, Virginia
Iglesia Nacional - Cancun, Mexico
Pine Island Presbyterian — Mattawan, Michigan

UNITED CHURCH OF CHRIST

Assyrian Evangelical (Congregational) - Chicago,Illinois

CONFERENCES and CONVENTIONS

Assyrian American National Federation National Conventions in Chicago, Illinois; Waterbury, Connecticut; Dearborn & Detroit, Michigan.
Christian Retreat Center - Bradenton, Florida
International Prophecy Conference - Tampa, Florida
Midwest Prophecy Conference - Omaha, Nebraska
Charismatic Business Men's Fellowship Convention - Lancaster, Penn.
Ministers Conference - Trivandrum, India
Blossoming Rose Symposium - Bridgman & Grand Rapids, Michigan
Calvary Ministries International (Exhibit) — Hebron, Kentucky
New Hope Christian Center Missionary Conference (Exhibit) — Waterloo, Indiana
World View Conference (Exhibit) — Rockford, Illinois

EVANGELISTIC MEETINGS

City Evangelistic Meeting -Mallapally, India
City Evangelistic Meeting - Kottayam, India
City Evangelistic Meeting - Chengannur,India

ORGANIZATIONS

Assyrian Cultural Center - Modesto, California
Assyrian Academic Society - Chicago, Illinois
Full Gospel International Businessmen's Fellowship - Middlebury, Indiana & York, Pennsylvania
Teen Challenge - Muskegon, Michigan
World Missionary Press - New Paris, Indiana
International Fellowship of Christian Businessmen Meetings in Charlottesville, Staunton, Harrisonburg, Mt. Crawford, Virginia
Christian Business Men's Committee Meetings in Tysons Corner & Reston & Leesburg, Virginia
United Assyrian Youth of Canada - Toronto, Canada
Assyrian Federation of West Europe - Giessen, Germany
Assyrian Babylonian Society - Jonkoping, Sweden
Assyrian Youth Federation - Linkoping, Sweden
Swedish Assyrian Democratic Organization - Norsborg, Sweden
U.S.Congress / Ambassadors Leadership Breakfast — Arlington, Virginia
International Foundation Staff - Arlington, Virginia
Assyrian National Assembly — Chicago, Illinois

CLUBS

Assyrian American Club - North HollyWood, California
Media Breakfast - Los Angeles, California
Exchange Club - Hillsdale, Michigan
Rotary Club - Three Rivers, Michigan
Assyrian Cultural Club - Vienna, Austria
Assyrian Cultural Center - London, Ontario, Canada
Mesopotamia Cultural Club - Weisbaden, Germany
Assyrian Mesopotamia Club - Gutersloh, Germany
Assyrian Mesopotamian Cultural Club - Enschede, Holland
Assyrian Club - Fitja & Jonkoping, Sweden

SCHOOLS

Northern Baptist Theological Seminary - Lombard, Illinois
Community Christian Academy - Shipshewana, Indiana
Indiana Christian University - South Bend, Indiana

TELEVISION & RADIO

TV Channel 54 - Jelico, Tennessee
Assyria Vision, KBSV, TV - Ceres, California
Sharokeen TV Broadcasting - Los Angeles, California
Action Sixties TV - Largo, Florida
The Good Life TV - Largo, Florida
Among Friends, WCFC TV - Chicago, Illinois
World Harvest Broadcast, WHME TV - South Bend, Indiana
Word Broadcasting Network TV - Louiville, Kentucky
Tri-State Christian TV - WTLJ - Allendale, Michigan
Radio KXGE - Glendale, Arizona
Radio WNZK - Southfield, Michigan
Radio WCTN - Potomac, Maryland
Assyrian radio broadcast - Weisbaden, Germany
The Assyrian Voice radio - Gutersloh, Germany

Short Wave Radio WINB — Red Lion, Pennsylvania

CHAPTER SEVEN

Newspaper sermons I have submitted and printed in the Three Rivers Commercial newspaper.

Love
Attitude of gratitude
"Faith Lift"
Silent Night
Valentine Day
April Fools
Dying is not for sissies
God's phone number
Go to heaven
Get Renewed
God loves you
Jesus loves the little children
Happy Father's Day
Spiritual Life Protection
Veteran's Day
The way to heaven
The best is yet to come
True Christianity
You got joy?
Highway 2009

A Spiritual Electrical System
The sweet P's of prayer
Reasons we want to go to heaven
Lessons from our Model Prayer
Power in Prayer
God's Valentine
Conditions to answered prayer
Faith lifted prayer
Who is your Father?
Your Will be done
Thanks-living
Why go to church?
The power of a praying mother
Honor your mother
No power in prayer?
Lord, teach us to pray
The Good News Gospel
The Gift of God
Believing Prayer
Happy St. Patrick's Day
How to talk to Father God
The place of heaven
Lord, teach us to pray
Christ's invitation to the laborer
Praise Yahweh for His great Name
To know God's Word is to know His Will
Jim's fellowship with Jesus
Prayer Meetings
Noah and the Ark

Love

Jesus said, You shall love your God with all your heart. . . and your neighbors as yourself.

On his 90th birthday, Dr Albert Schweitzer said, "I came here to Lambarene to put religion into practice. I think everyone should do some work for the coming of the Kingdom. We all should have the Spirit of Christ. Everyone can have his little Lambarene."

God's love binds us to all people. It makes each person our neighbor even though he may be from different race, creed, or language. The person across the street and the person across the ocean are both neighbors. Finding ways to be a real friend, a real neighbor, is a challenge. We can ask the Holy Spirit to reveal ways in which we can serve in love as good Samaritans. It may be hard work but we can trust the Holy Spirit to guide and help us.

I am told there is no word for love in the Japanese vocabulary, no endearing terms such as honey or darling. Japanese mothers teach their daughters that the tender emotions a woman feels for her family are so deep that it can be expressed only through actions.

While most of us believe that love should have verbal expression, we, too believe that to say "I love you" is meaningless unless our actions support our words.

When God gave his Son Jesus for our salvation, he expressed to us the deepest and greatest love that we will ever experience.

On the walls of an insane asylum were found words scrawled by some unknown inmate of the institution: "Could we with ink the ocean fill, and were the skies of parchment made, and every blade of grass a quill, and every man a scribe by trade: to write the love of God to man, would drain the ocean dry, nor could the scroll contain the whole, though stretched from sky to sky."

When we accept God's sacrificial love, we then can radiate it to others. We may not be asked to die for them, but we can give of ourselves to live for them.

When we love as Christ loves, selfish ambition and attitudes are crucified. Resurrected in their stead are our actions and attitudes that bear out our words of love.

Dear Lord, help us to express your love for others in the way we live each day. We want your love to fill us and to overflow to others. Give us some work of love to do for you today.

Attitude of Gratitude

The watchman of a fort in medieval times carefully observed all approaching visitors from his lookout tower to determine whether they were friends or enemies. If they were friends, the drawbridge was lowered across the moat to welcome them. If enemies, it was secured against them and the fort made ready for defense.

God has made us watchmen over own minds by giving us the privilege of deciding which attitude or thought can lodge there. Each day many thoughts, emotions and attitudes, some good and some bad, seek admission into our lives. They cannot force themselves upon us. (We can't say "the devil made me do it.") If they come in, it is because we have opened the drawbridge of our mind to them.

Wrong attitudes and thoughts cannot gain a foothold in our minds if our faith and trust in the Lord keeps the door barred against them. Accepting the good and refusing the bad is an everyday experience we all have. As long as we give hospitality to only healthful Christ-like attitudes, we are safe from all evil and are kept in the peace and fortress of God's love.

If sometimes the mailman delivers a package or letter that we do not care to receive, all we have to do is write "refused" on it and it will be returned to the sender. Satan often tries to send us undesirable packages of bad attitudes and thoughts. Return them to "sender" with an attitude of gratitude.

The story is told about the Swiss boy that hiked up the mountain to see what was there. When he reached the top he looked around and was disappointed that it did not look as good as he had thought it would. So as his emotion overcame him he yelled out "I hate you." He was surprised to hear a voice from across the hills answer "I hate you!" He ran home sobbing the story to his mother. He said he would not go back up that mountain because the mountain boy was mean. The wise mother suggested he try it once more, but this time to say "I like you." This new attitude made mountain climbing a happy pastime for him thereafter.

You see, our whole outlook on life is affected by our attitude. So, when doubts, fears, complaints try to come into our minds, close that gate and open the one that is gratitude for all that God has done and is doing in making "all things work together for good to those who love God."

God, help me to develop that attitude of gratitude.

A Faith Lift

Christ said "What things you desire, when you pray, believe that you receive them and you shall have them." (Mark 11:24)

A young housewife was tearfully relating her problems to an older friend. The friend asked "Have you prayed about them?" The young woman said "yes, but when I get through, my problems are still with me." The older woman smiled, "All you have done is worried in God's Presence. The next time you talk to God, BELIEVE He answers you and thank Him that He is taking care of the problem."

Often times our prayer time is spent not in actual praying, but in worrying on our knees. Believe that He will help. No situation is too impossible for Him to handle. With this awareness of His power and concern, you can leave each problem in His hands as you go on your way rejoicing, with the burden lifted and confident that the solution to your problem is on the way.

We need to know how to claim God's promises that are in the Bible. They are there for us to act upon them. Faith is not only a fact, but an act. For example, you have many demands on your time and energy. Proclaim this from Philippians 4:13, "I can do all things through Christ who strengthens me." Do you need health? Claim God's promise in II Kings 20:5,6, "I will heal you. . .and add unto your days." Do you desire relief from tension and worry? Relax as you declare Isaiah 30:15, "In quietness and confidence is my strength." Are you in need of the Lord's blessing on your finances? Confidently say "The God of heaven will prosper us," Nehemiah 2:20. (That is if you have been faithfully tithing and giving offerings.)

Remember that God's Word says, "faith without works is dead." God wants us to do our part so He can do His part. He wants to partner with us in our faith walk. Without us He will not, without Him we cannot!

Lord, I believe, help my unbelief. Teach me to not only believe Your word but to act upon it.

SILENT NIGHT

"Silent night! Holy night! All is calm all is bright. Round yon virgin mother and child.
Holy infant so tender and mild. Sleep in heavenly peace. sleep in heavenly peace

There is a beautiful story about "Silent Night" that took place during World War 1.

On Christmas Eve 1914, freezing troops were facing each other across a vast no-man's land. There was no shooting as British soldiers sat quietly listening to the sounds of men's voices singing. Finally, daring to raise their heads above the trenches, they saw the gleam of candles as German troops lit candles on small trees in their trenches. "Stille Nacht" could be heard as the German soldiers observed Christmas Eve.

That night on a battle-scarred landscape, the soldiers of both sides called a truce as they shared what they had of sausages and chocolates. Though the truce did not last:

For a few hours the war was forgotten and peace and good will prevailed.

On this Christmas Eve day of 2005 we want to remember in prayer our troops in Iraq, Afghanistan. South Korea. Japan. Germany and in other countries and states in the United States as they are away from their loved ones and are somewhat lonely.

I remember during World War II traveling in a troop train on Christmas Eve and the lonely feeling of the clickety clack of the train wheels on the tracks. But as I thought af Christ, my newly found Savior, His presence in my heart made me feel less lonely.

Let's pray for the greatest gift of peace to come to our world through Christ, the Prince of Peace.

Valentine Day

In the midst of sending gaily-colored cards and romantic messages to friends and loved ones, few of us are aware that the real meaning of St. Valentine's Day is sacrifice.

According to legend, Valentine takes its name from a young Christian who once lived in ancient Rome. Like so many of the early Christians, Valentine had been imprisoned because of his faith. Often and longingly he thought of his loved ones and wanted to assure them of his well-being and his love for them. Beyond his cell window, just within reach grew a cluster of violets. He picked some of the heart-shaped leaves and pieced them with the words "Remember your Valentine," and sent them off by a friendly dove. On the following days he sent more messages that simply said, "I love you."

Valentine died for his faith in Christ during the reign of Emperor Claudius. Years later, he was canonized by the Roman Church and February 14 was set apart as a day to commemorate his martyrdom. This is a day for paying tribute to a man who loved the Lord so much he was willing to die for Him.

Valentine's Day has become a day when special effort is made to express thoughts of love to one another.

In the New Testament, I Corinthians 13 is known as the "love" chapter. Here is a portion of it from the Contemporary language translation by Eugene Peterson. "Love never gives up. Love cares more for others than for self. Love doesn't want what it doesn't have. Love doesn't strut, doesn't have a swelled head, doesn't force itself on others, isn't always 'me first,' doesn't fly off the handle, doesn't keep score of the sins of others, doesn't revel when others grovel, takes pleasure in the flowering of truth, puts up with anything, trusts God always, always looks for the best, never looks back, but keeps going to the end. Love never dies."

God loves you. Love Him back and others too!

April Fools

Until the 16th century, I am told, the new year was celebrated on the first day of April. With the present calendar, New Year's Day was switched to January 1. In 1564, France became the first nation to adopt the new calendar. But a few stubborn folk insisted on continuing in their old ways, celebrating the new year on April 1, three months after everyone else had done so. These people soon became known as "April fools."

It is a good thing to be a determined person, one not swayed from a goal, when that goal is within God's will for us. But sometimes we don't consider God's purposes, only our own. We foolishly cling to our own aims and refuse to accept the possibility that the difficulties we encounter along the way may be God's way of showing us where we have been foolish.

The Book of Proverbs has a lot to say about being fools and foolish. It is written by King Solomon who was considered the wisest man of his time. This book is also called "The Book of Wisdom."

Here are some choice verses from proverbs for April Fool's Day:

1:7 – The fear of the Lord is the beginning of knowledge; but fools despise wisdom.

9:6 – Forsake the foolish and live; and go in the way of understanding.

10:1 – A foolish son is the heaviness of his mother.

10:14 – Wise men lay up knowledge; but the mouth of the foolish is near destruction.

10:18– He that hides hatred with lying lips and utters a slander is a fool.

14:9 – Fools make a mock of sin; but among the righteous there is favor.

15:20 – A wise man makes a glad father but a foolish man despises his mother.

18:2 – A fool has no delight in understanding.

18:6 - A fool's lips enter into contention and his mouth calls for strokes.

20:3 – It is an honor for a man to cease from strife but every fool will be meddling.

26:4 – Answer not a fool according to his folly lest you also be like him.

26:11 – As a dog returns to his vomit so a fool returns to his folly.

26:12 – See a man wise in his own conceit? There is more hope of a fool than of him.

29:11 – A fool utters all his mind but a wise man keeps it in 'till afterwards.

Jesus Christ said in Matthew 7:26 – Everyone that hears these sayings of mine and does not do them shall be likened unto a foolish man that built his house upon the sand.

The Apostle Paul said in Ephesians 5:15 – See that you walk circumspectly, not as fools.

Dying is not for Sissies

Hebrews 9:27 says, "It is appointed unto man once to die and after that the judgment.

What does it mean to die? To keep that final appointment? It means that you move. You leave the old house of your body you have lived in. You move on to the next state of life. Christ called that stage "paradise." Remember when Christ was dying on the cross and a thief that hung beside him said "Jesus, remember me when you come into your kingdom." Then Jesus said to him "today you shall be with me in paradise."

Dying is like moving out of a house. Some people have to move out early in life, some live in their houses many years. Reverently, we put the house the human body back into the dust from which it came. It has served its purpose. God did not design it to last forever. While we live in this body we have burdens, troubles, sickness, and death, but God made us to live with Him in a new and wonderful home what will last forever.

Here are the dying words of famous people without Christ:

Sir Thomas Scott, "Until now I thought there was no God or hell. Now I know there is both and I am doomed."
Talleyrand, "I suffer the pangs of the damned."
King Charles IX, "I am lost, I see it well."
Thomas Paine, "Stay with me, I fear to be alone."
Edward Gibbon, "All is now lost; finally irrevocably lost."

Here are the dying words of the saved people:

Moody, "This is my coronation day. If this is death, it is sweet."
President McKinley, "All is well, God's will is done."
Rutherford, "As sure as He ever spoke to me, His spirit says, 'fear not.'"
Thornton, the philanthropist, "Happy in Jesus, all is well."
George Washington, "It is well."

Susanne Wesley, "Children, when I am gone, sing."
Wesley, "The best of all is, God is with us."

When you are a devoted follower of Christ, you do not fear death, you can say with the Apostle Paul in I Corinthians 15:54-56.

"Death has been swallowed up in victory. Where, O death is your sting? Thanks be to God! He gives us the victory through our Lord Jesus Christ."

Many go to heaven without health-without wealth-without fame-without a great name-without learning-without big earnings-without beauty-without ten thousand other things-but none go to heaven without Christ.

God's phone number

Jeremiah 33:3 says, "Call to me and I will answer you."

God is saying here "call Me" so I consider this His phone number for prayer.

Isn't it awesome the way God answers our prayers? Here is an amazing true story of answered prayer.

A pastor was working late and decided to call his wife before he left for his home.

The pastor let the phone ring many times. He thought it was odd that she did not answer, but he decided to wrap up a few things and try again in a few minutes. When he tried again she answered right away. He asked her why she hadn't answered before, and she said that it hadn't rung at their home. They brushed it off as a fluke and went on their merry ways.

The following Monday, the pastor received a call at the church office, which was the phone that he had used that Saturday night. The man that he spoke with wanted to know why he had called on Saturday night.

The pastor could not figure out what the man was talking about. Then the man said, "It rang and rang, but I didn't answer." The pastor remembered the mishap and apologized for disturbing him, explaining that he had intended to call his wife.

The man said, "That's OK. Let me tell you my story."

"You see, I was planning to commit suicide on Saturday night, but before I did, I prayed, 'God if you're there, and you don't want me to do this, give me a sign now.' At that point my phone started to ring.

I looked at the caller ID, and it said, 'Almighty God'. I was afraid to answer."

The reason why it showed on the man's caller ID that the call came from "Almighty God" is because the church that the pastor attends is called "Almighty God Tabernacle."

Do you believe God answers prayer? Call on Him and thank Him for answering you.

Go to Heaven

A little girl was gazing at the sky one clear night. Her father asked her, "At what are you staring, my dear." She answered, "Oh daddy, I was just thinking that if the bottom side of heaven is so beautiful, how wonderful it must be on the other side."

Heaven must be wonderful. It is a comfort for folks to know there is a heaven to go to. Death does not end all. Jesus comforted His disciples with the thought of heaven when they were sad and discouraged about His coming death. He said "Let not your heart be troubled; you believe in God, believe" also in me. In my Father's house are many mansions, if it were not so I would have told you. I go to prepare a place for you. And if I go and prepare a place for you, I will come again, and receive you unto myself; that where I am, there you may be also." (John 14:1-3).

Christ tells us the facts about heaven.

1. The place. Heaven is somewhere in particular, and not just everywhere in general. Heaven is the place where God dwells — "In my Father's house," John 14:2. We say in the Model Prayer: "Our Father who art in heaven. . ." Heaven is the place where Christ has gone. Jesus arose in a body of flesh and bone, and ascended into heaven and is now living in heaven in that body. Those who have died in Christ are now "absent from the body and present with the Lord," II Cor. 5:8. They are with the Lord in heaven. '

2. The preparation. Heaven is being prepared for the Christian by Christ: "I go to prepare a place for you." There are many "mansions" or abiding places for us. Someone has said that if Christ could make the beautiful world that we live in in six days, what must heaven he like where Christ has been preparing it for us for over nineteen hundred years!

3. The promise. "I will come again." "To receive you unto Myself." "That where I am, there you may be also." We "born again" Christians will be with Jesus the Savior.

4. The people. We must be a prepared people. We must be ready for heaven while on earth. Jesus tells us that only those who have been "born again" through receiving Christ as Savior and Lord are the prepared people for heaven. "Verily, verily, I say unto thee, except a man be born again, he cannot see the kingdom of God," John 3:3.

Do you know the way to heaven yet? It is not by joining any church, nor being baptized, nor doing good deeds. It is only through Christ who said: "I am the Way, the Truth, and the Life, no man cometh unto the Father, but by Me," John 14:6.

Receive Christ now as your personal Savior and Lord of your life; and follow His teachings in the Bible, and you will be able to say as King David said in the Psalm: "Surely goodness and mercy shall follow me all the days of my life and I will dwell in the house of the Lord forever."

Get Renewed

Psalms 103:5 says,

"He satisfies my desires with good things, so that my youth is renewed like the eagle's."

The eagle lives to a very old age. As he grows old, his beak becomes so long that it hinders him from taking his food. Finally, he flies to the top of a cliff. Up there in his solitude, he peeks tirelessly on a rock until his beak is worn down little by little. All during this process the eagle is forced to fast, so he loses his feathers. When he is able to eat again, new feathers begin to grow, and his strength becomes like that of a young eagle. Then with a glorious sweep of his powerful wings he flies away from the cliff. He now is a thing of power and beauty again.

Everyone who is older would like to get their youth renewed. But youth is not just a time of life, but it is a quality of the mind. You are as young as your faith, your hope and your love. Sometimes, our problems and responsibilities may weigh us down and we may feel drained of all strength. When that happens, slip away as the eagle does to a quiet place. Then being alone with Christ, let our burdens drop off and our worries be subdued as Christ says "come to me all you who are weary and burdened, and I will give you rest," Matt 11:28.

As you rest in Christ's presence, He gives us new strength, fresh endurance and enough courage to carry us through. The Lord can renew our strength as He does the eagle's. I like how Isaiah 40:31 puts it: "Those who hope in the Lord shall renew their strength. They will soar on wings like eagle's, they will run and not grow weary, they will walk and not faint."

Dear Lord, thank you for your loving and encouraging words. I want to trust in you always. As I draw close to you in faith and quietness, renew me in my spirit, mind and body. And I believe that I shall rise up with new strength and fly like an eagle to new heights in my life. Amen.

God Loves You

Valentine's Day comes up on the 14th and it reminds us of love.

I John 3:1 says: 'Behold what manner of love the Father has bestowed upon us."

I am told of a picture that hangs in the National Gallery in London, which shows Christ hanging on the cross in utter darkness. As one keeps looking at the painting one gradually discovers another form in the background. There are other hands supporting Christ. There is another face more full of agony than the artist has pictured in the face of Christ Himself. It is the form and face of God the Father supporting His Son in infinite love, standing with Christ in the midst of His sufferings.

There are times when we cannot see God in the things that happen to us, but we may be assured that He is there. Sometimes it is only when we look back that we realize His presence was with us all the time, helping us in ways that we could not see or understand while we were going through the trial.

God stands by us, caring for us, loving us. He is always near, and nearest when we need Him most. Whatever or whoever else we may doubt, we can never doubt the love of God and that we are objects of that love.

Dr. Mantey, my Greek class professor, once told the class how he was once laid up for almost a year due to an accident. He was depressed that he couldn't get a job in order to make enough money to finish college. Then, his girl, "the sweetest one that ever crossed the pike" said she didn't want to go with him anymore. He felt terrible and he went into the woods and prayed out loud to God. A peace came into his heart as the line from the old hymn "The Solid Rock" came to him. "I dare not trust the sweetest frame, but wholly lean on Jesus' Name."

The words to the song "The Love of God" says it all: 'Could we with ink the ocean fill, And were the heavens of parchment made, were every stalk on earth a quill, and every man a scribe by trade, to write the love of God above would drain the ocean dry, nor could the scroll contain the whole, though stretched from sky to sky.

God loves you. Love Him back and others too.

JESUS LOVES THE LITTLE CHILDREN

Here are some religious comments and experiences of little children.

A parent said she had been teaching her three-year-old daughter The Lord's Prayer for several evenings at bedtime. Finally she decided to go solo. The mother said she listened with pride as she carefully enunciated each word, right up to the end of the prayer. She prayed: "Lead us not into temptation, but deliver us from Email."

One particular four-year-old prayed: "And forgive us our trash baskets as we forgive those who put trash in our baskets."

Another child prayed: "Our Father, who does art in heaven, Harold is His name. Amen."

A little boy was overheard praying: "Lord, if you can't make me a better boy, don't worry about it; I'm having a real good time like I am.."

After the christening of his baby brother in church, Jason sobbed all the way home in the back seat of the car; His father asked him what was wrong.' Finally, the boy replied, "That preacher said he wanted us brought up in a Christian home, and I wanted to stay with you guys."

Six-year-old Angie and her four-year-old brother Joel were sitting together in church. Joel giggled and talked out loud. Finally, his big sister had had enough and said: "You're not supposed to talk out loud in church." Joel asked, "Why? Who's going to stop me?" She said, "See those two men standing by the door? They're HUSHERS."

A mother was preparing pancakes for her sons, Kevin, 5, and Ryan, 6. The boys began to argue over who would get the first pancake. Their mother saw the opportunity for a moral lesson. "If Jesus were sitting her, He would say, 'Let my brother have the first pancake, I can wait." Ryan turned to his younger brother and said, "Kevin, you be Jesus!"

A wife invited some people to dinner. At the table, she turned to their six-year-old daughter and asked, "Would you like to say the blessing?" "I wouldn't know what to say," the girl replied. "Just say what you hear

Mommy say," the wife answered. The daughter bowed her head and said, "Lord, why on earth did I invite all these people to dinner?"

A Sunday school teacher asked her children, "and why is it necessary to be quiet in church?" One bright little girl replied, "Because people are sleeping."

Jesus said, "Let the little children come to me and forbid them not, for of such is the kingdom of God." And, "Except we become as little children, we will not enter the kingdom of heaven."

Happy Father's Day

Advice from the wisest father in the world (Solomon) from the greatest book in the world!

Proverbs 4:20-22 - My son, attend to my words; incline your ear unto my sayings. Let them not depart from your eyes; keep them in the midst of your heart. For they are life to those that find them and health to all their flesh.

8:13 – The fear of the Lord is to hate evil; pride and arrogance and the evil way and the froward mouth do I hate.

11:2 – When pride comes, then comes shame; but with the lowly is wisdom.

11:30 – The fruit of the righteous is a tree of life; and he that wins souls is wise.

13:22 – A good man leaves an inheritance to his children's children; and the wealth of the sinner is laid up for the just.

14:12 – There is a way that seems right to a man, but the end thereof are the ways of death.

14:34 – Righteousness exalts a nation, but sin is a reproach to any people.

15:1 - A soft answer turns away wrath; but grievous words stir up anger.

15:3 – The eyes of the Lord are in every place, beholding the evil and the good.

15:20 – A wise son makes a glad father; but a foolish man despises his mother.

16:18 – Pride goes before destruction and a haughty spirit before a fall.

16:32 – He that is slow to anger is greater than the mighty, and he that rules his spirit then he that takes a city.

17:6 – Children's children are the crowns of old men, and the glory of children are their fathers.

17:9 – He that covers a transgression seeks love, but he that repeats a matter separates good friends.

17:22 – A merry heart does good like a medicine; but a broken spirit dries the bones.

18:21 – Death and life are in the power of the tongue; and they that love it shall eat the fruit thereof.

22:1 – A good name is rather to be chosen than great riches, and loving favor rather than silver and gold.

22:6 – Train up a child in the way he should go; and when is old he will not depart from it.

23:7 – For as he thinks in his heart; so is he.

27:2 – Let another man praise you and not your own mouth.

28:9 – He that turns his ear from hearing the law, even his prayer shall be abomination.

28:13 – He that covers his sin shall not prosper, but whoever confesses and forsakes them shall have mercy.

28:20 – A faithful man shall abound with blessings.

29:1 – He that being often reproved hardens his neck, shall suddenly be destroyed.

29:18 – Where there is no vision the people perish.

29:25 – The fear of man brings a snare; but whoever puts his trust in the Lord shall be safe.

31:30 – Favor is deceitful and beauty is vain; but a woman that fears the Lord shall be praised.

Our Father who is in Heaven, hallowed be Your name.

Happy Father's Day

Words from the wisest father that ever lived (Solomon): "My son (and daughter), pay attention closely to my words. Do not let them out of your sight, keep them within your heart; for they are life to those who find them and health to a man's whole body." (parenthesis mine) Proverbs 4:20-22 NIV.

Words from another father on the:

7. Greatest hope – Heaven
8. Greatest catastrophe - Hell
9. Greatest book – Bible
10. Guarantee to heaven – New birth
11. Greatest knowledge – God's will
12. Greatest reward – God's commendation
13. Best question – What would Jesus do?
14. Worst enemy – Satan
15. Simplest prayer – "Help" and "Thank You."
16. Most worth- Friendship
17. Greatest success – Faithfulness
18. Best medicine – Laughter
19. Greatest joy – Giving
20. Greatest loss – Soul
21. Most satisfying work – Helping others
22. Ugliest personality trait – Selfishness
23. Most endangered species- Dedicated leaders
24. Greatest shot in the arm – Encouragement
25. Greatest problem to overcome – Fear
26. Greatest act – Forgiveness
27. Most effective sleeping pill –Peace of mind
28. Most crippling failure disease – Excuses
29. Most powerful force in life – Love
30. Most dangerous pariah – A gossiper
31. Worst thing to be without – Hope

32. World's most incredible computer-The brain
33. Deadliest weapon-The tongue
34. Two most powerful words- "I can."
35. Greatest asset- Faith
36. Most worthless emotion- Self-Pity
37. Most priceless possession – Integrity
38. Most beautiful attire – A smile
39. Most powerful channel of communication – Prayer
40. Greatest need – Trust in the Lord
41. Most contagious spirit – Enthusiasm
42. Most important in life – God
43. Greatest gift – Salvation through Jesus Christ
44. Greatest evidence- Faith
45. Greatest admission – Your mistake
46. **Greatest promise – Jesus Christ said "I will come again and receive you to Myself; that where I am there you may be also."**

SPIRITUAL LIFE PROTECTION

"Safety first" has been a key term in man's effort to protect person and property in the various places of life.

Special effort is made to protect our children from diseases. We protect them from ignorance and illiteracy by sending them to school. We protect them from evil influences and forces through the "protecting arm of the law."

But the greatest protection anyone can have is that of whom the Bible speaks. "The eternal God is our refuge and underneath are the everlasting arms," Deut.33:27. Here is the protecting arm of God without which there is no real protection. Have we committed ourselves to the strong, loving arms of God?

Is it not wonderful to have the privilege of the safety and protection of Almighty God? Is not a wonderful privilege and opportunity to go to church where we worship the Lord together and learn more of His ways?

As the children are planning to enter school, let us not deprive them of the privileges that are ours in God. Millions of children are not receiving any systematic spiritual instruction. Some may say "We will not influence our children in making decisions and choices in matters of religion." WHY NOT? The ads will, the press will, the TV will, their neighbors will, their peers will, their teachers will. We use our influence over flowers, vegetables and animals; shall we ignore our children in their spiritual life protection?

"Train up a child in the way he should go, and when he is old he will not depart from it, Prov.22:6.

VETERANS DAY

Tomorrow is Veterans Day though it is observed on Monday as a national holiday throughout the United States. Veterans Day has a relevance to each American Family in each town and city in our nation. In each generation, in each family there are those who have served their country. It may be a father, a brother, a grandfather, a cousin, or even a mother, a sister, a nephew or niece. It may have been in World War I, World War II, Korea, Vietnam, Iraqi Freedom or Operation Desert Storm. But whatever the conflict, whatever the service, the commitment to serve and protect our nation deserves our gratitude and a big "THANK YOU."

Some people may confuse Memorial Day and Veterans Day. Memorial Day is a day for remembering and honoring military personnel who died in the service of their country. While those who died are also remembered on Veterans Day, Veterans Day is set aside to thank and honor all those who served honorably in the military in wartime or peacetime. In fact, Veterans Day is largely intended to thank living veterans for their service and to acknowledge that their contributions to our national security are appreciated.

As a veteran myself, I pray that God can heal the hearts and bodies of so many veterans who have experienced unspeakable horrors in many wars, and lately, in Iraq and Afghanistan. I give thanks for their sacrifices and I pray that government leaders all over the world would do everything possible to avoid future conflicts and future loss of precious lives.

Also, on this Veterans Day observance, let us thankfully remember two men who died for us:

The service member who gave his life for our freedoms. "Greater love has no man than this, that one lay down his life for his friends," John 15:13.

Jesus Christ who died for our sins and was buried and rose from the dead on the third day that we may have a new freedom and be saved from hell and saved for heaven. "God so loved the world that He gave

His Only Begotten Son, that whoever believes in Him will not perish but have everlasting life. John 3:16

Prayer on Veterans Day from St. Joseph People's Prayer Book:

"Dear Lord Jesus Christ. . .Teach me to appreciate the virtue of patriotism — a true and Christian love of country. Let me love my country, not to follow it blindly but to make it the land of goodness that it should be. Let my patriotism be such that it will not exclude the other nations of the world, but include them in a powerful love of country that has room for all others too."

Let us always make the words of the following song our sincere prayer:

"God bless America, land that I love. Stand beside her and guide her through the night with the light from above. . . ."

THE WAY TO HEAVEN

The Apostle Thomas, commonly known as "doubting" Thomas, asked Christ "how can we know the way to heaven?" Jesus answered him with these words: "I am the way, the truth and the life; no one comes to the Father but by Me," John 14:6.

I wonder what answer Thomas would get today from the average person who would be asked "what is the way to heaven?" Some might answer:

"All ways (religions) lead to heaven."
"Do the best you can and you will make it."
"Be sincere in what you do."
"Keep the ten commandments."
"Go to church faithfully."
"Be baptized."
"Do good deeds."
"Nobody knows."

Jesus Christ gave the simple and sure way to heaven. He is the way. The word "way" means "road" or "path." Let me illustrate it this way. If someone were to ask you directions to Kalamazoo from Three Rivers, you would say "the way to get to Kalamazoo, is to take the road 131 and go north and you will get to your destination." The person that needs the direction then has to get on the road that gets to the destination.

So it is with Christ who is the way to heaven. You have to receive Him and trust Him to get you to heaven. Talking about the road will not get you anywhere and talking about Jesus will not either. It is accepting the "way" and getting on with it that gets you there.

You may be sincere in taking a different way and you will be sincerely wrong. Proverbs 14:12 says "There is a way that seems right to a man, but the end thereof is the way of death."

Heaven is a wonderful place. Besides no grief, sorrow or pain it is a place of joy, excitement, activity, exploration, discovery, fellowship with relatives, friends and heroes of the past, increased learning, artistic expressions, serving and ruling, receiving rewards for faithfulness on earth, face to face with Jesus and Father God and looking your best. I could also mention space traveling to the billions of galaxies of God's created universe or visiting and recreating on this new planet of ours. Wow! No wonder the Bible says in I Cor.2:9, "Eye has not seen, nor ear heard, neither has it entered into the heart of man what God has prepared for those who love Him." It surely will not be boring throughout eternity.

Jesus said "I go to prepare a place for you, that where I am there you may be also."

See you there and then I can tell you more what heaven is like.

The best is yet to come

Easter Sunday was celebrating the resurrection of Jesus Christ from the grave.

Isn't that what all the believers in Jesus Christ will experience one day? I believe it! Jesus said so in the Bible.

My son, Pastor Paul, told the following story in one of his sermons at Riverside Church that I would to pass on to you that shows faith in our own resurrection from the dead.

There was a woman who had been diagnosed with a terminal illness and had been given three months to live. So, as she was getting her things in order, she contacted her pastor and asked him to come to her house to discuss certain aspects of her final wishes. She told him which songs she wanted sung at the funeral service, what scriptures she would like read and what outfit she wanted to be buried in.

Everything was in order and the pastor was preparing to leave when the woman suddenly remembered something very important to her. "There's one more thing," she said excitedly. "What's that?" the pastor asked. She said "I want to be buried with a fork in my right hand." The pastor stood looking puzzled at the woman not knowing what to say. The woman explained: My grandmother once told me this story and from there on out, I have always done so. In all my years of attending church socials and potluck dinners, I always remember that when the dishes or the main course were being cleared, someone would inevitably lean over and tell us to keep your fork for the wonderful dessert that was coming.

So I just want people to see me there in that casket with a fork in my hand and I want them to wonder 'what's with the fork?' Then I want you to tell them: 'Keep your fork, the best is yet to come.' The pastor's eyes welled up with tears as he hugged the woman good-bye.

He knew this would be one of the last times he would see her before her death. But he also knew that this woman had a grasp of what heaven would be like. She knew that something better was coming.

At the funeral, people were walking by this woman's casket and they saw the fork placed in her right hand. Over and over, the pastor heard the question "What's with the fork?" And over and over he smiled.

During his message, the pastor told the people of the conversation he had with their woman friend shortly before she died. He told them about the fork and what it symbolized to her.

So, the next time you that you reach down for your fork, let it remind you that the best is yet to come for the devoted follower of Jesus Christ.

True Christianity

A real Christian is a devoted follower of Jesus Christ who has a personal relationship with Him.

It is the Christian person who has realized that he or she is a sinner, and that Christ died on the cross for our sins and that He rose from the dead so we can be forgiven of our sins and be saved for heaven and not go to hell.

Christianity is really a love story that can be condensed in one verse, John 3:16, "For God so loved the world that He gave is only begotten son, that whoever believes in Him should not perish but have eternal life."

Now let's make this personal: God so loved "__________" (put your name here) that He gave his son to die for "me," to pay for "my" sins; that by "me" believing (this means trusting) in Christ as "my" Savior and Lord, "I shall" not perish (be lost), but have eternal life(in heaven).

When you realize that God really loves you, then love Him back and show your love to Him. Talk to Him, read His word in the Bible and obey it. Let others see Christ's life in you. Let the Holy Spirit of God fill you as you yield your whole being to Christ.

Have you ever spoken to Christ about having a relationship with Him? If not, you may do it right now by saying: "Dear Lord, I confess that I am a sinner and want to turn away from my sinful ways. Thank you, Jesus Christ, for dying on the cross for my sins. Come into my life. Help me to live the life you want me to live, Amen." God's word says, "Everyone who calls on the name of the Lord will be saved," Romans 10:13.

It is simple as ABC to be a real Christian:

A – admitting you are a sinner.
B – believing Christ died for you.
C – calling on Him to come into your life.

Now thank your Lord that He is in you by His Holy Spirit. You are able to speak with the Lord anytime and to have him speak to you in your heart as you listen to Him.

One more thing that is very important in John 12:34-35. Jesus said, "A new command I give you: Love one another. As I have loved you, so you must love one another. By this all men will know that you are my disciples, if you love one another." Remember, our common enemy is the devil; fight him and not each other. Don't shoot your own soldiers.

You got joy?

A story is told of a depressed man who went to the doctor and was told to "snap out of it" and go to the theater and see the clown there and laugh at life. "He is amusing thousands of people." The despondent man answered "I am that clown."

There seems to a lack of joy even among so-called Christian people. A joyless Christianity is a starved Christianity, a powerless Christianity, an uninspiring Christianity. It is salt without its tang and a light under a bushel.

Think of the happiest person you know. Now if that person was anyone else but you, WHAT'S THE MATTER?

Before I became a follower of Jesus Christ, I was turned off by the lack of joy I saw in Christians. They seemed to be so negative, judgmental and critical. When I later received Christ into my life as my Savior and Lord, a joy came into my life that surprised me. I did not expect it and it sure beat anything else that I thought would bring me happiness. Didn't Jesus say that we would have joy and it would be full? (John 15:11)

Proverbs 15:13 says "A merry heart makes a cheerful face." Do we reflect the joy of the Lord in our lives? How can you tell if someone is sad, mad, or glad? By their actions!

"THE JOY OF THE LORD IS OUR STRENGTH" Nehemiah 8:10

The second shortest verse in the Bible is "rejoice evermore." (I Thess. 5:16)

I remember these lines from a chorus: "If you want joy, real joy, let Jesus come into your heart." Then sing: "I'm so happy and here's the reason why, Jesus took my burdens all away. . ."

You get JOY by putting:

Jesus first
Others next
You last

Highway 2009

This is the last Saturday of the year of 2008. New year 2009 is coming!

A new modern highway is being opened to us for traffic Jan. 1 Highway 2009 is a new way. None of us has traveled it before. It is different from route 2008, 2007, 2006 or any other route. For those who travel route 2009 will go over this highway only once.

This being true, we must not miss any blessings, beauties, opportunities and privileges along this new way. We will have many fellow travelers on this crowded thoroughfare, and some of them we will never see again.

On this road of life in 2009 what do we need most of all? We need guidance as we travel on Highway 2009. How can we get guidance? Here is what we need for the best guidance.

A good map, the Bible

Psalm 119:105 says "your Word is a lamp to my feet and a light to my path." The Bible is the only book which tells us what lies ahead. It shows the curves, dangerous intersections and treacherous places. It tells us about the devil, sin, temptations, trials and tribulations that we must face. It shows us the way to blessings and joys. Very importantly, it shows the way to be saved from the way to hell and for heaven.

A good guide, the Holy Spirit of God

The Holy Spirit is given to God's people for the very purpose of guiding us. Jesus said the Holy Spirit would guide us into all truth (John 16:13). The basic requirements for the guidance of the Holy Spirit are to desire and to submit to the will of God as found in the Bible.

Travel on this highway 2009 is a must. May it be a good way for you. A way of blessing and a way of growth. May you be a blessing to your fellow travelers every mile of the way for some will drop out by the way and not finish the journey.

Thank God for His guidance on this highway 2009. We don't know what the future holds, but we know who hold the future. Happy New Year!

A SPIRITUAL ELECTRICAL SYSTEM

Your prayers are like electrical wires. There is absolutely no power in an electrical wire when it is disconnected from the power source and is out of the electrical socket. It is only when you plug in that electrical wire into a "live" socket that the wire becomes hot and power comes out of it.

Your prayer must be connected — plugged into God — before any power can ever be released through your petitions.

God has created our universe so that we have the honor and privilege of addressing Him in the heavenlies through our prayers.

The prayer process is actually a miracle!

God waits for our prayers to come from somewhere, from some place, from someone on this planet called Earth. He waits until a certain prayer is directed toward Him so that He can respond to our needs, petitions and offerings.

Maybe you will be the next person who will lift up a prayer to Him. If you are, know that when He hears your prayer He will then move on your behalf. God has designed and arranged the spirit world in such a way that it takes you plus God, cooperating together, to make something happen. If I were to write it in a formula, it would look like this:

God + you = a happening

Without us, He will not. Without Him, we cannot.

The Sweet P's of Prayer

I believe that if you want to become really charged up spiritually through prayer — like being plugged into that electrical outlet — you need to begin to practice the following three P's in your prayer life.

The first P: Place

Find an appropriate place to pray, and make it your habitual place of prayer. This place is an extremely important decision. God has told us that we are to go into our prayer closets, so we must first select the place — the prayer closet — where we pray with some degree of thoughtfulness.

Once you start praying habitually at a certain place each day, and you do that for six months, I promise that you will never again stop seeking that time with the Lord.

Prayer is the process of getting yourself spiritually "charged". Once you have your battery fully charged, then you are ready and prepared to face anything the day might present to you.

The second P: Plan

Plan to pray and you will experience the most wonderful life you have ever experienced. Plan to draw closer to God in your prayer life, realizing that it is human nature and the nature of spiritual growth to start small.

At first, you might plan to pray only for five minutes per day. After that becomes comfortable, maybe you "graduate" to 10 or 15 minutes per day. Do not start off by declaring, "I am going to pray for a full hour." Just as a marathon runner starts by getting into shape,so too a prayer warrior must start with small sprints before being properly prepared to run the longer races.

Unless you just cannot seem to stop, start your prayer plan with small goals, and then let the Holy Spirit prompt you when it is time to adjust your prayer plan and pray for longer periods of time.

The third P: Persevere

Once you pick your place to pray, and allow the Holy Spirit to help you set your plan, then it is necessary to simply persevere and follow the plan that you have set in motion.

"Persevere" means that you "decide and determine" to stick with your prayers. Jesus encouraged us to pray continually, to never quit.

If you discover that perseverance in the mornings does not work for you, then find time in the afternoon, the evening, or even at bedtime (although I find many are too tired to routinely pray at bedtime). Once you get into the habit of going before God's throne, you will find yourself praying at a specific time each day, but also praying throughout the day.

In my own prayer life I have discovered that these three P's are basic if you want to have your spiritual life electrically recharged every day.

Reasons we want to go to Heaven

We will receive a changed body, I Cor. 15:52; Phil. 3:20, 21. An eternal body, never getting old.

No disease or sickness. No haircuts, shaving, brushing of teeth, etc.

We will have a custom, prepared house to live in, John 14: 2, 3.

We will meet Bible saints such as Adam and Eve, Abraham, Prophets, Priests, Apostles, and Angels. Matt. 8:11.

We will live in a perfect world of glorious light and brightness, Rev. 21, 22.

Time will be no more.

We will never again suffer loneliness, boredom, pain, fear, sorrow, suffering, I Cor. 15:26; Rev. 21:4.

We will receive rewards for being faithful and fruitful. Matt. 25:21, 23; I Cor. 3:14; II Cor. 5:10.

We will participate in awesome worship and praise, Rev. 5:11-14; 7:9-12. We will sing beautifully and perfectly.

We will see God, Job 19:26; I Jn. 3:2.

We will feel loved.

We will reign with Christ, Rev. 5:10; 20:4, 6: 22:15.

We will be space travelers exploring the universe like angels, Acts 1:10,11.

We will be filled with joy and pleasure, Psalm 16:11.

"No eye has seen, no ear has heard, no mind has conceived what God has prepared for those Who love him," I Cor. 2:9

Lessons from our Model Prayer

Over my lifetime I have used and encountered all types of prayer plans. Each one had its own benefits and drawbacks. Today, the prayer model I use is by all means not mandatory for you, but it has worked well for me.

As you apply this prayer model to your own life, you may decide to make adjustments and modifications. However, what I share here is the model I have now used for some years, and more importantly, I believe this is the biblical model that flows out of the Lord's Model Prayer.

Not the Lord's Prayer.

Notice that I wrote that this is the "Lord's Model Prayer," and not "The Lord's Prayer." Some call the Lord's Prayer the one that begins in God's Word with the statement, "Our Father which art in heaven."

Friend, I am now going to make an extremely controversial statement: What we call "The Lord's Prayer" is not THE Lord's Prayer.

Jesus did not pray that prayer because He did not need to pray that way. When His disciples asked Jesus to "teach us to pray," He essentially replied, "Pray like this." What He then taught them was what I call "our Model Prayer." The prayer of Jesus (the real Lord's Prayer) is contained in John 17.

The Model Prayer

For simplicity of terms here, I will call the prayer that Jesus taught us to pray "the Model Prayer," or, as some call it, "the Disciples' Prayer" because it was the pattern that Jesus gave for us to pray. This misnamed prayer is well known to almost every Christian in the world, and it goes as follows:

Our Father which art in Heaven, hallowed be Thy name. Thy kingdom come Thy will be done on earth as it is in Heaven. Give us this day our daily bread, and forgive us our debts as we forgive our debtors. And lead us not into temptation, but deliver us from evil. For Thine is the Kingdom, and the power, and the glory, forever. Amen.

As we look at this Model Prayer, there are certain absolute prayer lessons we can learn:

Prayer lesson #1

Start with praise.

The model prayer consists of starting out with praise and honoring God. "Our Father which art in heaven, hallowed by Thy Name." In other words, when we pray, the first thing we should declare is, "Lord, we reverence and honor Your name."

His name is Jehovah, but He also is known as Abba Father. He is known as "I Am that I Am." Moses said "Who shall I say has sent me?" He said, "Tell them it is I Am that I Am."

And so, as you start your prayer, spend some time honoring His numerous names, Everlasting Father, Eternal God, Faithful God, Gracious God. Call Him by His names. "Hallowed be Your name." Then go to the name of Jesus; go to the name of the Holy Spirit. In my prayer I say: "Oh, Holy Spirit, I am so thankful You are in me. I thank You, Holy Spirit for the fruit. I thank You for Your gifts. I bless Your name." Start out with praise as the model indicates, and give glory to His name: "Hallowed be Your name."

Power in Prayer

Remember, there is power in prayer, there is power in believing prayer when you are bringing your petitions to God.

In the satellite business, a signal goes up and hits a satellite, which can beam that signal anywhere in the world.

That is the way prayer has been designed by God. When you pray to the Lord, you are believing in Him, and you are believing He is hearing you. That prayer goes up to Him, and He is the power for the answered prayer anywhere in the world.

It is amazing and miraculous.

You can be in Three Rivers and shout up a prayer to God who can then touch someone in China or Russia.

No house or person is free from the penetration of prayer.

In your heart and mind you can shoot out a prayer toward somebody. Maybe at work there is somebody giving you a hard time, but shoot them with a prayer. God is waiting for a prayer to be created.

God waits because He wants to be in cooperation with His children. He waits for a prayer request to be made. He will not act upon the situation until someone makes the request. Otherwise, why would He say, "Ask and it will be given to you."

He wants us to ask so that we have cooperation with Him. Prayer, you might say, is the rail on which the train runs. Jesus said to never give up on prayer. And you know, God answers all prayer.

You, as a believer, are a child of God. So I can assure you, on the basis of God's Word, that He answers every prayer that is uttered.

Some people might say, "Brother John, God did not answer my prayer."

Then you do not understand the nature of prayer. When you pray, it is assumed you want His will to be done. That is our bottom line. Jesus said, "Not My will, but Yours be done." When you pray, God will answer with a yes or no according to His will.

Even "no" is an answer to prayer. He knows what is best for us. And if He says no, then that is an answer to prayer —that your prayer request is not the right thing for you to have at that time.

He answers with a yes, a no, or later. It is in that later that you think He has not answered the prayer. But just be patient. In His time, He will do the right thing.

God's Valentine

Valentine's Day, February 14, is a day set aside to remember those we like and love. Have you remembered what to give for your Valentine?

Do you know that Valentine's Day was named for Valentinus, a bishop of the church who became a martyr rather than deny his faith in God?

According to legend, while Valentinus was awaiting his execution, he befriended the blind daughter of the jailer and through his prayer her sight was restored. On the night before he died, Valentinus penned a farewell message to the girl who had meant so much to him and signed it "From your Valentine." This was the first Valentine.

The valentines we give are symbols of love; for that is what love is – a desire to give rather than take. Love gives and love forgives.

God gave when He wanted to show us how much He loves us. He wrapped His love up in the Person of Jesus Christ His Son and gave Him to the world.

Jesus Christ is God's love personified as John 3:16 says
"For God so lo**V**ed the word the world
That He g**A**ve
His on**L**y
Begott**E**n
So**N**
That whosoever
Believeth **I**n Him
Should **N**ot perish
But have **E**verlasting life.
47. John 3:16

This is God's valentine to you and me. Will you be His valentine?

Happy Valentine's Day this Sunday. Go to church and be God's valentine.

Read His love message to you in the Bible.

Conditions to answered prayer

"I will if you will."

Sometimes the answer contains a condition. If you will do something, then He will do it. It is cooperation with Him; God helps those who help themselves.

Sometimes He will give us the mind, the power, the wisdom, and the strength to do something that we are asking Him to do. He will enable us to accomplish it.

"I will if you will," He says.

One of my favorite stories that illustrates the active part of our prayer is about a young brother and sister. The sister was upset because her brother was making a device to trap birds, and she did not like that. She did not want him to be trapping any birds. So she said, "Mommy, I do not want my brother to be making a way to trap birds."

The mother replied, "What can I do about it? Why don't you pray?"

So she did.

The next day the girl came running to mother and said, "Mom, God answered my prayer. Brother will not be trapping any birds."

"How do you know that?" she asked, amazed at her little daughter's sudden faith.

"Because I went out in the yard and smashed the trap to pieces," the little girl replied.

"I will if you will."

That is believing prayer.

Prayer is where the power is, where the generator is. Intercessory prayer is a powerful force. Make it an extension of your life. Pray every day.

It is a calling of God to be a prayer warrior. You may not have come to that realization yet, but it is a call of God to be a prayer warrior. It is a privilege, a blessing, source of power.

Get in on the prayer power.

Jesus said, "If two of you shall agree on earth about anything that is touching the earth, it shall be done. Where two or three are gathered, there I am in the midst."

Faith Lifted Prayer

In Matthew 21:22, Jesus said: Whatever you ask in prayer..what is the next word? Believing! That is a faith prayer. Believing you will receive.

I John 5:14-15 is also a tremendous passage on prayer: Vs 14. This is the confidence we have in approaching God: that if we ask anything according to his will, he hears us. Vs 15. And if we know that he hears us — whatever we ask — we know that we have what we asked of him.

When we declare, "I know that You heard that, Lord," that is faith because He promised. And if we know that He hears us, "Then whatever we ask we will receive."

That is faith prayer.

If you pray in faith, prayer will unleash amazing things:

Healing: James 5:15 The prayer of faith will save the sick.

Thanksgiving: Philippians 4:6-9 Vs 6. Do not be anxious about anything, but in everything, by prayer and petition, with thanksgiving, present your requests to God. Vs 7 And the peace of God, which transcends all understanding, will guard your hearts and your minds in Christ Jesus. Vs 8 Finally brothers, whatever is true, whatever is noble, whatever is right, whatever is pure, whatever is lovely, whatever is admirable — if anything is excellent or praiseworthy — think about such things. Vs 9 Whatever you have learned or

received or heard from me, or seen in me — put it into practice. And the God of peace will be with you.

That is a prayer of faith; you received your salvation this way. When you heard that if you receive Jesus Christ as your Savior, if you call upon Him, "Whoever shall call on the name of the Lord shall be saved," and you wanted to turn from your sins and repent, you asked Jesus to come into your heart and accepted Christ as your Savior.

That is faith.

Who is your Father?

"Our Father."

The word "Father" in the Aramaic and in Hebrew is abba, or in the modern Aramaic, it is babba, If you say "Our Father," it is babben; "my father" is babbe.

What a way to open up a prayer, expressing that God is our Father. It is such an endearing word, this

Aramaic word. It is the same as what we would say today, "Daddy," or "Pappa," this Aramaic word babba.

Is God your father? You cannot call Him Father if He is not your father.

Do you know that there are two celestial fathers in this world?

There is Father God and father devil. Jesus said in John 8:44 "You are of your father the devil."

He said this to religious people. "And the desires of your father you want to do. He is a liar and the father of it." The devil is a father, and unfortunately, he has many kids too, who act like the devil.

Who is your father? If it is Father God, this comes about through being born again. In John 3:3, Jesus

said: "Unless one is born again, he cannot see the Kingdom of God."

You see, you are born the first time physically, and spiritually you are born again when you receive Christ

as your Lord and Savior, and you are born into His family so you become a born-again believer.

As John 1:12 says "As many as received Him (when you received Christ), He gives the authority to become the children of God."

You are in the family, so you can say, "Our Father." And in John 14:6, Jesus said: "I am the way, the truth

and the life. No one comes to the Father but by Me."

When you seek Christ, you are brought to the Father. He is your Father. And if you do not have God

as your Father, you automatically have the devil as your father.

It is as simple as that. There are only two fathers. If you do not have God as your Father, then you have the devil as your father.

There are two fathers and there are two kingdoms. There is a Kingdom of God, and a kingdom of the devil; a Kingdom of light and a kingdom of darkness.

There are two wills: the Father's will and the will of the devil. That is why it is so important, if you have

God as your Father, not to marry someone who has the devil as a father. Otherwise, you will have trouble with your father-in-law.

This Lord's Model Prayer represents you going straight to the Father, our Father. It is perfectly fine to pray occasionally to Jesus Christ, but Jesus said He came to lead us to the Father.

You come to the Father through Jesus Christ.

And so, go right to the Father in prayer, and start thanking Him that He is your Father. Praise Him that

He is your Father. Say, "I love You, my Father."

That is a great opening for prayer. Then say . . . . . "Our Father in Heaven"

This is very personal. In a crowd it is probably prudent to pray "Our Father," but when you are in your own prayer closet, than make it more personal, such as "My Father." Also, instead of saying, "Who art in heaven," you might consider praying "My Father who is in me."

Earlier I mentioned that the day of Pentecost was when the Holy Spirit came into the believers. Today,

when the Holy Spirit, the Spirit of God, comes into you, He is now in you. In John 14:23, Jesus declared: "If anyone loves Me, he will keep My Word, and My Father will love him, and We will come unto him and make Our home with him."

They will be in us — the Father, the Son, and the Holy Spirit. In Colossians 1:27, the Apostle Paul said: "Christ in you, the hope of glory."

And so, you can very well say, knowing that you are biblically on solid ground, "My Father in me." Do you see how that makes your prayer very personal, very intimate?

Yes, He is in heaven, but that is far off for our finite minds. "Father, You are in me," means much more to our understanding.

And, He is in you all day long, too, so you can be in touch with Him all day.

Your will be done

God's will is the same thing you would want for your children. Dads, moms, your will for your children is always the best. Jesus said: "If you know how to give good gifts to your children, how much more will your heavenly Father give good gifts."

We have a generous, giving Father; there is no need to keep begging for your needs. Just ask Him and then thank Him. I thank God this way: Lord, I thank You that your will is being done in my life, because I have asked for it. I thank you that your will is being done in my family because I have asked for it. I thank you that your will is being done with my relatives. I thank you that Your will is being done for the Church family. I thank you that your will is being done for all those in the ministry. I thank you that you are working your will regarding our country, our state, our city, our world.

You see, I made the request. After the request is made, thereafter, in faith, thank Him that He has heard it. Say "I thank You, Lord, that You are working on it."

Instead of keeping on begging, begging, and begging, throwing doubt, doubt, and doubt on all the other requests - remember that you are now in faith and operating on the high level of thanks. That thankful attitude pleases God: For without faith it is impossible to please God.

God likes faith.

When a son asks for a bicycle, most dads would reply, "Okay, I'll do the best I can to see about getting you a new bicycle." If, the next day there was no bicycle, the child might again say, "Dad, I want a bicycle," to which you would reply, "I told you that I am I going to give you a bicycle."

If that scene is repeated again and again, the dad might grow a bit angry and declare, "Hey, I told you I was going to give you a bicycle. Don't you believe me?"

The best response the child could say would be, "Thanks, Dad, you said you were going to give me a bicycle, and when you give it to me is up to you." The "when" is up to the heavenly Father. Thank Him!

The Word of God declares, "Whatever you ask according to His will," He will hear. That means He is going to do it. That is what it means when someone says "God heard me." It does not just mean that He listened, but it means, according to the Bible, that He heard it to do it, according to his will.

The best way to know what is God's will for your life is to know His word. That is why it is so important to be in the Word of God every single day.

To know His Word is to know His will!

If you know God's Word, then you know what to do. I am guided in what to do by knowing what God's Word says to do. It is as simple as that. So when I do it, I do not care much about the perceived outcome. If I did what was according to the will of God, I say, "Thank You, Lord." Even though it may not seem to be the outcome I expected, even though it may not seem very good at the time, it is going to work out for good because I am doing the will of God, and it is based upon the Word of God.

Thanks-Living

Every day should be Thanksgiving Day for us. We ought to celebrate Thanksgiving Day every day and set aside one day out of the year for grumbling.

A farmer was asked to have dinner with a man from the big city. The farmer did, and as it was his custom at home he asked the blessing at the table. When he had finished, his host said, "You are very old-fashioned. It is not customary now-a-days for well-educated people to pray at the table." The farmer said that it was customary for him, but some at his place never prayed over their food." "Ah," said the man, "they are sensible and enlightened. Who are they?" The farmer answered, "they are the pigs."

The priest called on an elderly Irish woman. "And how are you today?" "I'm bad enough, father. I've only got two teeth in the whole of my mouth, but thanks be to God they are opposite."

I read about the carpenter who started to slide down the steep high roof. He cried out "Oh, God, help me. O God, don't let me die." Just then his overhalls caught on a nail and stopped him."That's all right, God, don't bother, I'm ok now."

There is a legend of a man who found the barn where Satan kept his seeds ready to be sown in the human heart. He found that the seeds of discouragement were more numerous than others and those seeds could be made to grow almost anywhere. When Satan was questioned, he reluctantly admitted that there was one place in which he could never get them to thrive. "And where is that?" the man asked. Satan replied sadly, "In the heart of a grateful man."

When the children in our family were young, we began a tradition at the Thanksgiving Day table. Each of us gave thanks for something. We kept going on giving thanks until someone would not be able to think of something to be thankful about. I don't think anyone ever gave out, so we stopped before the turkey dinner got cold. Try it with you family this Thanksgiving Day.

Why Go To Church?

A Church goer wrote a letter to the editor of a newspaper and complained that it made no sense to go to church every Sunday.

"I've gone for 30 years now," he wrote, "and in that time I have heard something like 3,000 sermons.

But for the life of me, I can't remember a single one of them. So, I think I'm wasting my time and the pastors are wasting their time.

This started a real controversy in the "Letters to the Editor" column, much to the delight of the editor. It went on for weeks until someone wrote this clincher:

"I've been married for 30 years now. In that time my wife has cooked some 32,000 meals. But, for the life of me, I cannot recall the entire menu for a single one of those meals. But I do know this. They all nourished me and gave me the strength I needed to do my work. If my wife had not given me these meals,I would be physically dead today. Likewise, if I had not gone to church for nourishment, I would be spiritually dead today!" When you are DOWN to nothing. . . . . . God is UP to something!

Faith sees the invisible, believes the incredible and receives the impossible! Thank God for our physical AND our spiritual nourishment! I think everyone should read this! "When Satan is knocking at your door, simply say, "Jesus, could you get that for me?" SEE YOU IN CHURCH!

The Power of a Praying Mother

Personally, I am the result of my mother's prayers. Did I have a praying mother? Yes, I did. I wrote a book, 'Assyria, the Forgotten Nation in Prophecy', and I traveled all over the nation speaking on this subject. I dedicated my book on Assyria to my mother, and here is what I wrote:

To my Assyrian mother, Phoebe, who dedicated me, her first born, to God, from whom I learned the Assyrian language, and from whose lap I learned of the God of my fathers. By her intercessory prayers I was led to receive Jesus Christ as my Savior and Lord in the United States Navy.

Do you have a praying mother? Do you pray for your mother?

Let me address both mothers and fathers here who are reading this. If you ever come across the experience of having a child who is away from the Lord, make the request of the Lord for that child's need, and then thereafter, begin to thank the Lord that they are going to be saved, healed of an addiction, or whatever their particular need is.

Trust me, prayer works. I was the most unlikely one to be saved in our family. I was the oldest of five children, running around Chicago, and I never stepped inside of a church as a teenager. But in the Navy, the Lord got a hold of my life because of my mother's prayers, and what a joy she experienced when I called her and said, "Ma, I just got saved."

God got a hold of my life and here I am today, sharing this with you on prayer.

Praise God for praying mothers!

If you are reading this and you are away from the Lord, and your mother or father or both are alive, you might as well give up your resistance because they are praying for you! You will be nailed by their prayers! They are that powerful. I believe it. It happened to me, and I know it has happened to many, many others reading this.

The Miracle of Prayer.

There is a huge, mighty concept in believing prayer. Do you understand that prayer is miraculous?

Every time a prayer is heard, it is a miracle.

Think about it. God is able to communicate with any of the billions of people on this earth. He speaks over 5,000 different languages and dialects, understands all the different cultures and customs in all the 195 different countries of the world!

Do you see why prayer is miraculous?

God knows who you are and what you are thinking.

But the miracle of answered prayer is even more awesome! Whenever prayer is answered by God, that is a miracle. Imagine you can make a request and God answers it.

Amazing Grace!

'Honor . . . . your Mother'

(One of the Ten Commandments)

The first Mother's Day was celebrated in a Sunday School in Philadelphia. In 1910 Miss Anna Jarvis suggested that one day in every year should be set aside and celebrated in honor of all mothers.

President Wilson in 1914 asked that the American flag be put up on every government building on the second Sunday of May every year, which was set aside for Mother's Day.

President McKinley wore a white carnation in memory of his mother and it is now a custom for the people of the United States to wear a white carnation if the mother has died and a red or pink carnation if the mother is living.

England celebrated Mother's Day before the people in the United States did, but they called it Mothering Day. Everybody that was away from home tried very hard to get home to spend the day with their mother.

We should honor our mother because we owe her our own physical life. Think of how she bore us at her discomfort, pain and danger. Remember, teenager, you once had dirty diapers that mother had to take care of.

Mothers make a home out of a house. Dad provides what money will buy; Mom provides what money cannot buy.

We can best honor our mother by living the way she would want us to live. Let's make her proud of us.

Someone wrote: "Your mother is always with you. She's the whisper of the leaves as you walk down the street; she's the smell of bleach in your freshly laundered socks; she's the cool hand on your brow when you're not well. Your mother lives inside your laughter. And she's crystallized in every teardrop. She's the place you came from, your first home; and she's the map you follow with every step you take. She's your first love and your first heartbreak, and nothing on earth can separate you. Not time, not space not even death."

No Power in Prayer?

Remember, there is no power in prayer, but there is power in believing prayer when you are bringing your petitions to God.

In the satellite business a signal goes up, and hits a satellite which can beam that signal anywhere in the world. That is the way prayer has been designed by God. When you pray to the Lord you are believing He is hearing you. That prayer goes up to Him, and He is the power for the answered prayer anywhere in the world.

It is amazing and miraculous.

You can be in Three Rivers and shoot up a prayer to God who can then touch someone in China or Russia.

No house or person is free from the penetration of prayer.

In your heart and mind you can shoot out a prayer toward somebody. Maybe at work there is somebody giving you a hard time, but shoot them with a prayer. God is waiting for a prayer to be created.

God waits because He wants to be in cooperation with His children. He waits for a prayer request to be made. He will not act upon the situation until someone makes the request. Otherwise, why would He say, "Ask and it will be given to you"?

You, as a believer, are a child of God, so I can assure you on the basis of God's Word that He answers every prayer that is uttered.

Some people might say, Brother John, God did not answer my prayer." Then you do not understand the nature of prayer. When you pray, it is assumed you want His will to be done. That is our bottom line. Jesus said, "Not My will, but Yours be done." When you pray, God will answer with a yes or no according to His will.

Even "no" is an answer to prayer. He knows what is best for us. And if He says "No," then that is an answer to prayer - your prayer request is not the right thing for you to have at that time.

He answers with a yes, a no, or later. It is in that 'later' that you think He has not answered the prayer.

But just be patient. In His time He will do the right thing.

Conditions to answered prayer.

"I will if you will."

Sometimes the answer contains a condition. If you will do something, then He will do it. It is in

cooperation with Him; God helps those who help themselves.

Sometimes He will give us the mind, the power, the wisdom and the strength to do something that we are asking Him to do. He will enable us to accomplish it.

"I will if you will," He says.

One of my favorite stories that illustrates the active part of our prayer is about a young brother and sister. The sister was upset because her brother was making a device to trap birds and she did not like that. She did not want him to be trapping any birds. So she said, "Mommy, I do not want my brother to be making a way to trap birds." The mother replied, "What can I. do about it? Why don't you pray?" So she did.

The next day the girl came running to mother and said, "Mom, God answered my prayer. Brother will not be trapping any birds.

"How do you know that?" she asked, amazed at her little daughter's sudden faith.

"Because I want out in the yard and smashed the trap to pieces," the little girl replied.

I will if you will.

That is believing prayer.

Lord, teach us to pray

The disciples asked Jesus in Luke 11:1, "Lord, teach us to pray."

Is that also your heart's desire? Do you want this for your life? D o you cry out from the depth of your soul, "Lord, teach me to pray?"

Since you are reading this page, I believe you want that for your life. Remember, praying is about being in touch with God. That is the beautiful thing about prayer- you get in touch with Father God.

I am calling this prayer "the New Model of the Lord's Prayer" because things have happened since He gave that model to us, so there is indeed a New Model of the Lords' Prayer.

Let me emphasize that the New Model of the Lord's Prayer is a faith prayer, a thanks prayer. Keep that in mind because that is the transforming power of this prayer.

In Matthew 21:22, Jesus said: Whatever you ask in prayer. . .What is the next word? Believing! That is a faith prayer. Believing you will receive.

I John 5:14-15 is also a tremendous passage on prayer: 14: This is the confidence we have in approaching God: that if we ask anything according to his will, he hears us. 15: And if we know that he hears us – whatever we ask – we know that we have what we asked of him.

When we declare, "I know that You heard that, Lord," that is faith because He promised. And if we know that He hears us, "Then whatever we ask we will receive."

That is faith prayer. If you pray in faith, prayer will unleash amazing things: Healing: James 5:15 The prayer of faith will save the sick.

Thanksgiving: Philippians 4:6-9 6: Do not be anxious about anything, but in prayer and petition, with thanksgiving, present your requests to God. 7: And the peace of God, which transcends all understanding, will guard your hearts and your minds in Christ Jesus. 8: Finally, brothers, whatever is true, whatever is noble, whatever is right, whatever is pure, whatever is lovely, whatever is admirable – if anything is excellent or praiseworthy – think about such things. 9: Whatever you have learned or received or heard from me, or seen in me – put it into practice. And the God of peace will be with you.

That is a prayer of faith. You received your salvation this way. When you heard that if you receive Jesus Christ as your Savior, if you call upon Him, "Whoever shall call on the name of the Lord shall be saved," and you wanted to turn from your sins and repent, you asked Jesus to come into your heart and accept Christ as your Savior. That is faith.

The Good News Gospel

Think about this. Why is it called the Gospel of Good News? Because Jesus paid for it all – all that I owe!

Imagine if you owed a great financial debt, in excess of $1,900,000, and someone came up to you and said, "I have put one million dollars in the bank in your name into an account. All you have to do now is go and claim it."

Now, some would say, "Oh, no, I don't believe that. I'm not going to fall for that. Do you really expect me to go to my bank and try to claim one million dollars in some account? How ridiculous. How gullible do you think I am?"

Even though the money is in the bank in your name, and has been deposited to your account, you do not have it until you access it.

Yes, it has been deposited. There is a million dollars in the bank in your name. It is yours. All you have got to do is accept the "good news" of that reality and claim it.

In fact, Jesus is worth far more than a million dollars. But all you have got to do is accept Him and claim the promises He has given you for your life. In that wonderful, eternal package comes the forgiveness of sins. So, we say: Thank You, Lord, for forgiving our sins. And, I want to show my love and appreciation for You by living the way You would like me to live.

Now, here is another vital point: If we continue as believers to sin, then our fellowship is broken, and two other events will happen.

Event One: Abba Father is going to give His child a spanking.

Event Two: you will forfeit rewards.

There is a reward system God has prepared for us after this life is finished. Anything good you have done is rewarded. So, you cannot sin and expect to get away with it. No, our goal as Christians is to try and become "sinless." I like that word; I like to know that I am "sinning less" as I go on in my journey with God.

The gift of God

The celebration of Christ's birthday is a very unusual one. For when birthdays are celebrated, the age of the person is normally featured in the observance (except women). But in Christ's case, attention is still focused upon him as a baby, as though he had never grown up.

At birthdays, gifts are given to the one whose birthday it is. But on Christ's birthday He is little remembered by some.

One unusual thing about Christ's birthday is that the ones who celebrate the person's birthday bring gifts, but in Christ's case the ones celebrating His birthday are the recipients of a great gift.

At Christ's birthday, God gave everybody His greatest gift. Everyone is on God's gift list. Romans 6:23 "The wages of sin is death, but the gift of God is the gift of eternal life through Jesus Christ, our Lord."

What a wonderful gift this is to live forever in the presence of God, enjoying everything that makes existence worth having. It is God's Christmas gift to all.

This gift of God of eternal life resides in Christ Jesus, the Lord. It is wrapped up in Him.

When one looks back over the years to Bethlehem's manger, a proper view of Bethlehem is one that looks back through the cross on which Christ dies for our sins.

And the cross becomes the only lens which can give a clear and meaningful view of that first Christmas. This little babe in the manger is the God-man who dies on the cross for our sins that we may have the Christmas gift of eternal life. The baby hands and feet of Jesus will be pierced with nails 33 years later.

As we consider the babe in the manger, let us see Him as our Savior who died for us and rose from the dead and lives today in the hearts of all who have received Him.

Christ is the gift of God, freely given to everyone by God, and all one needs to do is receive this gift with thanks.

For God so loved the world (put your name here) that He gave His only begotten Son, that whoever (put your name here) believes in Him, will not perish, but have everlasting life – John 3:16.

Thanks be to God for His Christmas gift.

Do you know what Christ wants for His birthday present? You!

Believing Prayer

"This is the confidence we have in him, that if we ask anything according to His will, He hears us. And if we know that He hears us, whatever we ask, we will receive," I John 5: 14, 15.

In this article on prayer, my dear reader, I am trying to emphasize this matter of believing prayer, which is a matter of faith. People have told me, "Believing prayer revolutionized my prayer life." They have said, "I had a prayer life, but I have not thought of praying this way, in believing prayer. "

Turn you prayer around from a repetition to a thanksgiving prayer.

Someone else said to me, "Brother John, I have been praying for my child to be healed every day. I am asking, 'Oh, Lord, heal, heal, heal my child.'" Then he continued, "Now I am going to say thanks to God because I have already asked."

That is believing prayer, and it will revolutionize your prayer life. You will be positive. You will be praying in faith.

The Lord says He loves faith. The Bible declares, "Without faith it is impossible to please God."

Faith pleases God. Prayer helps you get to know the Lord better because you are in a relationship with God. You are talking to Him. Or, if you are not speaking, it is in your mind, talking to Him.

A little boy once said this: "Dear God, even when I am not praying, I am thinking about You."

Develop a prayer life for yourself as your spiritual thumbprint. I like that big thumbprint; it reminds me of God's big hand, His thumbprint is prayer, and it should be impressed upon us in our daily prayer lives.

One Christian song says it this way: "I want to know You, I want to hear Your voice."

When you are praying, once in a while, pause and say: "Lord, have you got anything to say about this?"

Let Him speak with you. He will put a thought in your mind. That is His answer.

If you give Him a chance to respond, it is beautiful. Believe He is responding because He does want to **talk to His children.**

Happy St. Patrick's Day

My great-grandson, Jack Booko, was born one year ago on St. Patrick's Day. May he grow up as a strong man of faith in Christ as St. Patrick did.

Patrick was born about A.D. 387 of noble and wealthy parents in Roman Britain. Patrick described himself in his Confession as a wayward youth who "knew not the true God." When he was 16 years old, he was captured, along with many others, by a band of Irish raiders and taken to Ireland, where he was sold as a slave.

In these days Patrick experienced a real conversion to Christ, and the consciousness of God's presence became the center of his life.

Six years after his capture and conversion at age 22, the Lord spoke to Patrick in a dream. "Soon you will go to your own country." In the strength of this word, Patrick escaped and traveled on foot for 200 miles to the port of the county and obtained passage on a ship. He finally arrived home where he was received with great joy by his parents. They begged him never to leave home again. But one night after nearly three years, Patrick had a dream in which he heard the voices of the Irish crying out to him. "We are asking you, holy youth, come and walk among us. . ." This would become "his heavenly vision" to which he would not be disobedient.

For 30 years Patrick labored as a true apostle among the Irish, preaching the Gospel, winning thousands of them to Christ, baptizing them and establishing them into churches.

St. Patrick, apostle to the people of Ireland, died on March 17th, A.D. 461 at nearly 75 years of age. Thirty years before, he had come to that very place to begin to minister the Gospel to a race that was almost entirely heathen. He left them almost completely Christian. His ultimate testimony was simply "Through Christ, with Him and in Him, to You, God the Father, in the unity of the Holy Spirit is all glory and honor." Amen and Amen!

Remember to wear some green for the Irish and St. Pat.

How to talk to Father God

We are going on a prayer safari, a journey, and I trust that it will make a big impact on all who take the journey.

The Lord's Prayer is really the Lord's Model Prayer. It is not meant to be a prayer that you just pray and repeat, and repeat, but it is a model prayer. The disciples asked Jesus to teach them. And He said, "Pray like this." He did not say, "Pray this," but He said, "Pray like this," or after this manner. '

Everybody seems to know the Lord's Prayer, even children say it. It was spoken in Aramaic. Jesus spoke the Aramaic language, which is the language of the Assyrians (of which I am one).

As you read this, say the Lord's Prayer out loud. Our Father in heaven, hallowed be Your name, Your Kingdom come, Your will be done on earth as it is in heaven. Give us this day our daily bread and forgive us our debts as we forgive our debtors. Let us not enter into temptation, but deliver us from evil. Yours is the Kingdom and the power and the glory forever.

That was spoken by Jesus in the Aramaic language. When Mel Gibson created the movie, "The Passion of the Christ," he used Aramaic. It was exciting to listen to that film in the Aramaic language. If you heard the Lord say the prayer, it would have sounded like this in Aramaic: (Here we will write out the Lord's Prayer in Aramaic.)

The Lord's Model Prayer (NKJV)

In the language of Jesus Christ — Aramaic/Assyrian language.
Babin bi shmeya — Our Father in heaven
Pa-esh m'kootsha shimookh — hallowed be Your name.
Etya Melkootookh, — Your kingdom come.
Hawi rizi-yookh— Your will be done.
Dakhi bi shmeya, oop uhrah — On earth as it is in heaven.
Hulun luckhma sun-kahnin idyo yoma — Give us this day our daily bread

Shuklun Khobayn dakhit oop ukhnan shweklun daynun dahrun —And forgive us our debts as we forgive our debtors.

La moritlun ul jurahba — Do not let us enter temptation *(Lamsa)

Illa poseelun min beesha -but deliver us from the evil one.

Sahbip deyookh eela melkewta oo khela oo tishbukhta —— For Yours is the kingdom and the power and the glory.

Hul ahlum, ahbadeen, ahmeen—forever. Amen.

To properly understand this prayer, you need to comprehend a little bit about the Middle East mentality. To help you understand more of the Lord's Model Prayer, I will put down some foundational groundwork. This was a BC prayer — meaning that it took place before the crucifixion of Christ, before He died on the cross as an atonement for our sins.

And finally, as I have shared before, this is not the Lord's Prayer. Jesus did not pray this prayer for Himself. He could not have prayed this for Himself, because the words in this prayer ask for the forgiveness of sins. This is really the disciples' prayer.

The Lord's prayer is in John 17.

The place of Heaven

Heaven is fun; a place of unlimited pleasure, happiness and joys. (Ps. 16:11, 1 Cor. 2:9; Rev. 14:13)

Heaven is dynamic. It is bursting with excitement and action. It is the ultimate playground. God invented it. It is Disney World, Hawaii, Paris, Rome and New York all rolled into one. It is a vacation that never ends. It is all-inclusive.

We don't lose our identity in heaven (a spiritual body like Christ). Our changed body will obey the commands of the mind. (We will travel faster than light throughout God's universe.)

In heaven we will experience a whole new variety of sights, sounds, smells, feelings, and tastes. God is a great artist and inventor and creator. Pleasurable sensations are retained in heaven and God may substitute something better.

Our reunions and relationships in heaven are going to be fabulous with our spouses, children, relatives and friends.

Even our animals (Why not: Ps. 36:6 says God cares for people and animals alike). And don't forget your heavenly assistants, the angels.

"Rest in peace" means going on from what you were doing to greater things: free from worries, suffering, sickness and pain.

Heaven will not be boring, ever, will it? It will be discoveries and works that never end. With singing, dancing, playing instruments, learning to be an artist, or any other interest.

The highlight of heaven is seeing God! Worshiping and praising Him. He will then have the answers to all of our questions.

"When we all get to heaven, what a day of rejoicing that will be! When we all see Jesus, We'll sing and shout the victory."

Christ's Invitation to the Laborer

There are three verses in the Bible of which it may be said that there are few passages more important than this in Matthew 11:28-30."Come to me all you who LABOR and are heavy laden, and I will give you rest. Take my yoke upon you and learn from Me. . .and you will find rest for your souls. For My yoke is easy and My burden is light."

Christ extends a gracious invitation to the laborer as Monday is Labor Day honoring the laborer. When Christ says "come to Me," He promises rest, meaning He will refresh you. Christ is speaking about rest for your soul which includes your emotions, intellect and will.

When Christ says "take My yoke upon you and learn from Me," He is talking about you being in a yoke (a bar or frame of wood by which two animals are joined at their necks for working together), where He will be pulling with you and for you.

Where Christ says "His yoke is easy and His burden is light," He is comparing it to the yoke that is of one having a yoke apart from Christ which is not easy and light.

Christ wants you to cast all your worries and burdens of sins upon Him for He cares for you.

Jesus said whoever comes to Me, I will not cast out. So, come to Him and trust in Him and love Him and have a happy Labor Day.

Praise Yahweh for His Great Name

I remember an instance where a small child came running home from her Sunday School lesson and reported to her parents, "Mom and Dad, I know Gods name." They asked, "You do? What is it?"

"Harold," she replied. "How did you come up with that, honey?" her parents asked, trying not to be skeptical or put down her enthusiasm. "My teacher was praying," she replied, "and she said, 'Harold be your name.

Harold — hallowed. What is God's name?

"God" is not his name; "God" is his title. His name is not "Allah." What is his name? Do you know his name? If you get nothing more out of this article, then get ready to treasure what you are about to read, because it is something that 99.9 percent of believers do not know — the answer to the question, "What is the name of God?"

Of course, there are many attributes listed in the Bible to describe God, but His name is hallowed and special, and is found in Psalm 68:4 "Sing unto God, sing praises to His name,"

Psalm 68:4 identifies His name as Yah. "Extol Him who rides upon the clouds, by His name, Yah, and rejoice before Him."

The New King James has it "Yah," or "Jah," pronounced Yah, and you find that in the word "hallelujah," meaning, "praise the Lord."

His name is Yah.

Now you have something to share with others.

My dear wife, Burnell, came from the Upper Peninsula of Michigan, and for some reason, her word for "yes" always sounds like "yah." She is always on the phone saying; "yah." The Swedes and the Finns use

"Yah" "for yes.

Sometimes, I joke with her and say "Honey, say yes, not yah. After all, you do not want to take the name of the Lord God in vain."

"Yah" is the short form of Yahweh, which is the Aramaic-Hebrew name of God. Now, in the Greek it is pronounced Jehovah, and they translated it Yah, or Yahweh. Unfortunately when it is translated into

English, it becomes "Lord," but it is really "Yah."

Psalm 68:4 says His name is “Yah.” Thank and praise Yahweh for His great name.

To know God's Word is to know His will

If you know God's Word, then you know what to do. I am guided in what to do by knowing what God's Word says to do. It is as simple as that. So when I do it, I do not care much about the perceived outcome. If I did what was according to the will of God, I say, "Thank You, Lord." Even though it may not seem to be the outcome I expected, even though it may not seem very good at the time, it is going to work out for good because I am doing the will of God, and it is based upon the Word of God.

Anything in the Word of God that He has spoken as a command or advice, do it, and you are in the will of God. For instance, in I Thessalonians 5:18, it says:

For this is the will of God in Christ Jesus concerning you, in everything give thanks.

What is the will of God? To give thanks!

So I give thanks "in everything." Not for everything, but "in everything." It may not be that you are able to give thanks for everything, because sometimes trouble comes, and none of us is really "thankful" for trouble. But, when you are in trouble, say, "Thank You, Lord, in this trouble You are with me. In this trouble, You are going to make it work out for my good."

II Peter 3:9 is another example of enabling Scripture to help you understand God's will for your life, and for the lives of others.

The Lord is not willing that any should perish, but that all should come to repentance.

It is not His will that any should perish. When you pray for someone to be saved, you are praying in

God's will. God wants them to be saved more than you do. Isn't that beautiful? I believe, actually, that if

you are praying for someone in your family, you only need to pray it one time for salvation, and then start thanking Him. Say once:

Lord, I want my son,(my daughter, father, mother). . .I want that one to be saved. I pray for that one to be saved for heaven, and saved from hell.

If you believe God has heard your prayer, if you believe in the truth of God's Word, if you believe the

Holy Spirit will work on that request (which He will), what do you do after you have prayed that prayer? Even though you see the person acting like the devil, you do not say, "Oh, God, save that person." You already have prayed that, so here is what you say: "Thank You, Lord, for working on them."

Jim's Fellowship With Jesus

A minister was driving past his church in the middle of the day and decided to stop and check inside to see if anyone had come to pray. As he stood in the empty church, the back door opened and a man came down the aisle. The minister frowned as he saw that the man had not shaved in a while, his shirt was kind of shabby, and his coat was worn and frayed. The man knelt down, bowed his head a short period of time, then rose and walked away.

In the days that followed, every day at noon this same fellow came down the aisle, knelt just for a brief moment, with a lunch pail in his lap, then rose and walked away.

Well, the minister's suspicions grew, with robbery as a main fear, so he decided to stop the man and ask him, "What are you doing here?"

"I work down the road," the man replied. "My lunch time is only a half hour, so lunchtime is my prayer time, my time for finding strength and power. I only stay for a few moments because the factory is so far away. I just kneel here and briefly talk to the Lord, praying:

I just came again to tell you, Lord, how happy I have been since we found each other's friendship, and since I learned how you took away my sins. I don't know much about how to pray, but I think about you everyday. And so, Jesus, this is Jim checking in today. Amen."

The minister felt foolish as he heard the man's explanation, and feebly replied, "That's fine. You are welcome to come and pray anytime." "Thanks," Jim replied. "Well, it's time to go."

Jim then hurried out the door. As he left, the minister knelt at the altar as if he had never knelt at that altar before. His cold heart melted, warmed with love, and he met with Jesus there. As the tears flowed down his cheeks, in his heart he repeated Jim's humble prayer:

"I just came again to tell you, Lord, how happy I have been since we found each other's friendship, and since I learned how you took away my sins. I don't know much about how to pray, but I think about you everyday. And so, Jesus, this is me checking in today. Amen."

One day, as noon past, the minister noticed that old Jim had not yet come in. As more days passed without Jim, the minister began to worry some, so he decided to visit the factory down the road and ask about Jim. There he learned that Jim was ill.

The minister went to the nearby hospital, where the staff explained that they were worried about Jim, even though he always gave them a thrill. The week Jim was with them, he brought about positive changes in the ward. His smiles and joy were contagious. His attitude changed people.

The head nurse could not understand why Jim was so glad and joyful since he received no flowers, no calls or cards, and not even a single visitor until the minister appeared by his bed. The minister diplomatically voiced the nurse's concern to Jim.

"Jim, the nurse told me that you haven't been visited by anyone. Do you have any family here?"

Looking surprised, old Jim spoke up with a winsome smile. "The nurse is wrong. She couldn't know that He is here all the while, everyday at noon. He is here, a dear friend of mine. You see, He sits right down, takes my hand, leans over and says to me:

I just came again to tell you, Jim, how happy I have been since we found each other's friendship, and I took away your sins. I always love to hear you pray, and I think about you everyday. And so, Jim, this is Jesus checking in today. Amen."

Many people will walk in and out of your life each day, but only true friends will leave footprints in your heart. May God hold you in the palm of His hand and may angels watch over you.

PRAYER MEETINGS

The most important and most neglected meeting in churches is the Prayer Meeting. Most churches have no regular prayer meetings where the people can come together to pray. The few churches that do have regular prayer meetings have a very small attendance. Some prayer meetings are considered boring. Pray that the prayer meetings are worth attending.

Prayer meetings in the New Testament:

Matthew 26: 40,41 — Could you not keep watch with me for an hour? Watch and pray so that you will not fall into temptation. The spirit is willing but the flesh is weak..
Acts 1:14 — They all joined together constantly in prayer.
Acts 2:1,4 — They were all together in one place. . .All of them were filled with the Holy Spirit. . . .
Acts 4:31 — After they prayed, the place where they were meeting was shaken and they were all filled with the Holy Spirit and spoke the word of God boldly.
Acts 6:4 —(The Apostles) We will give our attention to prayer and the ministry of the word.
Acts 12:12b — Many people had gathered and were praying.
There is power in numbers, Matthew 18: 19,20 - If two of you on earth agree about anything you ask for, it will be done for you by My Father in heaven. For where two or three come together in My Name, there I am with them.
Leviticus 26:8 — Five of you will chase a hundred, and a hundred of you will chase ten thousand.

What you do in prayer meetings as Intercessors:
Share praises to God and answers to prayer.
Give thanks to God and sing praises.
Pray for healings.
Pray for unsaved and unchurched people to come to the Lord.

Pray for spiritual, emotional, physical and financial needs among us.
Pray for all of the leaders and workers in the church.
Pray for the Sunday services and other ministries of the church.
Pray for those in spiritual and political authority.
Pray for missions and missionaries.
Pray for peace in our city, state, country and the world.
Pray for the unity and love of believers in Christ.
Allow the Lord to direct in what else should be prayed according to His will.
Jesus Christ and the Holy Spirit are also Intercessors for us.

NOAH AND THE ARK

This story of Noah in the Bible (Genesis 6-9) is mind-boggling to me. If it were not in the Bible I would have a hard time believing it. A boat being built by Noah and his three sons was 450 ft long, 75 ft. wide and 45 ft. high with three decks. Then he boarded 2 animals of all species and 7 of some special animals.

Jesus Christ believed this and referred to it, so I believe it too.

Genesis 6:5-8, The Lord saw how great man's wickedness on the earth had become, and every inclination of the thoughts of his heart was only evil all the time. The Lord was grieved that he had made man on the earth, and his heart was filled with pain. So the Lord said, "I will wipe mankind, whom I have created, from the face of the earth — men and animals, and creatures that move along the ground, and birds of the air for I am grieved that I have made them." But Noah found favor in the eyes of the Lord.

God, in His grace, gave the people on earth many years to repent of their evil ways while Noah built the ark. On the day of the flood, Noah, his wife, and his three sons and their wives entered the ark. No one else had the faith to get in. So, the floods came and all outside of the ark perished.

Today, God has warned of a coming judgment (read II Peter ch.3). He has made provision for our salvation. Our Ark is Jesus Christ and whoever is in Christ is saved.

It was not believing about the Ark that saved Noah, but getting into the Ark saved him. So, it is not just believing about Christ that saves you, but receiving Him as your Savior and Lord. So, get on board, there is room for you and your family. Don't miss the boat!

CHAPTER EIGHT

LAUGH A LOT

FAMILY LIFE: A SENSE OF HUMOR

One thing that God wants to bless all His children with is a sense of humor. Laughter is something that the Bible says is good for us. And there is no better place for humor than in the family. As parents we cannot take ourselves too seriously. We must be able to laugh at ourselves as well as at our children. And, let's face it, children can be funny. Yes, there are other times, but there are also times when you just have to have a good laugh.

Ecclesiastes 3:4 says there is 'a time to weep and a time to LAUGH. Some of our problems come when we don't know the difference — when to weep and when to laugh. But God says there is a time for everything. The Bible says that when God breaks us out of any captivity something joyful comes over us:
"When the Lord brought back the captives to Zion, we were like men who dreamed. Our mouths were filled with laughter, our tongues with songs of joy. . . The Lord has done great things for us, and we are filled with joy." Psalm 126: 2-3

Proverbs 1 5:13 says that "a happy heart makes the face cheerful.' And, "all the days of the oppressed are wretched, but the CHEERFUL heart has a continual feast' (Proverbs 15:15). Further, "a cheerful heart is good MEDICINE' (Proverbs 17:22). There is no doubt that we all need some good medicine from time to time. And God says that a cheerful heart is a good medicine for us. Dan Wolfe

Below are examples of content that makes me laugh. Perhaps it can do the same for you.

I HAVE LEARNED TO LAUGH A LOT

Proverbs 17:22, A merry heart does good like a medicine.
GIVE US A SENSE OF HUMOR, LORD
GIVE US THE GRACE TO SEE A JOKE,
TO GET SOME HUMOR OUT OF LIFE,
AND PASS IT ON TO OTHER FOLK.

On the church bulletin board: "Don't let worry kill you, let the church help."
The reason they have fences around cemeteries is because so many people are dying to get in.
When the bald man got a comb for his birthday, he said he would never part with it.

What went through the bumble bee's mind when it smacked into the car's windshield? It's rear end.

A bear without teeth is a gummy bear.

Do you know how many dead are in your cemetery? All of them.

Cross a canary with a lawnmower and you have shredded tweet.

Cross a rattlesnake with a horse and if it bites you, you can ride it to the hospital.

Cross a tiger with a parrot and I don't know what happens but when it talks everybody listens.

The cookie went to the doctor because it was feeling crummy.

Cross a cow and a duck you get milk with quackers.

Cross a duck with a lawnmower and get shredded quackers.
Applicant applying for a job was asked "Where did you get your training?" Answer: "At Yale." "Good, and what is your name?" "Yim Yohnson."

Confucius say: "One who eats many prunes, sits on pottie many moons.

A duck flying upside down "quacked up."

"Despair" is de tire you keep in da trunk of da car.

DEFINITIONS: Woodpecker = knocking bird
Earth's pull = grabity
Ex=Lax: chocolate candy bar with fluid drive.
Opposite of "hot dog" — "cool cat."

Difference between Bird Flu and Swine Flu: for bird flu you need "tweet-ment" for swine flu you need "oinkment."

He goes to see a psychologist and says "I can't make any friends, can you help me you fat slob?"

You know that you always put your left foot on last, don't you'?
The Sunday School teacher asking, after saying the ten commandments, "Is there a commandment that teaches you how to treat your brothers and sisters"? "Yes" said the boy, "thou shalt not kill."

What happened when the owl lost its voice? It didn't give a hoot.

WHY is it that doctors call what they do "practice?"

WHY is the man who invests all your money called “a broker?”
WHY isn’t there a mouse flavored cat food?
WHY do they sterilize the needle for lethal execution?
WHY if flying is safe they call the airport “the terminal?”

Seniors Hymns:
Blessed insurance
Just a slower walk with Thee
Give me the old-timers religion
Precious Lord, take my hand, help me up
Nobody knows the trouble I have seeing

If a turtle doesn’t have a shell, is it homeless or naked?
If a deaf child signs swear words, does the mother wash the hands with soap?
Would a fly without wings be called “a walk?”
Can vegetarians eat animal crackers?
What is a free gift? Aren’t all gifts free?

There’s a knock at the front door and a man open it and looks down to find a snail sitting on the stoop. He picks up the little snail and throws it as far as he can. Three years later, there’s a knock and the man opens the door, looks down and there sits the same snail. The snail looks up and says “What on earth was that about?”

Restaurant and waiters:
Customer: “What’s this fly doing in my soup? Waiter says, “the back stroke.”
Customer: “Why is my donut all smashed?” Waitress says, “you wanted a cup of coffee and a donut, and to step on it.”
Customer: “Why are you putting your thumb on my steak?” Waiter says, “I didn’t want to drop it again.”
Angry customer about his steak: “I said, well done.” Waiter, “thank you, sir, I seldom get a compliment.”

THE ECONOMY IS SO BAD:
CEO's are now playing miniature golf.
A truckload of Americans got caught sneaking into Mexico.
Motel 6 won't leave the light on.
The mafia is laying off judges
They can only afford to throw one shoe at the president.
The father tells his kids when the ice cream wagon plays the music it means it has no ice cream.
Shop lifters have stopped coming to the store.
The panhandler has to close his branch office.
They are cutting the pizza into six slices instead of twelve.

Teacher to student: "Sam, what is the outside of a tree called?" Sam "I don't know." Teacher: "Bark, Sam, bark." Sam, "Bow, wow, wow."
The pastor asked those with special needs to come forward to the front for prayer. Leroy joined the line and at his turn he was asked "what do you want me to pray about for you?" Leroy said, "Preacher, I need you to pray for help with my hearing." The pastor puts one finger in his ear and the other hand on the head and prayed fervently. The pastor than asked "how is your hearing now?" Leroy answered, "I don't know, it ain't 'till next week."

SLOGANS:
Radiator shop: "Best place in town to take a leak."
Veterinary's waiting room: "Be back in 5 minutes. Sit! Stay!
On maternity room door: "Push, push, push."

UNEMPLOYED BECAUSE:
Worked in an Orange Juice factory — got canned, couldn't concentrate
In Muffler Factory — too exhausting.
Shoe Factory — couldn't fit in.
As Historian — no future in it.
At Starbucks — same old grind.
Professional Fisherman — couldn't live on my net income.

ELDERLY PEOPLE ASK:
Why do banks charge a fee due to insufficient funds when they already know you are broke?
Why doesn't Tarzan have a beard?
Why does Superman stop bullets with his chest, but ducks when you throw a revolver at him?
If people evolved from apes, why are there still apes?
Why is it that no matter what color bubble bath you use, the bubbles are always white?
Why is it that whenever you attempt to catch something that is falling off the table, you always manage to throw something else over?
How come you never hear father-in-law jokes?

The statistics on sanity say that one out of every four persons is suffering from some sort of mental illness. Think of your three best friends. If they are ok, then it is you.

"If you add 5 q + 5 q, what do you get?" "10 q.". . . . . "You're welcome."
Business is so bad even the shoplifters stopped coming.

What do you get when you cross a duck with a firecracker? A firequacker.

Confucius says: "Crowded elevator smell different to midget."

Which month has 28 days? All

How many days in a week begin with "T"? 4

How many seconds in a year? - 12

Cross a godfather with an attorney and you get an offer you can't understand.

Ad in newspaper - Lost dog: left ear cut off, crippled right front leg, blind in left eye, bobbed tail, neutered by mistake, answers to the name "Lucky."

Escaped criminal photographed from four different angles and copies sent out. The ambitious sheriff of a small town sent in the report: "pictures received, all four men shot while resisting arrest."

Dad was so cheap he told his child that when the ice cream wagon rang its bell it means they were out of ice cream.

He said "Last night I got double rest. I dreamed I was sleeping."

"Doctor, I've broken my arm in two places." "Well don't go back there again."

The dentist of the year got a little plaque.

Do you know why I exercise and take vitamins every day? So I will look good when I am dead.

The economy is so bad in Iraq now, Iraqis can only afford to throw one shoe.

How can you drop an egg six feet without breaking it? By dropping it seven feet — it won't break for the first six.

Cross 50 German female pigs with 50 male deer and you get a hundred sows and bucks.

"I'd like a large pizza," said the customer. "Would you like me to cut it into six or 12 slices?" asked the waiter. "just six, please," responded the diner. . . . . . "I could never eat 12 slices."

Q: Why did the suggestible man stare at the frozen orange juice can for two hours? A: The label said, "Concentrate"

The father of the bride should realize he isn't losing a daughter but gaining a bathroom.

Grateful child: "I thank you from my bottom to my heart."

I read they now have a pill that is half aspirin and half glue. It's for people who get splitting headaches.

Italian boy volcano to the Italian girl volcano: Do you lava me like I lava you?"

Indian sending smoke signals and seeing the atomic mushroom explosion saying "I Wish I had said that!"

A joint checking account is never overdrawn by the wife; it is just under-deposited by the husband.

The low self esteem group will meet Thursday 7pm in the church basement. Please use the back door.

Newly recruited policeman was asked in an exam, "What would you do if you had to arrest your mother?" He said, "Call for back up."

Lady holding cookie above Fido's head: "Speak!" Dog: "What shall I say?"

You know what the Indian said when his dog fell over the cliff? "Dog-gone."

Man driving the wrong way on a one way street was stopped by a policeman, When asked where did he think he was going, answered, "I must be late, everybody is coming back."

What happens to ducks when they fly upside down is that they quack up.

If you put a family of ducks in a box, you get a box of quackers.

A blind man goes into the K-Mart with his seeing eye dog and takes his dog by the tail and swings him around over his head. When asked by the manager what he was doing he said, "Oh just looking around."

What did the boy octopus say to the girl octopus? I want to hold your hand, hand, hand, hand, hand, hand, hand.

A centenarian's advice on how to live to be a hundred: "Get to 99 and then be very, very careful."

<u>Top pick-up lines for singles</u>. . . . . 1. My prayer is answered. 2. Hi angel 3. How about coming over to my place for a little devotional? 4. I'm Episcopalian. What's your sign? 5. Read any good Bible passages lately? 6. You must be tired. Why? You've been running through my mind all the time.

"Pilot to tower, pilot to tower. Out of gas at 8000 feet, 30 miles over the Atlantic Ocean. Give instructions." "Tower to pilot, tower to pilot. Repeat after me: 'Our Father which art in heaven. . . .'"

A Sunday school teacher asked her class: "Who decreed that all the world should be taxed?" The little girls answered: "The Democrats."

What did the porcupine say to the cactus? "Is that you, mama?"

What did the nearsighted porcupine say when he backed into the cactus? "Pardon me, honey."

One prison inmate to another: "You know, we're very lucky." Second inmate: "Oh? Why's that?" First inmate: "How many people can say: "Just our being here makes the world a better place?"

How to catch a unique rabbit? Unique up on it. How to catch a tame rabbit? Tame way.

Why does the rabbit rest in the refrigerator? Because it's a westing house.

I haven't slept for ten days and I'm not even tired at all. . . . . I sleep nights.

I try to pay my taxes with a smile but they keep insisting on money.

Customer asking waitress why her donut was smashed. The waitress said you asked for coffee and a donut and to step on it.

Putting on weight is the penalty for exceeding the feed limit.

"I'll have to have a raise, sir, "said the young bookkeeper. "There are three companies after me." "What three?" demanded the boss. "Light, telephone, and water," was the reply.
Comment by fifth of eight speakers on a program:"I feel like an Egyptian mummy-pressed for time."

Manager: "Didn't you get my letter firing you?" Doris: "Yes, sir, but on the letter it said, 'Return in five days.'"
What did the hat say to the necktie? "You hang around while I go on a head."

"Aren't you the fellow who sold me this car a few weeks ago?" inquired a man who stopped at a used-car lot. "I sure am," said the smiling salesman. "Well, tell me about it again," said the buyer. "I get so discouraged!"

Hans and Fritz and their mama were mountain climbing. Hans fell off and Fritz said, "Look, Ma, no Hans."

"When I was a child," said Aunt Polly, "my mother told me that if I made ugly faces, I would stay like that." "Well," said little Adelaide, "you can't say you weren't warned."

Children asked by Sunday School teacher, "Where is God"? One said "In Heaven", but another said "In the bathroom. In the bathroom?, the teacher replied. How is that? The child responded that his father says so because he says every morning outside of the bathroom door, "My God, are you still in there?"

What's the difference between boogers and broccoli? The kids won't eat the broccoli.

Here's a thought: Had it been Wise Women instead of Wise Men, they'd asked for directions, arrived on time, helped deliver the Baby, cleaned the stable, made a casserole, and brought diapers and other practical gifts!

During a Bible study review one Sunday a teacher asked her class if anyone knew who the twin boys were in the Bible. "That's easy," Paul said, "First and Second Samuel." Any triplets in the Bible? 1, 2, 3rd John

Redneck church - People think rapture is when you lift something too heavy and the collection plates are really hub caps from a '56 Chevy.

Two elderly ladies in church service. One says to the other 'her butt is falling asleep'. The other said "I know, I heard is snoring 3 times."

A pastor bowed his head and solemnly said in church, "Let us pray for those who are sick of this congregation."

Why do we sing "A-men" instead of "A-women?" Because we sing hymns, not hers.

Some school children were discussing their parents' jobs in class. One new youngster said that he was the son of a pastor. Another youngster asked: What abomination do you belong to?

Woman went to the post office to buy stamps for her Christmas cards. The clerk asked "What denomination?" "Oh, good heavens! Has it come to this? Well, give me 50 Catholic and 50 Baptist ones."
The family seated in a restaurant had finished their dinners when Father called the waiter over. "Yes, sir?" said the waiter. "My son has left a lot of meat on his plate," explained Father. "Could you give me a bag so that I can take it home for the dog?" "Gosh, Dad!" exclaimed the excited boy. "Do we have a dog now?"

The Fayetteville couple were having a big fight. The woman shouted, "Aw, yew're so dumb yew think Barnum and Bailey are married to each other!" The husband said, "What difference does it make, long as they love each other."

The judge had just awarded a divorce to Lena, who had charged non - support. He said to Olie, "I have decided to give your wife $400 a month for support." "Well, dat's fine Judge," said Olie. "And vunce in a while I'll try to chip in a few bucks myself."

There was a pretty nurse named Carol who broke her engagement to a doctor. She was explaining everything to a friend. "Do you mean to say," exclaimed Cindy, "that the bum asked you to give back the ring AND all his presents?" "Not only that," said Carol, "he sent me a bill for 37 visits."

Papa ghost asked Mama ghost "What are we having for breakfast?" Mama: "Ghost toasties." Sister: "I want shrouded wheat." Brother: "How about 'grave nuts." They all sang "I ain't got no body."

"You know, dear," said the beleaguered husband, in an attempt to appease his bewildered wife, "I've been thinking over our argument and — well- I've decided to agree with you after all." "That won't help you a bit," she replied. "I've changed my mind."

The ship was sinking fast. The captain called out "Anyone here know how to pray." One man stepped forward and said, "I do, captain." The captain said, "Good, you pray. The rest of us will put on life preservers. We're one short."

Great religious truths — 1. Muslims do not recognize Judaism as a religion. 2. Jews do not recognize Jesus as the Messiah. 3. Protestants do not recognize the Pope as the leader of the Christian faith. 4. Baptists do not recognize each other at Hooters.
And, just a thought for all the women out there. . . . .MENtal illness, MENstrual cramps, MEN tal breakdown, MENopause. . . . . . .Ever notice now all of women's problems start with men?. . . . . .And when We have real trouble it's HISterectomy!!!

DAFFYNISHIONS
ILLEGAL- a sick eagle
PARADOX — two doctors
GRUESOME - a little bit taller

"He who hesitates is last"

He is so lazy he thinks manual labor is the President of Mexico.

Modern definition of outhouses — "The Unflushables."

What did one casket say to the other casket? Hey, is that you coffin?

If all the college students in America were laid end to end they would be more comfortable.

If all the automobiles in the United States were placed end to end it would be Sunday afternoon.

Creation - A man said to his wife one day, "I don't know how you can be so stupid and so beautiful all at the same time." The wife responded, "Allow me to explain." God made me beautiful so you would be attracted to me; God made me stupid so I would be attracted to you."

A preacher is buying a parrot. "Are you sure it doesn't scream, yell, or swear?" asked the preacher. "Oh absolutely. It's a religious parrot," the storekeeper assures him. "Do you see those strings on his legs? When you pull the right one, he recites the Lord's Prayer, and when you pull on the left he recites the 23rd Psalms." "Wonderful," says the preacher, "but what happens if you pull both strings?" "I fall off my perch, you idiot.", screeched the parrot.

A Texas GI, playing poker with some English soldiers, drew four aces. "One pound," ventured the Englishman on his right. "I don't know how you-all count your money," drawled the Texan, "but I'll raise you a ton." Pastor in Germany is called a German shepherd.

Knock, knock! Who's there? Old lady. Old lady who? I didn't know you could yodel!
He who laughs last is a slow thinker.

He who laughs, lasts.
Turtle found — dad says it is dead - children decide to gather around and have a funeral. In the middle of the service the turtle stuck his head out . . . . . . after hesitation about what to do, the boy says, "let's kill him and go on."

Two Roman galleys are lined up side by side for the start of the Emperor's annual race down the Tiber. One galley slave tums to another and says, "Let's win this one for the Whipper!"

Good news and bad news — Galley slave master in the AM makes an announcement: "For lunch, an extra ration of bread and wine. . . . . After lunch, the skipper wants to go Water skiing.

We all have our peculiarities: do you stir your cup with your right or left hand? I use a spoon.

Weight watchers will meet at 7PM at the F.P. Church. Please use the large double doors at the side entrance.

Worry does me good. 90% of the things I worry about never happen.

Angry Quaker wife to husband who was out too late and controlling her anger said: “When thou get home to thy kennel tonight, I hope thy mother bite thee.”

John was furious when his steak arrived too rare. “Waiter,” he shouted, “didn’t you hear me say ‘well-done?” “I can’t thank you enough, sir,” replied the waiter. “I hardly ever get a compliment.”

What’s red, sits in trees and says “meow, meow?” A crazy apple.

Cross an ant with a parrot and you get a walkie talkie.

What animal has two humps and is found at the North Pole? A lost camel.

During a chess convention at a local hotel, the manager became extremely annoyed when the conventioneers stood around the lobby, discussing the game and blocking the way. Finally ordering them to their rooms, he said, “If there’s one thing which makes me furious, it’s chess nuts boasting by an open foyer!”

Parents sent their son to college and spent $50,000 on his education and all they got was a quarterback.

A Dieter’s Prayer- The Lord is my shepherd, I shall not want; He maketh me to lie down on vinyl-covered gym mats. He leadeth me to flavored calorie-free waters; He restoreth my goals, He diverteth me from the path of midnight snacking for my health's sake. Yea, though I walk through the alley of Vendors of Pastry, I will fear no weevil; for thou art with me; My diet and exercises, they confort me. Thou preparest a table before me spread with veggies and low-fat protein; Thou steameth my fish in foil, My resolve runneth over. Surely, if I follow this living plan all the days of my life, My hips will be slim forever. Amen.

The snake got an extra job on rainy days. He was a Windshield viper.

A golfer having a bad day, on the last hole, went into a tantrum; he swore, broke his putter and said "I've got to give it up." "Give up golf?" asked the caddie. "No, "he said, "give up the ministry."

Unfortunately a man fell out of a plane. Fortunately there was a haystack below. Unfortunately there was a pitchfork in the haystack. Fortunately he missed the pitchfork. Unfortunately he missed the haystack.

A guy went to a full service gas station and asked for a dollars worth of gas. The gas attendant belched in his face.

SONGS OF THE OPEN ROAD
At 45 miles per hour, sing "Highways are Happy Ways."
At 55 miles per hour, sing "I'm But a Stranger Here. Heaven Is My Home."
At 65 miles per hour, sing "Nearer My God To Thee."
At 75 miles per hour sing, "When The Roll Is Called Up Yonder. I'll Be There."
At 85 miles per hour sing, "Lord I'm Coming Home."

What did the Martian say to the gas pump? "Take your finger out of your ear and listen to me."

Boss: "You're the laziest man I've ever seen. Don't you do anything quickly?" Clerk: "Yep, I get tired fast."

An Englishman went into a restaurant in a New England town and was served a delicacy unknown to him. When he asked the waiter what it was, the waiter replied, "It's bean soup, sir." Upon this the Englishman answered quite peeved, "I don't care what it's been, I want to know what it is now."

Prosecutor: "Now tell the court how you came to take the car." Defendant: "Well, the car was parked in front of the cemetery so naturally I thought the owner was dead.

The best way to double your money is to fold it.

Son knocks over the out- house. The father asks the son if he did it - son says" yes" and gets a spanking. The son then refers to George Washington who told the truth about chopping down the cherry tree and not being punished for telling the truth. The father says, "But George Washington's father was not up in the cherry tree."

Two morons were building a house. One, examining each nail as he picked it up, threw away about half of them. The other asked, "What's the matter?" First Moron—About half of them have heads on the wrong end. Second Moron — You fool, those are for the other side of the house.

"What is your age?" asked the Magistrate. "Remember," he cautioned, "you are under oath." "Twenty-one and some months," the woman answered. "How many months?" "One hundred and eight."

Man calling on telephone: "Hello Bill, this is Joe." "Louder. I can't hear you." "Joe! J as in John, O as in Otto, E as in Eddie." "You must have the wrong number, I don't know any of those fellows."

Husband: "I hate to mention this my dear, but you are getting fat." Wife: "Well, aren't you the lucky one. Remember you once told me I was worth my weight in gold."

When my grandson Billy and I entered our vacation cabin, we kept the lights off until we were inside to keep from attracting pesky insects. Still, a few fireflies followed us in. Noticing them before I did, Billy whispered, "It's no use, Grandpa. The mosquitoes are coming after us with flashlights."

My wife walked into the den and asked "What's on the TV?" I replied "Dust." And that's how the fight started. . . .

The thief broke into the store and stole everything but two boxes of soap. The dirty crook!

Wanted: Human cannonball. . . . . . . Must be willing to travel.

I'm not old, I'm chronologically gifted.

The snap, crackle, pop in the morning aren't my freaking rice crispies.

'When I was younger, all I wanted was a BMW. Now, I don't care about the W.

I'm so old that whenever I eat out, they ask me for my money up front.

Higher Education

A dog is so smart that his master decides to send him to college. Home for vacation, his master asks him how college is going. "Well," says the dog, "I'm not doing too great in science and math, but I have made a lot of progress in foreign languages." "Really!" says the master. "Say something in a foreign language." The dog says "Meow!"

Foreign Language

A mother mouse and a baby mouse are walking along, when all of a sudden, a cat attacks them. The mother mouse goes, "Bark!" and the cat runs away. "See?" says the mother mouse to her baby. "Now do you see why it's important to learn a foreign language?"

Paddy was in New York. He was patiently waiting and watching the traffic cop on a busy street crossing. The cop stopped the flow of traffic and shouted, "Okay, pedestrians." Then he'd allow the traffic to pass. He'd done this several times, and Paddy still stood on the sidewalk. After the cop had shouted, "Pedestrians!" for the tenth time, Paddy went over to him and said, "Is it not about time ye let the Catholics across?"

Life After Death

"Do you believe in life after death?" the boss asked one of his employees. "Yes, Sir." the employee replied. "Well, then, that makes everything just fine," the boss went on. "After you left early yesterday to go to your grandmother's funeral, she stopped in to see you."

Rude Parrot

A lady was walking down the street to work and she saw a parrot on a perch in front of a pet store. The parrot said to her, "Hey lady, you are really ugly." Well, the lady was furious! She stormed past the store to her work. On the way home she saw the same parrot and it said to her, "Hey lady, you are really ugly." She was incredibly upset now. The next day the same parrot again said to her, "Hey lady, you are really ugly." The lady was so upset that she went into the store and said that she would sue the store and kill the bird. The store manager replied, "That's not good," and promised he wouldn't say it again. When the lady walked past the store that day after work the parrot called to her, "Hey lady." She paused and said, "Yes?" The bird said, "You know."

Six guys were playing poker when Smith loses $500 on a single hand, clutches his chest and drops dead at the table. Showing respect for their fallen comrade, the other five complete their playing time standing up. After

the game Mr. Roberts looks around and asks, "Now, who is going to tell the Wife?" They draw straws. Rippington, who is always a loser, picks the short one. They tell him to be discreet, be gentle, don't make a bad situation any worse than it is. Rippington says, "Gentlemen! Discreet? I'm the most discreet man you will ever meet. Discretion is my middle name, leave it to me." Rippington walks over to the Smith house, knocks on the door, the wife answers, asks what he wants. Rippington says, "Your husband just lost $500 playing cards." She hollers, "TELL HIM TO DROP DEAD!"
Rippington says, "I'll tell him."

The Bathtub Test

During a visit to the mental institution, a visitor asked the Director how do you determine whether or not a patient should be institutionalized. 'Well,' said the Director, 'we fill up a bathtub, then we offer a teaspoon, a teacup and a bucket to the patient and ask him or her to empty the bathtub.' 'Oh, I understand,' said the visitor. 'A normal person would use the bucket because it's bigger than the spoon or the teacup. . .' 'No.' said the Director, 'A normal person would pull the plug. Do you want a bed near the window?'

Lawyer: Now would you please tell the jury the truth. Why did you shoot your husband with a bow and arrow? Defendant: "I didn't want to wake up the children."

Dumb Sky Diver

An idiot was taking sky-diving lessons. The instructor explained that it was time for his first jump, and all he had to do was jump from the plane, count to six, and pull the rip cord. A truck would be waiting for him in the field where he would land. The man jumped from the plane when he was told to, and counted to six.When he pulled the rip cord, the parachute wouldn't open. He tried the reserve chute and that didn't open. Frustrated, he muttered to himself as he fell, "I bet the truck won't be waiting for me either."

BAKED STUFFED CHICKEN

6-7 lb. baking chicken
1 cup melted butter
I cup stuffing (Pepperidge Farm is good)
I cup uncooked popcorn (ORVILLE REDENBACHERS LOW FAT)
Salt/pepper to taste
Preheat oven to 350 degrees. Brush chicken well with melted butter, salt, and pepper. Fill cavity with stuffing and popcorn. Place baking pan with the neck end toward the back of the oven. Listen for the popping sounds. When the chicken's behind blows the oven door open and the chicken flies across the room, it is done. . . . . And you thought I couldn't cook.

God Loves Drunks Too!

A man and his wife were awakened at 3:00am by a loud pounding on the door. The man gets up and goes to the door where a drunken stranger, standing in the pouring rain, is asking for a push. "Not a chance," says the husband, "it is 3:00 in the morning!" He slams the door and returns to bed. "Who was that?" asked his wife. "Just some drunk guy asking for a push," he answers. "Did you help him?" she asks. "No, I did not, it's 3am in the morning and it's pouring rain out there!" "Well, you have a short memory," says his wife. "Can't you remember about three months ago when our car broke down, and those two guys helped us? I think you should help him, and you should be ashamed of yourself! "God loves drunk people too you know." The man does as he is told, gets dressed, and goes out into the pounding rain. He calls out into the dark, "Hello, are you still there?" "Yes," comes back the answer. "Did you still need a push?" calls out the husband. "Yes, please!" (the reply from the dark) "Where are you?" asks the husband. The drunk says: "Over here on the swing."

What's the difference between a sewing machine and a kiss? One sews nice, the other seems so nice.

A baker should stop making donuts when he gets tired of the hole business.

Some tortures are physical and some are mental, but one that's both is dental.

<u>Children's definition of love:</u>

Love is when you go out to eat and give somebody most of your French Fries without making them give you any of theirs. Chrissy — age 6

Love is when my mommy makes coffee for my daddy and she takes a sip before giving it to him, to make sure it is OK. Danny — age 7

If you want to learn to love better, you should start with a friend who you hate. Nikka - age 6

Love is when Mommy gives Daddy the last piece of chicken. Elaine — age 5

Love is when Mommy sees Daddy smelly and sweaty and still says he is handsomer than Brad Pitt. Chris age 7

I know my older sister loves me because she gives me all her old clothes and has to go out and buy new ones. Lauren — age 4.

Dear God: In Sunday school they told us what You do. Who does it when You are on vacation? Jane

Dear God: I read the Bible. What does beget mean? Nobody will tell me. Love, Alison

Dear God: Are you really invisible or is that just a trick? Lucy

Dear God: Is it true my father won't get in Heaven if he uses his bowling words in the house? Anita

Dear God: Did you mean for the giraffe to look like that or was it an accident? Norma

Dear God: Instead of letting people die and having to make new ones, why don't You just keep the ones You have now? Jane

Dear God: Who draws the lines around the countries? Nan

Dear God: I went to this wedding and they kissed right in church. Is that okay? Neil

Dear God: What does it mean You are a Jealous God? I thought You had everything. Jane

Dear God: Did you really mean "do unto others as they do unto you"? Because if you did, then I'm going to fix my brothers. Darla

Dear God: Thank you for the baby brother, but what I prayed for was a puppy. Joyce

Dear God: Why is Sunday School on Sunday? I thought it was supposed to be our day of rest. Tom

Dear God: Please send me a pony. I never asked for anything before, You can look it up. Bruce

Dear God: My brother is a rat. You should give him a tail. Ha ha. Danny

Dear God: Maybe Cain and Abel would not kill each other so much if they had their own rooms. It works with my brother. Larry

Dear God: I want to be just like my Daddy when I get big but not with so much hair all over. Sam

Dear God: You don't have to worry about me. I always look both ways. Dean

Dear God: I think about You sometimes even when I'm not praying. Elliott

Dear God: I bet it is very hard for You to love all of everybody in the whole world. There are only 4 people in our family and I can never do it. Nan

Dear God: Of all the people who work for You, I like Noah and David the best. Rob

Dear God: My brother told me about being born but it doesn't sound right. They're just kidding, aren't they? Marsha

Dear God: If You watch me in church Sunday, I'll show You my new shoes. Mickey

Dear God: I would like to live 900 years like the guy in the Bible. Love, Chris

Dear God: We read Thomas Edison made light. But in school they said You did it. So I bet he stole your idea. Sincerely, Donna

Dear God: The bad people laughed at Noah — "You made an ark on dry land, you fool." But he was smart, he stuck with You. That's what I would do. Essie

<u>Grandma's Letter</u>

She is eighty-eight years old and still drives her own car. She writes:

Dear Grand-daughter:

The other day I went up to our local Christian book store and saw a "Honk if you love Jesus" bumper sticker. I was feeling particularly sassy that day because I had just come from a thrilling choir performance, followed by a thunderous prayer meeting. So, I bought the sticker and put it on my bumper.

Boy, am I glad I did, what an uplifting experience that followed. I was stopped at a red light at a busy intersection, just lost in thought about the Lord and how good He is, and I didn't notice that the light had changed. It is a good thing someone else loves Jesus because if he hadn't honked, I'd never have noticed. I found that lots of people love Jesus. While I was sitting there, the guy behind started honking like crazy, and then he leaned out of his window and screamed,
"For the love of God! Go! Go! Go!, Jesus Christ, Go! What an exuberant cheerleader he was for Jesus!
Everyone started honking! I just leaned out my window and started waving and smiling at all those loving people. I even honked my horn a few times to share in the love. There must have been a man from Florida back there because I heard him yelling something about a sunny beach. I saw another guy waving in a funny way with only his middle finger stuck up in the air. I asked my young teenage grandson in the back seat what that meant. He said it was probably a Hawaiian good luck sign or something. Well, I have never met anyone from Hawaii, so I leaned out the window and gave him the good luck sign right back. My grandson burst out laughing. Why even he was enjoying this religious experience. A couple of the people were so caught up in the joy of the moment that they got out of their cars and started walking towards me. I bet they wanted to pray or ask what church I attended, but this is when I noticed the light had changed. So, I waved at all my brothers and sisters grinning, and drove on through the intersection. I noticed

that I was the only car that got through the intersection before the light changed again and felt kind of sad that I had to leave them after all the love we had shared. So I slowed the car down, leaned out the window and gave them all the Hawaiian good luck sign one last time as I drove away. Praise the Lord for such wonderful folks!
Will write again soon, Love, Grandma

NEVER GOT A DINNER:

Adam, the first man, when Eve asked him if he loved her said "who else?" — Never got a dinner. "

Noah, the greatest financier in the Bible, who floated his stock when the whole world was in liquidation, - never got a dinner.

Moses, when he went to the Red Sea, said, "I was only going for a dip; I didn't expect this." - Never got a dinner.
Abraham Lincoln who said "a house divided, is not a house but a condominium, - never got a dinner.

Benjamin Franklin who said "the best way to double your money is to fold it, - never got a dinner.

Captain John Paul Jones, when he was going down with his sinking ship said, "why do I have to be Captain," - never got a dinner.

David, the first insurance agent in the Bible who gave the giant a piece of the rock, - never got a dinner.

The Martian who landed from outer space said to the gasoline pump, "Take your finger out of your ear and listen to me," - never got a dinner.

Most of us have now learned to live with voice mail as a necessary part of our lives. Have you ever wondered what it would be like if God decided to install voice mail? Imagine praying and hearing the following: Thank you for calling heaven: For English press 1. For Spanish press 2. For other languages press 3. Please select from one of the following options: Press 1 for request. Press 2 for complaints. Press 3 for all others.

I am sorry, all our angels and saints are busy helping other sinners now. However, your prayer is important to us and we will answer it in the order it was received. Please stay on the line.

If you would like to speak to God, press 1. Jesus, press 2. Holy Spirit, press 3. To find a loved one who has been assigned to heaven, press 5, then enter the social security number followed by the # sign. If you receive a negative response, please hang up and dial code 666. For reservations to heaven, please enter JOHN followed by 316. Our computers show that you have already been prayed for today, please hang up and call again tomorrow. The office is now closed for the weekend to observe a religious holiday. If you are calling after hours and need emergency assistance, please contact your local pastor.
Thank you and have a heavenly day.

THE ASSYRIAN AMBASSADOR

Ladies and gentlemen, I am the Assyrian Ambassador who come from Iraq to America to talk about the restaurants. Excuse my broken English. As I look at your radiator faces, I am about to undress you on this subject.

You know, I got a restaurant in Iraq; it is called "Parkyourcarcas #1." It is number one because it is the only one.

We have got a nice menu with good deserts. We got two kind of mimps pie: mimps and peppermimps; two kinds of apple pie: apple and pine-apple; two kinds of cake: chocolate cake and stomach ache.

But when you come to my restaurant, don't make a mistake and go across the street. They have a place called the Greasy Spoon. It is not like my place. They got flies all over the tables. But not at my place. I got a special table for the flies. My place is one restaurant where you can eat dirt cheap.

One ting I got which is only at my place. I got a special reducing menu. Here it is:

Breakfast:
1/2 peeled grape (save skin for lunch)
One cornflake dipped in milkweed juice
1/2 teaspoon of crumbs shaken out of toaster

Lunch:
Two pickle pimples (dill or sweet)
One finely chopped chicken ear
One medium-sized goldfish fin
One blanched grape leaf

Supper:
Three frog warts
Prime rib of guppy
One baked sesame seed
Stewed stains from the cook's apron

One fellow tried it faithfully and completely disappeared in two months.

I think I will disappear now, too.

Thank you, and God bless America and Iraq
FINALLY; How to make it to 100 years old. Go to 99 and be very careful! Or, have a lot of birthdays!

CHAPTER TEN

MY PRAYER LIFE

For many years, since 1982, I have had the privilege of being the Regional Representative of Intercessors For America, an organization encouraging and equipping believers to intercede for America, with prayer and fasting.

I faithfully spend one to two hours each morning before breakfast, five days a week, along with my physical work-out schedule. I also listen to recorded Christian music during this time. On Saturday I have an intercessory prayer group meeting in our Riverside Church from 9:00 - 10:00 am. On Sunday, I count my time in church as my devotional time. I also pray with people in the church service who Come forward for prayer.

I am a prayer warrior. I have a SLDC degree (short legged demon chaser).

Over my lifetime I have used and encountered all types of prayer plans. Each one had its own benefits and drawbacks. Today, the prayer model I use is by all means not mandatory for you, but it has worked well for me.

As you apply this prayer model to your own life, you may decide to make adjustments and modifications. However, what I share here is the model I have now used for some years, and more importantly,

I believe this is the biblical model that flows out of the **Lord's Model Prayer.**

<u>Not</u> the Lord's Prayer

Notice that I wrote that this is the "Lord's Model Prayer," and not "The Lord's Prayer." Some call the Lord's Prayer the one that begins in God's Word with the statement, "Our Father which art in heaven."

Friend, I am now going to make an extremely controversial statement: What we call "The Lord's Prayer" is not THE Lord's Prayer!

Jesus did not pray that prayer because He did not need to pray that way. When His disciples asked Jesus to "teach us to pray," He essentially replied, "Pray like this." What He then taught them was what I call "Our Model Prayer." The prayer of Jesus (the real Lord's Prayer) is contained in John 17, which I have included later In the book.

The Model Prayer

For simplicity of terms here, I will call the prayer that Jesus taught **<u>us</u>** to pray "the Model Prayer," or, as some call it, "the Disciples' Prayer" because it was the pattern that Jesus gave for us to pray. This misnamed prayer is well known to almost every Christian in the world, and it goes as follows:

***Our Father which art in heaven, hallowed be Thy name. Thy Kingdom come, Thy will be done on earth as it is in heaven. Give us this day our daily bread, and forgive us our debts as we forgive our debtors. And lead us not into temptation, but deliver us from evil. For Thine is the Kingdom, and the power, and the glory,forever.* Amen.**

As we look at this Model Prayer, there are certain absolute prayer lessons we can learn:

Start With Praise

The model prayer consists of starting out with praise and honoring God. "Our Father which art in heaven, hallowed be Thy Name." In other words, when we pray, the first thing we should declare is, "Lord, we reverence and honor Your name."

His name is Jehovah, but He also is known as Abba Father. He is known as "I Am the I **Am."** Moses said,

"Who shall I say has sent me?" He said, "Tell them it is I Am that I Am**."**

And so, as you start your prayer, spend some time honoring His numerous names. If you cannot remember any of His names, just go through the alphabet and some of these names should pop back into your mind.

Abiding Presence,
Almighty Father,
Blessed One,
Great Creator,
Our Deliverer,
Everlasting Father,
Eternal God,
Faithful God,
Gracious God,
Healer of every disease,
Master Lord,
Peace in the Storm,
Provider of all,
My Righteousness,
Sanctifier of my life,
Shepherd of my life,
Supplier of our needs.

Call Him by His names. "Hallowed be Your name." Then go to the name of Jesus; go to the name of the Holy Spirit. In my prayer I say:

Oh, Holy Spirit, I am so thankful You are in me. I thank Your Holy Spirit for the fruit. I thank You for Your gifts. I bless Your name.

Start out with praise as the model indicates, and give glory to His name: "Hallowed be Your name."

Since Psalm 68:4 in the NKJV says "extol Him who rides on the clouds, by his name YAH, and rejoice before Him," I use His name and pray praising Him with the following list of words, using a different letter of the alphabet each day.

YAHWEH, YOU ARE:

ADMIRABLE, AFFECTIONATE, ALL IN ALL, ADVOCATE, ALMIGHTY, ANSWER, A-OK, ARK, AWESOME, ASTRONOMICAL, ATONEMENT, ATTRACTIVE, AUTHORITY, ADMINISTRATOR, AFFLUENT, ADORABLE, AUTHOR OF LIFE

BALM, BEAUTIFUL, BEST, BLESSER, BOSS, BOUNTEOUS, BRILLIANT, BULWORK, BUOY

CREATOR, COMFORT, CHIEF, CAPTAIN, CARE GIVER, CARETAKER, CAUSE, CHASTISER, CHEER, CHOICE, CHRIST, CEO, COMMANDER, COMPASSION, CONDUCTOR, CONGENIAL, CONSTANT, CONSISTANT, CONSULTANT, CONTROL, CONVERTER, CONVICTOR, COUNSELOR, COURAGE, COVER, CURE, COMING KING

DELIVERER, DEITY, DELIGHTFUL, DOCTOR, DESIGNER, DEVELOPER, DISCIPLER, DIVINE, DOMINION, DOOR, DURABLE, DYNAMIC

ETERNAL, EVERLASTING, ECSTASY, ECUMENICAL, EFFECTIVE, EFFICIENT, ELECTOR, EMINENT, EMPATHIC, EMPOWER, ENABLER, ENCOURAGER, ENERGIZER, ENLARGER, ENJOYABLE, ENORMOUS, ENOUGH, ESTABLISHER, EXALTER, EXCELLENT, EXHILERATING, EXPEDITER, EXPERT, EXTRA, EVERYTHING I NEED

FAITHFUL, FIRST, FIXER, FORCE, FORTRESS, FAITH, FRIEND, FULLNESS, FUN, FUND, FATHER

GOD, GOOD, GRACE, GREAT, GLORIOUS, GIVER, GENERATOR, GENTLE, GORGEOUS, GRAND, GRATIFYING, GUARDIAN, GUIDE

HEAVENLY FATHER, HELPER, HOLY, HAPPINESS, HARBOR, HEALTH, HEALER, HERO, HIGHRISE, HIGHWAY, HOLD, HOPE, HOST

IMMORTAL, INVISIBLE, INSCRUTIBLE, IDEAL, IDENTITY, ILLUMINATION, I AM, IMPORTANT, IN, INCARNATE, INCOMPARABLE, INDISPENABLE, INFALLIBLE, INFINITE, INSPIRATIONAL, INTEGRITY, INTELLIGENCE, INTERESTING, INVALUABLE, INVIGORATING, IRREFUTABLE, IT, INHERITANCE

JEHOVAH JIREH, JESUS, JOY, JEWEL, JUDGE, JUST

KING, KIND, KEEPER, KEY, KEYSTONE

LORD, LOVE, LIVING, LEADER, LIBERAL, LIBERTY, LIFE, LIFTER, LONGSUFFERING, LOVER

NEAR, NEAT, NECESSARY, NEEDED, NEEDFUL, NEVER FAILING, NICE, NIFTY, NOBLE, NONE LIKE YOU, NOTABLE, NUMBER ONE

OMNIPOTENT, OMNISCIENT, OMNIPRESENT, OK, ORDERLY, OUTSTANDING, OVERALL

PARDON, PARTNER, PATIENT, PEACE, PERFECT, PERPETUAL, PILOT, PLEASING, PLEASURABLE, PASSION, POSSIBILITY, POTTER, POWER, PRAISEWORTHY, PRAYER ANSWERER, PRESENT, PREDESTINATOR, PROMISE KEEPER, PRICELESS, PRIME, PROBLEM SOLVER, PROFOUND, PROMOTER, PROSPERITY, PROVIDENCE, PROVIDER, PUNISHER, PURGER, PURPOSE, PROTECTOR

QUALITY, QUALIFIER, QUESTION ANSWERER, QUICK, QUEST, QUIETUDE

RECOVERER, RECTIFIER, REDEEMER, REFUGE, REIGN, REJUVENATOR, RELIABLE, RELIGION, RELATIONSHIP, REMARKABLE, REMEDY, REPOSE, RESCUER, RESOURCE, RESPONDER, REST, RESTORER, RESURRECTION, REVIVER, REWARDER, RIGHT, RIGHTEOUS, ROCK

SABBATH, SACRIFICE, SAFETY, SAFEKEEPER, SALVATION, SAVIOR, SANCTIFIER, SANCTUARY, SATISFYER, SPIRIT, SPECIAL, STRENGTH, SUFFICIENT, SUPREME, SYMPATHETIC, SWEET, SUPER

TEACHER, TENDERHEARTED, TRUTH, TIMELESS, TOPS, TRANQUILIZER, TRANSPORTATION, TRANSMITTER, TREAT, TREMENDOUS, TRUIMPH, TRUIMPHANT, TROUBLE SHOOTER, TRUE, TRUST

ULTIMATE, ULTRA, UNDEFEATED, UNDERSTANDING, UPPER TAKER, UNITY, UNIFYING, UNIVERSAL, UNIQUE, UNPARALLELED, UPLIFTING

VALUABLE, VERITY, VICTOR, VICTORIOUS, VIRTUE, VITAL

WAY, WEALTH, WILLING, WINNER, WISE, WITH US, WITHIN, WONDERFUL, WOW, WORSHIPFUL, WORTHY

XTRA, XCELLENT, XTRAVAGENT, X RAY EYES, XALTED, XCITING, XHILARATING, XQUISITE

YEA, YES, YIELDED TO, YOKED WITH, MY YOUTH

ZEAL, ZEALOUS, ZENITH, ZEST, ZIPPY

Affirm His Kingdom

The next line declares, "Thy Kingdom come, Thy will be done." This too is to put us into the praise mode. When those words were first prayed, it was a request, and it became fact: the Kingdom has now come! Do you know that in your spirit?

His Kingdom has come, and will is being done on the Earth!

When you pray for God's Kingdom to come, you are praying for His rule in your life.

Jesus spoke of the Kingdom when He first came on the Earth. John said, "Repent, the Kingdom of God is at hand". . . it is close. You know the Kingdom is close when it is at hand. Then He added, "The Kingdom of God is within you." So the Kingdom came, and it now dwells in you and me. When you let Jesus come into your life, that is when the Kingdom came into your life.

There are hundreds of millions of people who have Jesus in their lives, and those people collectively comprise His Kingdom. When you let Him rule in your life, and you join hundreds of millions of believers who have Christ rule in their lives, that becomes a pretty good-sized Kingdom.

His Kingdom has come!

So at this point in my prayer I declare: *Lord, I thank You that Your Kingdom has come. I thank You, Lord, that Your Kingdom is in me. Lord, Your Kingdom is growing.*

Do you know there are millions and millions of people getting saved every month in the world? His Kingdom is coming into more and more places, and more and more hearts. So I say: Lord, I thank You that Your Kingdom has come. I thank You, Lord, that Your will is being done throughout the world.

Is the Lord's will being done in your life? His will is being done in hundreds of millions of lives, and His will is being done on earth as it is in heaven. Then I add: But, Lord, I thank You that when You come again, it will culminate. You will then have Your Kingdom full. You will fully be ruling over Your Kingdom on the Earth.

In that mode of praising the Lord that His Kingdom has come, and His will is being done, I additionally say this:

Lord, I thank You that Your will is being done in my life.

You know how I know His will is being done in my life, and how you can know the same?

Number one: I asked Him.

Number two: I am not doing anything to hinder it. I want it. I am not living in sin to hinder His will. So I say:

Thank You, Lord, Your will is being done 1n my life.

I have prayed for my family in the past, and I have made certain requests, so now I say:

Thank You, Lord, that Your will is being done in my family, with my wife, and with my children. I praise You that Your will is being done. And I thank You that Your will is being done with my relatives. I thank You, Lord, that Your will is being done with my entire church family.

How do I know it is being done?

Because I asked.

It says in the Bible that if you ask anything that is according to His will, He will do it. So I know to ask for His will to be done, and if it is according to His will, He is doing it. So I pray:

Notice that we are still in the praise mode with thanks. This pleases God, and it does us some good as well.

Praise and thanksgiving produce power. There is power in praise. We are talking about prayer power, and there is praise power. If you have put that into your prayer, there is power in praise.

Give thanks that His Kingdom has come and His will is being done.

Share Your Needs

Now it is time to say something about your needs. "Give us this day our daily bread." In that context, I pray:

Thank You, Lord, that You are providing for my daily needs.

I put my needs into the "thank" mode. I say:

Thank You, Lord, that day by day You are meeting my needs.

How do I know that?

Because I have prayed it. Now, I can pray it again if I want to, but I would rather put it into praise and thanksgiving mode. You know, you will receive the things of God as you approach His throne with thanks and praise.

Thank and Confess

The next line is, "Forgive us our debts," or trespasses, or sins, "as we forgive those who sin against us." In this part of the prayer I say: Thank You, Lord, for forgiving my sins.

I am still in the thanks mode. I thank You, Lord, for the blood of Jesus; I thank You, Lord, that my sins are all forgiven.

Now, if the Holy Spirit convicts me of some sin in my life, I confess it here. Did you know a Christian - one who has been born again is never asked in the New Testament to pray for the forgiveness of your sins?

You may not have noticed that as you read the New Testament. But think about it. Have you ever seen it in the New Testament?

God's Word never says to ask for the forgiveness of sins!

Why? Because your sins have already been forgiven!

Why are you asking for something that you have been already granted? You have been forgiven, so thank Him for it.

You might ask, "But Brother John, what about when I slip and sin?"

That is covered by confession. If we confess our sins, He is faithful and just to forgive them! You do not have to ask and ask and ask for forgiveness with each sin. Instead, Jesus essentially tells us, "Confess your sins and you are forgiven."

So I thank the Lord, and if He shows me any sin in my life, I will confess that sin and thank Him some more. I mean, if there is something I have to confess, I will confess it on the spot. I do not like to wait five minutes, or even a single minute. I do not want to wait until the end of the day and say, "Let's see, what did I do during this day?" By then I would have forgotten, anyhow, unless it was a big, bad sin.

In the thank mode I say: *I thank You, Lord, for forgiving me of my sins, and I thank You, Lord, for giving me the grace* to *forgive others.*

Forgive is what He does.

The model is, "Forgive our debts as we forgive those," so I say: Thank You, Lord, for Your grace that enables me to forgive. It is Your grace that enables me to forgive anybody, because I cannot do it by my own grace.

In my flesh, I am a vengeful type of person. When I was unsaved, if you crossed me, you were in deep trouble. I was looking out for a way to get even with you. That is the way we did things in Chicago. If I was not saved, I would probably be a mobster, and probably be dead too.

Thank Jesus we never remain the same when He enters into and takes over our lives.

Thank Him for the grace He gives you to forgive. Thank Him for the times when you can say: "1 cannot think of anyone to forgive, I cannot think of anyone I am holding anything against."

This process builds up my faith and helps me get spiritually charged.

It helps me; it could help you.

Do Not Enter Temptation

"Lead us not into temptation" is a wrong statement.

Why are you asking God not to lead you into temptation? Since when is God going to lead His children into temptation? Did that contradiction ever cross your mind? People who pray that are saying, "Lead us not into temptation."

The Aramaic translation, in the Assyrian language that Jesus spoke, which is the language of Jesus, is translated into English this way: "Do not let us enter temptation." (The Holy Bible from ancient Eastern Manuscripts)

That is considerably different than, "Lead us not into temptation."

It is literally saying, do not let us enter. So I pray:

Thank You, Lord, for not letting me enter into temptation.

I tell you, it has been amazing how that prayer has reduced more and more the temptations in my life. I realize that I am not tempted as much as I used to be when I started praying:

Thank You, Lord for not letting me enter temptation.

Please understand, **temptation by itself is not a sin.**

Temptation only turns to sin when you yield to the temptation. But, I do not want to even enter into temptation, so I say, "Thank You, Lord, for not letting me enter temptation."

Preserve Me From Evil

For the phrase "Deliver us from evil" I pray:

Thank You, Lord, for delivering me from evil, and the Evil One.

That evil means the Evil One, the devil. So I add:

Thank You, Lord, for delivering me from evil and the Evil One, the devil.

I am making these terms turn into praise and thanks.

Begin and End With Praise

Notice how the Lord's Model Prayer ends: "For Thine is the Kingdom and power and glory forever."

The Lord's Model Payer begins with praise, "Hallowed be Your name," and ends with praise. So when I come to that part of my prayer, I say:

Thank You, Lord, Yours is the Kingdom, and the power, and the glory.

Then I start praying in the Holy Spirit. I say: Lord, I thank You for Your Holy Spirit and the gift of Your Holy Spirit of tongues, the unknown language.

Then I add: *Lord, in case I have missed anything, I want* to *intercede, I want* to *praise, I want* to *make requests, I want* to *express my needs, I want* to *express my desires in the heavenly language.*

Then I go into the heavenly language to end my praying. This is devotional prayer. The Apostle Paul, in Ephesians 6:18 when he was talking about praying, said: *Pray in the Spirit on all occasions, with all kinds of prayers.*

Pray in the Spirit. . . that means in the Holy Spirit. Praying in the Holy Spirit means you are praying in tongues.

If you pray this way, you will be spiritually charged!

Now look carefully at I Corinthians 14:2

For anyone who speaks in a tongue does not speak to *men, but* to *God.*

This Scripture is speaking about what I call a devotional tongue. This is not a tongue to be spoken in church, which is a tongue that needs interpretation. This is a devotional tongue because it says you are not speaking to men, or to people, but to God.

Look at verse 4: He who speaks in a tongue edifies himself.

"Edify" means "to build up, to get strengthened."

One of the great ways to be spiritually charged is to pray in tongues. That is what it declares in verse **4.** Praying in tongues edifies, or builds himself up!

Some stiff-necked people say, "I do not need to speak in tongues." You do not need to be built up? You do not need to be strengthened?

But I do understand where they are coming from in their thinking because there were years when I was a Baptist and I hated tongues. I did not like tongues, did not believe in tongues, and even thought that tongues were of the devil. But today I am so thankful that I was cracked enough that a little light came in and now I love tongues. I thank the Lord for tongues. I thank the Lord for the language of the Holy Spirit.

I pray in tongues, and in that, I am experiencing what Romans 8:26 says. You see, I do not always know everything to pray about, and when I am not sure if I am praying properly for all of the issues, or even if I mention everything I can think of, I still pray in tongues according to Romans 8:26**:** *In the same way, the Spirit helps us in our weakness. We do not know what we ought to pray for, but the Spirit himself intercedes for us with groans that words cannot express.*

Do you see it?

We do not always know how to pray, so the Spirit Himself intercedes through us and for us. Imagine - the Holy Spirit Himself is interceding on our behalf! That is through tongues; it is the gift of the Holy Spirit.

Notice that the Scripture describes praying with groans. If you cannot speak in tongues, why not just try groaning? Or, do not you believe in what the Bible says? I am talking to those who are too closed to go in the Spirit in prayer.

If that is you, why not groan? Believe me, some people do.

Sometimes there are times during the day when you do not know what to say, but all you do is sigh or groan. That is the Holy Spirit too. With groans He helps us.

God is kind and gracious and good to help us in our prayer lives. I love tongues because it is so easy. I do not have to use my brain; it allows my brain to relax. And, it is the perfect prayer because of the Holy Spirit.

CONCLUSION

MY LIFE VERSES

I Samuel 12:24 — Only fear the Lord and serve Him truth with all your heart; for consider What great things He has done for you.

Psalm 112:1-3 - Blessed is the man who fears the Lord, who delights greatly in His commandments. His descendents will he mighty on earth; the generation of the upright will be blessed. Wealth and riches will he in his house, and his righteousness endures forever.

Galatians 5:6. . . faith working through love. . . .

Jeremiah 29:11 - I know the plans I have for you, declares the Lord, plans to prosper you and not to harm you, plans to give you hope and a future.

Matthew 6:33 - Seek first the kingdom of God and His righteousness and all things shall be added to you.

Job 36:11 — If they obey and serve Him, they will spend the rest of their days in prosperity and their years in contentment.

I Corinthians 13:8 - Love never fails.

"Senior Version of 'Jesus Loves Me'"

Here is a new version just for us who have white hair or no hair at all. For us over middle age (or even those almost there) and all you others, check out this newest version of Jesus Loves Me.

JESUS LOVES ME
Jesus loves me, this I know,
Though my hair is white as snow
Though my sight is growing dim,
Still He bids me trust in Him.
(CHORUS)
YES, JESUS LOVES ME..
YES, JESUS LOVES ME..
YES, JESUS LOVES ME,
FOR THE BIBLE TELLS ME SO.
Though my steps are oh, so slow,
With my hand in His I'll go
On through life, let come what may,
He'll be there to lead the way.
(CHORUS)
When the nights are dark and long,
In my heart He puts a song..
Telling me in words so clear,
"Have no fear, for I am near."
(CHORUS)
When my work on earth is done,
And life's victories have been won.
He will take me home above,
Then I'll understand His love. (CHORUS)

MY FINAL WORDS – BE BORN AGAIN

As The Scripture Speaks Of it

It is wonderful to be saved, isn't it'? Have you ever made an inventory of what one does have when he is saved, converted, "born again," as the scripture speaks of it? Think of it! Sins are forgiven when one is saved; one has a new nature, having a Father in Heaven, promises of answered prayers. This does not mean that those who are not Christians do not get answered prayers. They may get a few of them answered by God's grace. They do not have the promise of answered prayers as those who are saved. Those who are saved have eternal life. They have love and joy.

I would like to pause for half a minute on joy. I said, "those who are saved have joy." If there is anything that does not attract someone else to Christ, it is the long, sour, sad face of one who calls himself a Christian. One of the greatest hindrances to the Christian life is a sad face because the Christian has joy. If you are a Christian and you do not have joy on your face, why don't you have your heart notify your face about it and have joy?

One who is saved also has peace. The Holy Spirit is in the life of the Christian. The soul is saved. There is the promise of resurrection and eternity in Heaven. These uncalculated riches and many more belong to the one who is saved and has become a child of God.

Longfellow, it is said, could take a worthless sheet of paper, write a poem on it, and make it worth $6,000. That's genius! Rockefeller could sign his name to a piece of paper and make it worth $1,000,000. That's capital! Uncle Sam takes silver, stamps it, and makes it worth a dollar. That's money! A mechanic takes material worth $5.00 and makes an article worth $50.00 out of it. That's skill! An artist can take a piece of canvas, paint a picture on it, and make it worth $1,000. That's art! God can take a worthless sinful life, wash it in the blood of Christ, put his Spirit in it, and make it a blessing to humanity. That's salvation!

Now in order to become a child of God, one must accept Christ as his personal savior. We want to emphasize this truth, to those who may not be sure that they are saved. This should be emphasized for Christians, so that they may know what is necessary in speaking to someone without Christ. The Bible says that in order to become a Child of God one must accept Christ as personal Savior and Lord. We find in John 1:12 that it has the term "Received Him." "Receiving Him," is a term expressing this truth of the need of accepting Christ as savior. To those who received Him (Christ), He gave the power to become the sons of God.

The word "receive" is a passive term. When you do nothing, you are passive. This word "receive", in the Bible, in the active voice; (in the Greek) when you do the act. It is not passive. Those who receive Him can see that there is some action involved. To them, He gave the power or right or authority to become the sons of God. So, you see this doesn't mean simply believing the information about Christ. There are too many church members. who feel that they are saved because they believe in their mind some information about Christ. That is passive. Believing is passive. You can believe things and not do anything. That is not receiving, and one becomes a Child of God, remember, by receiving Him.

To illustrate this point I have just given, how intellectual assent, or believing something, really doesn't get you anywhere, I would like to have you think with me about a trip that I might want to take to Chicago. I call the Grand Trunk Depot and ask the man when the train is going to be leaving for Chicago. He gives me the time and I go at that time, say three o'clock in the afternoon, and purchase a ticket. This ticket is for the train that takes me to Chicago. Soon the train pulls into the station, some people get off and some get on. You ask there, "Are you going to Chicago?" "Yes, this is the train that is going to Chicago." You ask the conductor. "Is this train going to Chicago?" "Yes." You have got the ticket, you believe all these things, and your faith is strong in the fact that this train goes to Chicago. All of a sudden the train starts to pull away and you are still there at the depot believing all of these things. Yes, you believe all of these facts about that train and you even have your ticket, but you are not on the way to Chicago because you have had this passive belief. One may believe all these creeds about Jesus Christ and say, "Yes, I believe that Jesus Christ died for the world and His blood was shed on the cross," but unless you receive him and he receives you at the same time, you don't get to Heaven.

That is in the Bible. Just as you don't get to Chicago unless you get on that train, until you receive it and it receives you. This is what is meant by believing in Christ. We have heard too much "easy believism" in the past where there are many persons who think they are saved but they are not; that all you have to do is believe. The Demons believe, and tremble, the Bible says, and are not saved. I'm afraid that is why we don't have many out and out Christians, witnessing Christians, because they haven't had this active believing and receiving. Now to prove beyond a shadow of a doubt that believing is receiving, God has put those two words in this one verse. "As many as received Him (Christ), to them gave He power to become the sons of God, even to them that believe on His name, which means, in the end, that those who are receiving, are the ones who are doing the real believing. So this is one term the Bible names, expressing this truth of the need of accepting Christ as personal Savior and Lord.

There is another term, "letting Him come in" (Rev. 3:20). Jesus says, "Behold I stand at the door and knock, if any man hear my voice and open the door I will come in to him and will sup with him and he with Me." Christ is pictured as knocking at our life's door, wanting to be let in. "Behold I stand at the door," the life and heart, and He knocks. He knocks, but He does not break open the door. We again have to be the active agent. If we do nothing, He will not come in. We have to be active. "if any man hear my voice and open the door," (There it is — activity). He will come in. He knocks at our heart's door in many ways. He is knocking right now by His words. When one hears the Word of God, that is God knocking at that one's life, wanting entrance. He also knocks in His providence or in various circumstances. I find one of the most effective ways the Lord knocks, when persons do not listen to His word, is when He really knocks them on their backs. When they are knocked on their backs, say by an accident, they have a chance to really think about the Lord and say, "Why, what do the material things in this life matter?" You work at two jobs, work your head off trying to accumulate the necessary material things. One doesn't have time for the spiritual things and he is knocked flat on his back and it dawns on him, "Why, what good is all of the material now?" Sometimes God has to bring you to that point where you see that the things of this world don't really count, and only having Christ is what counts. He knocks in His various ways to enter into the life. We have to let Him come in to be saved. If Christ is kept outside, something must be wrong inside. Christ comes in when we open the door. He says He stands at the door knocking. If any man hears His voice and opens the door, He will come in. That is one of the best verses for assurance of being saved. That is one of the best ways one can know that he is saved, by having faith in this verse. Notice what Christ said. If anyone hears His voice and opens the door, He will come in. No one who opens the heart's door to Christ needs to question whether Christ came in because He said He would, didn't He? All we have to do is open the door. He will do the rest. He will do His part of coming in.

Many times when I have the wonderful privilege of leading someone to Christ, I ask the person, "Are you saved?" The person says "yes" and I say, "Suppose someone were to ask you, 'how do you know you're saved?'" Now the most frequent answer is, "Well, I feel real good inside", and I say, "That is wonderful, you should feel good, but if you're basing your assurance that you're saved on how good you feel, what if you wake up the next morning and you don't feel too good? You might feel a little sick—maybe a little indigestion and you just don't feel very good -then what's going to happen to your assurance if you're depending on how you feel?"And I say now let's look at this verse, Rev. 3:20. You opened your heart's door to Christ," and the person says "yes". "What did Christ say He would do? Christ says, "I will come in." Now according to this verse, how do you know Christ came. into your life?" Sometimes they still don't get it, and after pressing so that they may get hold of that truth, it dawns on them that the reason they may know they're saved and Christ came in is because He said He would, and He cannot lie, and that is our assurance that we're saved.

There is a true story about a home where someone left an almanac at the door of a little cottage. In the center of this almanac was a picture of the Lord Jesus knocking at the door of the hearts. Some of you have a picture of Christ knocking at the door. This was like that. The mother hung this almanac in the kitchen and when the little boy came home from school he asked about it. But mother was getting supper ready and she didn't take time to answer his questions, and pretty soon his father came in and the boy said, "Daddy, who's knocking at the door?", and the father said, "Well, that's Jesus knocking at the door." The little boy said, "why is He knocking at the door?" The father didn't answer the question, and the boy kept asking about it, "Why is Jesus knocking at the door?" Finally the father said, "He wants to get in." This father, unsaved, answered him shortly and didn't go into it anymore, and the boy said,

"Why don't they let Him come in'?" Dinner came and the father changed the subject, and again and again this little heart. was touched by that scene in that incident, and he kept asking, "Why don't they let Him in?" Soon that question was ringing in this father's ears and in the father's heart. At last, two days later, this father fell on his knees and cried, "Lord Jesus, I know you are knocking at my heart. Please forgive me for keeping you outside and keeping you waiting so long. Lord Jesus, the door is open. Won't you come in right now?" And Christ came in and saved that father and used him in that home.

Jesus said, "I stand at the door and knock, if any man hear my voice and open the door I will come in to him and sup with him and he with me."

Now the third term that I want to mention, emphasizing the same thing, the need of accepting Christ the Savior, is the term "taking Him", Rev. 22:17 says, "And the Spirit and the Bride say, Come. And let him that heareth, say Come. And let him that is a thirst come. And whoso-ever will, let him take the water of life freely." Taking the water of life is taking Christ. This expresses the truth of the need of accepting Him, the Savior. A thirsty man must take the water in order to have his thirst quenched. Christ said that if we come to Him and drink we will have our spiritual thirst quenched, and we will have the Holy Spirit in us. Water is also the symbol of the Spirit, and when the Bible says, "Take the water of Life", this again shows the need of doing something about Christ in order to have the promised result. Doing something about it! Taking Him - not just looking at Him. Not just believing about Him, but taking Him into the life and having a relationship made. I want to illustrate this matter of taking Christ as Savior by a personal illustration, and you will know what I'm talking about because it's happened to some of you. There was a time I was introduced to a young lady and I thought she was a nice girl, and we chatted for a few minutes at a church party. We happened to see each other again on Sunday and we talked a little more. Soon I found that I was deeply interested in that young lady in more than a friendly way, for I began to build a kind of belief about her, you might say. I began to believe she was a very sincere Christian. I began to believe she possessed qualities and abilities God could use in His service. I began to believe her tastes were very similar to mine and I began to believe that, incredible as it was, she really liked me, and I began to believe that I was falling in love. Now in my mind I had this long creed and belief about that girl and I subscribed to that creed honestly, and yet that creed, that belief, made no difference regarding our personal relationship until there came that never forgotten time in church when I said, as we exchanged our marriage vows, "I take thee to be my wife". That definite act, when I said, "I take thee to be my wife", established a life-transforming relationship when I became her husband, and every other relationship was altered when I took that person. That is the way it is with Jesus Christ. Again, there may be a lot of belief about Him, you may even say you love Him, but you have to take Him into your life and say, "I take you as my Savior and Lord", which involves responsibilities. "I take you as my Savior and Lord." Lord means Lord of the life, when one makes the decision. On that basis, then, a relationship is established just as in marriage. We assumed quite a responsibility from then on that we didn't, have before. It comes from taking something, someone, that changes our relationship, and any others are forever altered.

Now, have you accepted Christ as your personal Savior and Lord? You are not a child of God in the spiritual sense until you do so, for the Word of God which I have been giving you, says, "As many as received Him, to them, (the ones who receive) gave He power (or the right) to become the sons of God" (or children of God). No one else is a child of God but the one who receives Christ as Savior.

Salvation is a gift. Now what two actions can one take when offered a gift? "The wages of sin is death, but the gift of God is eternal life through Jesus Christ our Lord." A gift - what two actions can you take? Either receive or refuse. It's as simple as that - to receive or refuse. There are these only two alternatives in this matter of receiving Christ.

One receives or refuses, and one who does not receive Christ cannot say, "Well, I'm not rejecting Him." Yes, the one who has not received Christ is rejecting Christ. If you had a gift and you were to offer it to someone. . . . if that person did not receive that gift, that person's action, that person just being passive, will tell you he or she is rejecting that gift. And so, you may make no move to accept Christ the Savior, but by that very act you show that for the present you are rejecting Him. And why would someone reject Jesus, Christ the Savior, who gives us salvation, which, the Bible said, brings us all those riches which we talked about earlier? It doesn't make sense, does it, that persons are rejecting the Savior in this country of ours? But they are. It seems incredible that they are rejecting Christ when so much could be theirs by accepting Him. It is much worse than the news item that came from Belleville, Illinois, where the Belleville National Bank had a stunt featuring its celebration of its silver jubilee. This bank gave the radio announcer, Bill Bailey, 40 silver dollars and authorized him to sell them at 50 cents each. He was equipped with his portable microphone and he roamed the block in front of the bank for 30 minutes. His approach was to offer a silver dollar in his out - stretched hand and just ask, "Will you give me 50 cents for this silver dollar?" His first potential customer was an elderly retired farmer, and he examined the coin gingerly and scrutinized the date and handed it back with a glare, and said, "I think you are a racketeer from St. Louis", and he hurried away. The next man approached by Bill Bailey recoiled and threatened to call a policeman. A housewife did make the first purchase and she said, "it looks like a good deal to me", and she opened her purse for 50 cents and said, "In these times, I'm willing to take a chance on anything." Another woman told Bailey hesitantly, "I've only got a quarter," and another woman pushed the price down to 11 cents before buying it. But after the program, and this was being broadcast on the radio, Bailey turned back 36 unused silver dollars, Before calling the people of Belleville foolish for hesitating to purchase silver dollars at half price, stop and ask yourself if you are not doing something even more foolish in refusing to accept the Lord's offer of eternal life as a free gift. Strangely enough, because it's a free gift, some people think there is a catch to it, and I've heard them say that it seems that it's just too cheap, this. being saved through receiving Christ the Savior. But the Scripture says "The gift of God is eternal life through Jesus Christ our Lord."

I want to close with a wonderful letter of witness a girl sent to a G. I. This G. I. had received a blood transfusion and it saved his life. The blood donor's name was sent with this blood and he wrote her a letter of thanks. She wrote this letter back that so well emphasized this truth and fact of receiving Christ the Savior. She wrote, "Dear G. I. Joe, How nice of you to write a personal letter of thanks for the help my Red Cross blood donation was to you. We can both thank God that blood was on hand when and where you needed it. I trust your strength will be returning rapidly and that someday soon I may meet you back home. In the mean time I am wondering if you have ever expressed your thanks for a blood donation far more costly and needful than any I could give. I mean, of course, the precious blood which Christ gave for the sins of the world 2,000 years ago. What a gift it is. While mine to you caused only brief inconvenience, His gift cost untold agony. I gave what I could easily spare. He gave His life to die and rise again, that lost men might be saved from their sins - my blood helped prolong your physical life. How thankful I am I did it, but because of His death and resurrection for you, you can have eternal life. My blood helped heal your body; His heals and cleanses the soul. Mine aided you only, but His is effective for all of the world. In one respect His gift and mine are similar, both must be accepted personally. My blood helped you only when you received it. Christ's sacrifice for you will not give you spiritual life unless you accept Him as your Savior. I know it would have seemed unthinkable when you were in desperate need to have refused the blood I was so glad to send your way. I trust that it will seem far more unthinkable to refuse His gift, given with much greater love to meet an infinitely greater need. I would be so glad to hear that you have done this and are trusting Christ as your savior.

Sincerely yours, Wilma Hiscock."

Yes, "as many as received Him, to them gave He power to become the sons of God, even to them that believe on His name. Behold, I stand at the door and knock. If any man hear my voice and open the door, I will come into him. And the Spirit and the Bride say, Come. And let him that is a thirst come. And whosoever will, let him take the water of life freely."

Shall we bow our heads in prayer?

Dear God, thank You for your love and the gift of salvation through Your Son, Jesus Christ.

I realize that I am a sinner and that Jesus Christ died for me that I may be saved from my sins and from hell and for heaven.

I turn away from the devil and my sinful ways and turn to Christ to receive Him as my Savior and Lord of my life.

Thank You for the assurance of Your Word that in doing this I am saved and born again by Your Holy Spirit who comes into my life now.

I yield completely to Jesus Christ now to be filled with Your Holy Spirit. I want to be a devoted follower of Christ by obeying Your words in the Bible.

Praise be to You, Lord, now and forever

Amen

ADDENDUM

MY SON, PASTOR PAUL, SHARES ABOUT HIS DAD

When raising a child it has been said: "more is caught than taught" and this was definitely true of my relationship with my dad. Our home growing up was filled with a lot of activity being a family of six, but Love ruled and because of that there came a feeling of stability. Every Friday night was "Family" night, which consisted of watching the Flintstones on TV while eating a candy bar, followed by a game like hide-and-go seek in the dark or wrestle on the floor with Dad! We were taught to respect both mom and dad but also to laugh and have fun together.

The amazing thing is my father did not have that type of home or family growing up. Not once did he hear the words "I love you" from his father lips. He grew up on the streets of Chicago selling newspapers and then learned to gamble and became a tough guy. He could have easily ended up in jail but God had other plans for his life. After joining the Navy he had a genuine conversion experience. At boot camp he decided to open the Gideon Bible and read it. He invited Jesus into his life and that changed the whole course of his life. After the navy he went to Moody Bible Institute and went full-time into the ministry. Even though he did not have a good example of a loving father he was that and more to his children.

As a young boy, I watched my Dad live out an authentic walk with God. He was the "real deal". . .his private and public lives were the same. He taught me you could always tell what a man is like by how treats his wife and manages his money. Dad was devoted to my mother and theirs was a love story that lasted 61 years. He tenderly cared for her up to her final day. He was known for the saying, "Happy Wife, Happy Life".

Growing up we lived frugally but comfortably on a pastor's salary and his side jobs of student teaching on the side to help with the bills. He paid cash for everything and never went in debt.

My father loved the bible and he committed to memory over 2,000 verses! When I was 15 years old I went through a year of depression. My Dad said to me, "We will meet daily and I will help you through this.". . . .and he did. It was during this time that God was shaping me for the ministry. I pressed into God, prayed with my Dad and accompanied him when he visited the needy. I learned when you are going through hard times; you need to reach out to someone else that is hurting and God will bless you in return. I loved being at his side.

In 1975 my father was voted out of the Baptist Church for his strong beliefs. It was hard to watch my parents rejected and lose everything; even the home they lived in since it was a parsonage. All the time I saw a strength and courage as they took it on as a challenge and adventure, trusting that God would take care of their every need. He even had humor during this time. He would explain by saying, "I left because of illness. They got sick of me."

I watched him pioneer a "new" work and was proud of his willingness to take risks and follow his heart. I observed his humility as he invited other pastors into his life for accountability and I learned the important principle that in order to have authority you need to be under authority. Riverside Church was birthed and they never looked back.

After graduating from college, I told my Dad I was interested in serving full-time in the ministry. He told me I could go to

seminary or be trained and disciple under him. He said he could not promise me a position and that I would have to get a job while being trained. I accepted his offer and met with him weekly for hours of prayer, training and study. He gave me different responsibilities in the church where I served as a volunteer. I saw Jesus' principle of leadership that says "Faithful with little, faithful with much; faithful with another man's things, faithful with my own" (Luke 16:10)

After 3 years of training and serving, my father laid his hands on my head and prayed for a double anointing of everything he had been given to be passed on to me. That is a day I will never forget. Today if you ask me what seminary I went to, with a smile on my face I proudly say that I graduated for the J.B. Bible School at the top of my class!

Eventually my dad went on to trans-local ministry and traveled around the world and I became the Senior Pastor of Riverside Church. The church was passed from father to son. I am now standing on his shoulders and he is a spiritual father and consultant to me. He sits in the front row every Sunday and is one of my biggest cheerleaders. The church is continually growing and lives are being changed every Sunday through God's love and power.

I will forever be grateful to God for the gift he gave me in my father. He is a "piece of work", a "one of a kind". . .to know him is to love him! He has been my father, mentor, friend and it's been an amazing adventure doing life with him.

CPSIA information can be obtained at www.ICGtesting.com
Printed in the USA
BVOW06s1143010813

327536BV00002B/9/P